Sexual Violence and Predatory Journalism in India

Sexual Violence and Predatory Journalism in India examines unethical editorial practices in the reporting of sexual crimes against women in India, introducing the term Predatory Journalism.

This book conceptualises and analyses predatory practices that commodify sexual crimes against women, examining how it is facilitated and motivated by online spaces and social media channels and how it can often result in further harm to victims and their families. It argues for editorial intervention, more regulation, policy measures and legal frameworks that will help build a sensitive and ethical media landscape and rebuild public trust. Key issues examined include sexism, sensationalism, invasion of privacy, victim blaming, media trials, media manipulation of information, armchair reporting, explicit sexual imagery, the usage of unreliable sources and a lack of responsibility and accountability.

Providing a comprehensive analysis of the issue and offering a framework for ethical practice, *Sexual Violence and Predatory Journalism in India* will be essential reading for scholars and students of media and cultural studies, journalism and sociology interested in the intersection of media and crime in India and its associated ethical challenges.

Francis Philip Barclay is an Assistant Professor of Media and Communication at the Central University of Tamil Nadu, India. He is the founding editor of the *Journal of Media and Communication* and co-editor of *Social Media in India: Regulatory Needs, Issues and Challenges* (2022) and *Gender and Popular Visual Culture in India: 'Benevolent' Sexism and Disguised Discrimination* (Routledge, 2023).

Kaifia Ancer Laskar is an Assistant Professor of Journalism and Mass Communication at Aliah University, India. She is co-editor of *Gender and Popular Visual Culture in India: 'Benevolent' Sexism and Disguised Discrimination* (Routledge, 2023).

"A multifaceted analysis of unethical media practices in reporting sexual violence in India, this book reveals a disturbing reality through rigorous reflection and research. Insightful for anyone committed to ethical journalism and understanding the media's impact on societal perceptions and the exploitation of ensuing trauma."

Syeda Afshana, *Professor of Media Studies, Media Education Research Centre, University of Kashmir, India, and Visiting Fellow, Centre of International Studies, University of Cambridge, UK*

"Barclay and Laskar's data-driven analysis of 'Predatory Journalism' addresses how sensationalist reporting has seeped into and tainted the mainstream news cycle and causes harm to victims and their communities. As the authors stand up to abusive journalistic tactics to restore public faith in news across print, radio, television, streaming platforms and social media, concerned citizens and ethical editors may be inspired to support victims of sexual crimes and the journalists who provide accurate and respectful reporting."

Artemis Preeshl, *Director, Center for Diversity and Inclusion, Buena Vista University, USA*

"This important book examines the reporting about crimes against women in India and the ethical challenges that journalists face. It also addresses the impact of those challenges on the victims of crimes, focusing on privacy, sensationalism and victim blaming. The authors apply the important concepts of critical theory and feminism as part of the moral obligation that journalists face when covering difficult crimes and the impact on the women who are victims. It adds to the growing scholarship about the coverage of crimes against women. I highly recommend this book."

Kimberly Voss, *Professor of Journalism, University of Central Florida, USA*

Sexual Violence and Predatory Journalism in India

Emerging Unethical Practices

Francis Philip Barclay and Kaifia Ancer Laskar

Routledge
Taylor & Francis Group
LONDON AND NEW YORK

First published 2025
by Routledge
4 Park Square, Milton Park, Abingdon, Oxon OX14 4RN

and by Routledge
605 Third Avenue, New York, NY 10158

Routledge is an imprint of the Taylor & Francis Group, an informa business

British Library Cataloguing-in-Publication Data
A catalogue record for this book is available from the British Library

ISBN: 978-1-032-58695-3 (hbk)
ISBN: 978-1-032-74191-8 (pbk)
ISBN: 978-1-003-46804-2 (ebk)

DOI: 10.4324/9781003468042

Typeset in Times New Roman
by KnowledgeWorks Global Ltd.

For

Mrs. Maud Jones,

my grandmother and first teacher

who knew only to love me till her last breath.

For

Ma (Mrs. Nazlee Begum Laskar), Baba (Mr. Ancer Ahmed Laskar),

Mr. George Jones, Mrs. Anusha Venkat,

Mr. Rakib Kausar Barbhuiya,

Zia, Zara and Ziyan.

For the knowledge that kills ignorance.

For democracy.

Contents

List of figures *ix*
List of tables *x*
Foreword *xi*
Acknowledgements *xiii*
Content warning *xiv*

Introduction: Foregrounding Predatory Journalism in Reporting Sexual Violence 1

PART I
Introduction 7

1 What Makes Sensational Sexual Crime Stories? Topical Bias and News Prioritisation 9

2 Predatory Journalism: Conceptualisation 22

PART II
Unmasking the Predator 41

3 Headline Horrors: Losing Sense for Sexist Sensationalism 43

4 Prejudicial Reporting and Media Trials: Case Studies 61

5 Eroticism and Exhibition: Editorial Exploits in Rape Reporting 77

6 Churnalism: How "Spiced-up" Sexual Crime News Stories Are Cooked Up in Minutes 89

PART III
Taming the Beast 111

7 The Social Dilemma: Rise and Impact of Social Media News Channels 113

8 Predatory Journalism: Consolidation, Criticism and Consequences 127

9 The Way Forward: Building a Sensitive and Ethical Media Landscape 138

Index *153*

Lists of figures

1.1	Google News search trends	10
2.1	Predatory Journalism: A model	29
6.1	Google News search trends for 12 months	93
6.2	Time-series plots for the three cases: Search trends and articles published	95
6.3	Cross-correlation between search trends and article counts	96

List of tables

1.1 Variables and measurement 13
1.2 Characterisation of the accused and victims 14
1.3 Period-wise prevalences of sexual crime 16
1.4 Associations among the crimes 17
1.5 Patterns of prevalences of news values 17
1.6 Editorial top priorities 18
3.1 Topics and grammatical structure 49
3.2 Frames and measurement 50
3.3 Devices and measurement 50
3.4 Illocutions and measurement 51
3.5 Period-wise descriptives: Topics and grammatical structures 52
3.6 Word-phrase frequencies 53
3.7 Period-wise descriptives: Frames and devices 54
3.8 Period-wise descriptives: Illocutions 55
3.9 Characterising the illocutions 56
4.1 News frames and discursive themes 64
6.1 Discordant locus and dissonant composition 92

Foreword

Drs. Barclay and Laskar critique the predatory practices that commodify sexual crimes against women to expand the reach of journalistic copy. The authors argue for increased editorial intervention to prevent the exploitation of victims of sexual assault. In this foreword, I consider the purpose, method and frame of this study in the context of the #MeToo Movement and resultant consent- and trauma-informed practices. As an intimacy director, choreographer and writer of books on consent-based practice, I affirm that the "outing" of victims of sexual assault violates their rights. Consent is an affirmative and enthusiastic agreement to engage in a specific practice. Tacit compliance is not consent. Therefore, unless survivors of sexual violence agree to have details about the incident or contact information for themselves and their families released, it is incumbent upon the journalists to respect their privacy.

I first met Dr. Francis Barclay at the "Future Communications: Rethinking Societies, Cultures and Governance" international conference at Pondicherry University in India in April 2024. Barclay presented his assessment on reporting on sexual violence against women in India. His data provoked the most robust discussion of the session. As he fielded questions from a diversity of viewpoints, Dr. Barclay steadfastly framed his data within the scope of this powerful study, thereby providing a model for ethical journalism. Thus, Barclay and Laskar's approach speaks to the data-driven analysis of this most pressing problem to ensure the rights of victims.

The new terms introduced and close reads of numerous high-profile incidents centre the reader in the midst of the multifaceted dilemma. A quantitative assessment of themes underscores how content on sexual violence baits the public to the detriment of the survivors. The introduction of the term "Predatory Journalism" addresses how sensationalist reporting has seeped into and tainted the mainstream news cycle.

The Manipur sexual violence in 2023 that went viral exemplifies this study. Even after sexually explicit videos and reports were ostensibly withdrawn, victims continued to be subjected to re-traumatisation by continued circulation online. The journalistic treatment of high-profile cases has degraded over the past decade despite the Protection of Children from Sexual Offences Act 2012 among other legal processes and outcomes.

Further, eroticism and exhibitionism of the survivors' plight are stoked by the influence of digital media. The usage of titillating headlines and graphic descriptions profits the media outlets at the emotional expense of the survivors. Thus, the survivor's right to privacy is traded in for the public's supposed right to know about criminal behaviour. This journalist balancing act frequently errs on the side of revealing humiliating details that compromise the welfare of the victims, their families and their communities. The coining of the term "churnalism" points to the misuse of information through the investigation of alternative angles of the sex crime stories to maintain public interest regardless of the accuracy of the information in this post-truth age.

The authors take care to address the proliferation of predatory churnalism. Skilful data collection of news samplings compares how sexual violence is presented across social media sites. By identifying techniques used to saturate the news cycle, the authors uncover how revealing intimate details about sexual crimes promotes readership. Finally, the authors envision a more ethical approach to fact-checking, editorial oversight, regulation and legal frameworks to rebuild public trust in media accounts.

Churning of stories by different media outlets day after day jeopardises the health and safety of the victims, their families and their communities. Journalists capitalise on the salacious hype to intrigue their readers through hyperbolic accounts of sexual battery, assault and rape. These repeated invasions of privacy re-traumatise women with every article that directly or indirectly exposes their identities without their consent. This volume sheds light on how news stories cause harm to victims and their communities. Further, when a news event becomes associated with a particular city, state or region, the homogenisation of the crime leads to stereotyping all persons in that region, which extends the reach from the initial harm caused by the inciting incident to impact the community at large. The reader may confront discomforting truths across these mediums. As the authors stand up to abusive journalistic tactics to restore public faith in news across print, radio, television, streaming platforms and social media, concerned citizens and ethical editors may be inspired to support victims of sexual crimes and the journalists who provide accurate and respectful reporting.

Artemis Preeshl
Director, Center for Diversity and Inclusion,
Buena Vista University, USA

Acknowledgements

As always, our first thanks go to our spouses for their inspiration and support, from understanding the importance of this book and providing encouragement to reading the early drafts and offering "expert" suggestions. We also thank our parents and children for their love.

We extend our heartfelt gratitude to the publisher, editors and reviewers for their faith and investment in our idea. We especially thank Routledge Editorial Assistants Chris Parry and Gemma Rogers, Senior Publisher Helen Pritt and former Senior Editor Neil Jordan. Their positivity, invaluable feedback, guidance and continued support have helped shape this book into what it is today. We express our sincere indebtedness to Prof. Artemis Preeshl for her valuable contribution to this book's foreword section.

We record our faithful gratitude to the Indian Council of Social Science Research (ICSSR) for funding a major research project titled "Sexual Crimes Against Women and Sensationalist-Exploitative Journalism: Emerging Unethical Trends and Practices in India". Data collected as part of the project was useful for analysis conducted in Chapters 1 and 3.

We also thank Dr. C. Pichandy and Prof. K. V. Nagaraj for being our guiding lights in media research. We post our gratitude to colleagues Dr. Boobalakrishnan N., Dr. Akila S., Prof. Ravindran G. and Dr. Mohammad Reyaz for their goodwill and support.

We also thank our scholars Dr. Akhila S., Dr. Malavika Sunil K., Dr. Showkat Ahmad Jan, Ms. Haritha Harilal, Mr. Ram Kumar Dhar, Ms. Harini D., Ms. Harini J., Ms. Rieugleen R., Thrisha T., Mr. Kirupakaran R., Ms. Solaipriya M., Ms. Preethi J. and Ms. Sana Tabassum for their help in data collection. We also thank our institutions Central University of Tamil Nadu and Aliah University and their administration for their encouragement, resources and support.

Finally, we thank you, the reader, for your interest in this book. Your curiosity and willingness to engage with alternative perspectives make writing and publishing books like this one a worthwhile endeavour. Thank you for joining us on this journey and contributing to media criticism in good faith. We hope that this book will enlighten and inspire you. Thank you!

Content Warning

As the title suggests, this book deals with sensitive topics such as rape and molestation, among other forms of sexual violence. It presents excerpts and points to imagery from news published on sexual crimes against women to conduct in-depth analyses and engage in discussions. The decision to include those excerpts was not taken lightly. The book examines how these crimes are covered in the news media and offers critical but constructive criticism, aiming to improve journalistic practices and public understanding. Your life experiences (along with the way you perceive and process information) may be unique. Some of you may have also experienced similar trauma, and some of the published material may be upsetting or triggering for some of those readers, though those contents, generally, do not come with a warning in the news. In any case, reader discretion is advised.

Introduction

Foregrounding Predatory Journalism in Reporting Sexual Violence

Perhaps, sexual violence (against women) could be common far more than we could count, for a majority of it go unrecorded—the National Sexual Violence Resource Center statistics stated that one in five US women would be raped at least once in her lifetime (NSVRC, 2015) and the Indian National Family Health Survey concluded that about 99 per cent of sexual violence were not reported to the police (Bhattacharya & Kundu, 2018, April 24). To such a degree, the true scale of sexual violence has remained concealed. *Why?* Prejudiced civilisations—and their unequivocal social norms formalised with recurrent reinforcements—place immense emphasis on the modesty of a woman and acts that insult or outrage that modesty are adjudged grave offences—at times, even casting a shadow of shame and blame on the victim (or survivor). Even after the sexual assault *per se*, a survivor's ordeal is far from over. When—sexual gratification aside, as a show of power and domination aimed at controlling and humiliating—her privacy is invaded, body violated and modesty outraged, the traumatic event could engender enduring sociological and psychological sequelae (Kalra & Bhugra, 2013). It could depress self-esteem and make the survivors vulnerable to further violence, thereby instilling a sense of fear, restricting their freedom and obstructing occupational opportunities. Thence, sexual violence could be more extensive in patriarchial (or hypermasculine) cultures (World Bank, 2022, October 1).

Even the count of recorded cases of sexual violence is staggering. On an average Indian hour, at least three rape cases (86 a day) and close to 70 cases of crime against women (1,664 a day) are registered (NCRB, 2022). Seeking justice means navigating a gauntlet of legal scrutiny, (in the worst cases) media spectacle and societal judgement. Though just a minuscule fragment of them reach the newspapers (about 8.4 per cent make it to the front pages, according to (Sreedharan & Thorsen, 2021), those stories are, at times, sensationalised. Too often, even the most courageous and determined efforts end in acquittals, with the perpetrators of crime evading accountability (according to NRCB data, the conviction rate for rape is 39 per cent [TNN, 2021, September 16]). As a source of credible information and social institution that can harness (and use) people power, the news media plays a critical role in shining a light on these tragedies and ensuring the guilty face consequences. *But is it upholding its moral obligation?*

DOI: 10.4324/9781003468042-1

This book foregrounds unethical editorial practices (practised in a section of mass and news media) that exploit the readers (or media audience) and victims for gain—classified under the aggregate of Predatory Journalism—while reporting sexual violence against women, analysing an assortment of recent cases reported in India.

Predatory Journalism is viewed as a media culture cultivated in a competitive environment with the abuse of its power. Critical theory and a feminist point of view are used to identify and analyse the indices of this phenomenon, as sensationalised news content could have sexual, sexist and sectionalist (intersectional) undercurrents aimed at appeasing (and feeding) the patriarchal mindset (of the media audience).

This book is unique in its comprehensive conceptualisation and analysis of Predatory Journalism, widening its scope beyond mere sensationalism to include a range of other editorial issues such as prejudicial reporting, media trials, privacy invasion, manipulation of information while engaging in armchair reporting, the rise of social media news channels, media hyping, explicit imagery and hyperdetailing of sexual crime in the news, problematic source citation and the generic lack of responsibility and accountability.

By exploring a plethora of formal and pragmatic issues in a range of news media from print and television to websites and social—and combining qualitative and quantitative research methodologies—this book offers a theoretical framework to analyse Predatory Journalism and provide empirical evidence to support the assertions. Characterising this contemporary media malady and raising awareness about the importance of responsible and ethical reporting during such challenging times, this book becomes an essential reading for anyone interested in understanding the intersection of media and the popular topic of sexual crime against women in India and the ethical challenges and dilemmas that arise.

This book is divided into three parts.

In the first introductory part, the reporting trend of sexual violence against women in India is examined and Predatory Journalism is conceptualised.

Chapter 1 on "What Makes Sensational Sexual Crime Stories? Semantic Microstructures and News Prioritisation" underscores that though sexual crimes against women are widespread in India, most of them go unreported in the mainstream media. Certain cases, nevertheless, hog the media limelight and it is critical to answer why and what news ingredients influence this scrupulous election to the front pages.

To empirically understand reporting trends of sexual crimes against women in India, this Chapter analyses the front pages of the *Times of India* (New Delhi edition) published during 1 June—31 December 2023, covering seven months and 213 days. Several factors, such as the type of sexual and allied crime reported, information available about the accused and victims, news values that the news stories featured, forms and presentation of the articles and the subtopics covered, that could potentially influence news prioritisation and placement are examined. Manual quantitative content analysis is used to identify semantic microstructures (subthemes and news values) popular within this news topic and relate space allocation and news prioritisation with them.

What is conceptualised as "Predatory Journalism" in Chapter 2 and accounted for in the subsequent parts of this book is not a phenomenal peculiarity hot off the press but an editorial eyesore that has dotted and daunted the history of news. Even so, what had been perceived as a perimetric problem has now become mainstream—extensively explicit and extreme—warranting a receptive nomenclature and theoretical exposition that encompass the incitements and implications of an ultraist form of journalism prominent in the present times. Where does the concept of "sensationalism" fall short in sufficiently describing the destructive form of journalism perceptible in a section of the news media at a time when online social media hold sway? How can Predatory Journalism be conceptualised when the audience is overwhelmed with apparently unlimited news mediums and sources? What are the needs for such a conceptualisation? With a conceptual review of existing terms and a succinct spotlight on contemporary editorial eccentricities and anomalies, this chapter attempts to answer these critical and timely questions.

In the second part of this book aimed at "Unmasking the Predator", several concepts identified under Predatory Journalism are empirically examined.

Chapter 3 on "Headline *Horrors*! Losing Sense for Sexist Sensationalism" discusses the contemporary-rancorous need for sensationalism in news headlines and its implications. Performing a manual content analysis of a sample of 254 digital news headlines published on the 2023 Manipur sexual violence (during the examination window of 20–28 July 2023), this chapter uses the pragmalinguistics framework to identify sensationalist, sexist, sexual and sectionalist illocutions embedded within or implied by those headlines.

These illocutions are associated with locutionary topics and frames. Further, this chapter examines how lexical choices are deployed to support illocutionary discourse acts to offer empirical evidence and specifically theorise on sensationalism in the reporting of extreme sexual crimes against women in India. It also demonstrates how sensationalism is instantiated through specific linguistic devices and argues for the need to balance the demand for attention-grabbing headlines with sensitive news reporting.

In Chapter 4 that focuses on prejudicial reporting and media trials, television coverage of two recent cases of sexual crimes against women in India (the 2019 Hyderabad gangrape-murder and the 2017 Kerala actress abduction-molestation case involving actor Dileep) is analysed to review the gimmicky news media tendency to engage in prejudicial reporting and conduct media trials—overstepping their role as a watchdog and defender of democracy through information dissemination. Using a critical discourse analysis, this chapter identifies cues of prejudicial reporting that could potentially hinder legal action or influence judicial evaluation and biassed media trials that could skew public opinion and create an emotional outpour that may be misinformed or misdirected. This CDA approach also offers the scope to discuss power struggles (or the misuse of power) and inherent sexism.

Chapter 5 of this book tackles two editorial exploits in rape reporting, eroticism and exhibition, conducting a multimodal analysis of text and imagery in news reports of the 2023 Manipur sexual violence, the 2018 Kathua rape case and the 2017 Unnao rape.

This chapter unfolds the exhibitionist hyper detailing in the textual descriptions of sexual crimes and explicitness in the gory news imagery to explain how contemporary news reporting tactics are trained to send shockwaves.

Exhibitionism of sexual crime in the news refers to an excessive focus on graphic or lurid details (unwarranted information about the crime that can re-traumatise the victim) appearing in some way gratuitous or exploitative, eroticising or sexualising the crime (through direct descriptions of the sexual acts and avoiding euphemisms) often narrating the crime (as a first-person account [or witness] while it is not the case). It also discusses how this trend exploits and stimulates the readers, evoking emotional and erotic responses marking the ideological biases of sexism and classism behind such reporting.

Analysing three cases of sexual violence against women, Chapter 6 looks into two critical concepts that are used to characterise Predatory Journalism: Discordant Locus and Dissonant Composition. Using these concepts, issues such as churnalism—or engagement in armchair reporting or recycling content—misinformation, lack of proper mention of sources of information in news reports and privacy invasion are tackled.

Churnalism is a desk-bound phenomenon that curtails the possibility of field investigations, fact-checking and verification of sources. Erroneous reports are constructed based on imagined conspiracy theories or recycling of unverified claims and sources. To present news stories as amazing and at a great speed, predatory journalists end up recycling news, at times adding a new angle to them. In the conceptualisation of Predatory Journalism, Locus alludes to the distance from where (or the position from which) information is gathered for news stories. Under the concept of Discordant Locus, problematic obscure and obtrusive reporting practices are explored and privacy invasion is discussed. To draw readers or viewers, often invasive journalism is employed—especially in the context of reporting sexual crimes against women—for exclusive and emotional content.

Three chapters feature in the third part of this book.

The rise of social media news channels has transformed the media landscape in India, with millions of people now turning to platforms such as Instagram, Twitter and YouTube for news and information. Online imagery also contributes to the overall understanding of news events as, in contemporary times, the readers approach diverse mediums, from news websites and YouTube to image and video search engines, to piece together bits of information scattered across the Internet. Chapter 7 explores the impact of social media news channels on the reporting of sexual crimes in India and the ethical challenges posed by these platforms, such as the lack of regulation and editorial oversight. Unlike traditional media, social media platforms are not subject to the same ethical and legal standards and are often driven by profit. This can spread inaccurate (mis)information. Social media and search algorithms that control what users read can manipulate how news spreads, creating filter bubbles or echo chambers. This chapter reviews relevant literature to explore how online social media propagates and can be used as a constructive tool to check Predatory Journalism.

In Chapter 8, the findings of the previous chapters are summarised and the causes, emerging trends and implications of Predatory Journalism are discussed. It explores concepts such as exploitation, desensitisation of media audiences, normalisation of sexual violence, victim-blaming, shaming and rape culture. Aiming to build a sensitive and ethical media landscape, the conclusionary Chapter 9 offers informed and specific policy recommendations. It identifies ways in which the practice of Predatory Journalism can be checked.

This chapter argues for a comprehensive regulatory framework for promoting responsible reporting that will be based on a balance of legal mechanisms, independent regulatory bodies and self-regulation and be designed to promote greater accountability, transparency and public trust in the media. It will also prescribe ethical guidelines and codes of conduct that can guide journalists and media organisations in their reporting. We believe that this book will be a wake-up call and an essential reading for a wide range of people.

References

Bhattacharya, P. & Kundu, T. (2018, April 24). 99% cases of sexual assaults go unreported, govt data shows | Mint. *Mint*. https://www.livemint.com/Politics/AV3sIKoEBAGZozALMX8THK/99-cases-of-sexual-assaults-go-unreported-govt-data-shows.html

Kalra, G. & Bhugra, D. (2013). Sexual violence against women: Understanding cross-cultural intersections. *Indian Journal of Psychiatry*. *55*(3), 244–9.

NCRB. (2022). *Crime in India 2022: Statistics*, vol. 1. National Crime Records Bureau, Ministry of Home Affairs, Government of India. Retrieved from https://ncrb.gov.in/uploads/nationalcrimerecordsbureau/custom/1701607577CrimeinIndia2022Book1.pdf

NSVRC. (2015). *Statistics about Sexual Violence*. National Sexual Violence Resource Center. Retrieved from, https://www.nsvrc.org/sites/default/files/publications_nsvrc_factsheet_media-packet_statistics-about-sexual-violence_0.pdf

Sreedharan, C. & Thorsen, E. (2021). *Sexual violence and the news media: Issues, challenges, and guidelines for journalists in India. UNESCO*. Retrieved from https://eprints.bournemouth.ac.uk/35830/7/MAAR%20REPORT%20PDF%20Online%20.pdf

TNN. (2021, September 16). NCRB: At 39% and 41%, rape & murder see poor conviction rate. *The Times of India*. https://timesofindia.indiatimes.com/india/ncrb-at-39-and-41-rape-murder-see-poor-conviction-rate/articleshow/86249857.cms

World Bank. (2022, October 1). Violence against women and girls – what the data tell us | World Bank Gender Data Portal. Retrieved from, https://genderdata.worldbank.org/en/data-stories/overview-of-gender-based-violence

Part I

Introduction

1 What Makes Sensational Sexual Crime Stories?

Topical Bias and News Prioritisation

On average—according to 2022 NCRB data—about 86 rapes among 1,664 cases of crime against women and children are registered in a day in India, but most of them go unreported in the mainstream media. Certain cases, nevertheless, hog the media limelight and it is critical to answer why and what news ingredients influence this scrupulous election to the front pages.

In 2022 alone, 31,516 rape and 3,288 attempt cases were registered, as per the 2022 NCRB records. As many as 4,45,256 cases of crime against women were registered in 2022, posting an increase of four per cent from 2021 (4,28,278).

A majority of those cases were pertaining to "cruelty by husband or his relatives" (31.4 per cent), kidnapping and abduction of women (19.2 per cent), "assault on women with intent to outrage her modesty" (18.7 per cent) and "rape" (7.1 per cent). Similarly, 1,62,449 cases of crime against children were registered during 2022—posting an 8.7-per cent increase over 2021 (1,49,404 cases) (NCRB, 2021). About 45 per cent of these cases were kidnapping and abduction, while cases registered under the Protection of Children from Sexual Offences Act, 2012, including child rape, accounted for 39.7 per cent (NCRB, 2022).

As many as 248 cases were categorised as murder with rape or gangrape and the Indian state of Uttar Pradesh alone registered 62 of them (Sharma, 2023, December 4). This apart, 124 cases of acid attacks involving 140 victims were registered across the nation during 2022.

If these staggering numbers were not distressing enough, government estimates indicated that 99.1 per cent of cases of sexual assaults go unreported (Kundu, 2018, April 24).

Quite frequently, bold news headlines of extreme sexual violence strike us from the broadsheet front pages and social media links lead us to the webpages exhibiting breaking news with exclusive imagery. Caught up in this melee of competitive-rigorous reporting, we mostly fail to look beyond the episodic events, critically read the persistent patterns and realise how those coverages limit or expand our understanding about the long-term sociopolitical effects.

Even while the news media hypercoverages of popular cases of gangrape, such as the 2012 Delhi, 2017 Unnao, 2018 Kathua, 2019 Hyderabad and 2020 Hathras events, have triggered nationwide activism and created rabid readership for sexual violence, they have raised the threshold for avid coverage, prioritising the violent,

DOI: 10.4324/9781003468042-3

gruesome and those with other essential ingredients—such as the availability of micro-details and appalling imagery or the incorporation of a political angle or caste card—for the broadsheet front pages or the prime-time television.

Though such hypercoverages of sexual violence—along with the allied expert debates on televised shows and mixed public judgments posted on online social media—could mean more distress than support, at least for the survivors and their families, it is still crucial to understand the factors that affect news prioritisation to iron out underlying issues. In an article on "Sexual Violence in India's Headlines", Langston (2016, August 15) writes:

> In recent years, news coverage of sexual violence in India has increased, but the Indian press's coverage has serious flaws—including a tendency to ignore victims from underprivileged backgrounds and to print sensationalistic depictions of rape.

Analysing India's leading English-language newspapers, Jolly (2016, July 20) showed that the 2012 Delhi gangrape case triggered a significant increase in rape coverage in India.

Drache and Velagic (2014) performed a media monitoring exercise of rape reporting before and after the Delhi incident on four leading Indian English language publications: *The Hindu, India Today, The Indian Express and Tehelka.* Their study results indicated a substantial increase in rape reporting. Google News search trends also indicate an increase in demand for news on sexual violence, including rape and gangrape, post the 2012 phenomenon.

Google News search trends for the topic "rape" in India are presented in Figure 1.1.

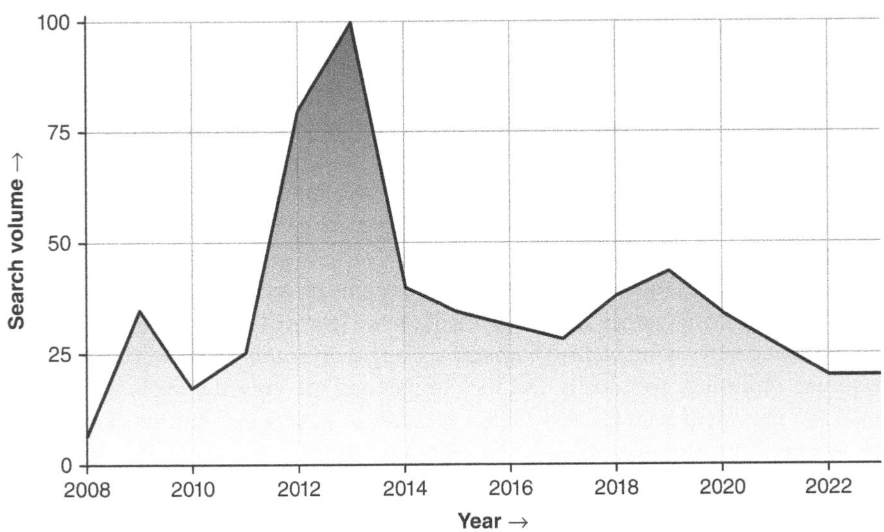

Figure 1.1 Google News search trends.

Source: Created by the authors using the Google Trends API

In her analysis, Jolly quotes former *The Times of India* reporter Smriti Singh as saying:

> There is this term we use called PLU–it means 'people like us'. Whenever there is a murder or rape case involving a female, in your head you have a checklist as to whether the story qualifies to be reported or not.
>
> (Jolly, 2016, July 20)

Jolly (2016, July 20) points out that factors such as the socio-economic class of the victim, the geographical location where the crime has occurred and the extremity of the violence determine whether the story will be picked up and highlighted by the press.

Similarly, analysing 10 Indian newspapers across six languages, Sreedharan and Thorsen (2021) observed that about 8.4 per cent of the rape and sexual violence stories reported made it to the front pages, mostly focussing on the "outlier" cases. Gangrape contributed to 20 per cent of those front-page stories on sexual violence and a regional bias was also identified. Their analysis of 1,635 news articles revealed that about 40 per cent of them detailed the crime, apart from impressions of victim-blaming and politicising the crime. Sreedharan and Thorsen (2021) also showed that the social (or celebrity) status of the accused and victims and the brutality of the crime influenced editorial decisions. Examining the coverage of sexual violence in English and Malayalam newspapers for a month after the Delhi gangrape case was reported. Joy (2022) found that of the 550 news articles on sexual violence identified in *The Times of India, The Hindu, Malayala Manorama and Mathrubhumi*, 74 occupied the front pages.

Similarly, analysing the front pages of top-selling Hindi and English dailies, Singh (2022) found rape-related news stories covering about 8 per cent of the news space, on average, appearing every fourth day and about 43 per cent of those stories identified to be being problematic with issues such as sensationalism, trivialisation and victim-blaming. Underscoring that "newspapers are considered important platforms to mobilise and sensitise the people regarding different social issues" and that the "issues of the women, their rights and atrocities meted out against them need to be raised in various forums including the newspapers", Ahmad (2019) examined how *The Indian Express and The Times of India* covered cases of sexual violence against women to find out that these newspapers failed to prioritise cases of sexual harassment and observed negativity thriving in the news reports that cover women's issues.

Echoing similar views in a study that examined the editorial coverage of atrocities against women in the Indian newspapers, Gangopadhyay, Bandopadhyay and Chatterjee (2012) observed generic low prioritisation and crimes such as rape and sexual harassment fetching prime space.

On a commentary on "Media Sensationalism and Mob Mentality in India: Which Rapes Cause Outrage?", Singh (2020, October 30) identified several factors such as caste, brutality, death of the victim and acquaintance of the accused with the victim as factors influencing editorial decisions while reporting cases of sexual violence against women in India.

What makes sensational sexual crime stories?

Galtung and Ruge (1965) conceptualised "news values" to answer the "deceptively-simple" question of "what is news?" In simple terms, news values went on to be understood as news-selection criteria. While most seminal studies on news values had focussed on traditional journalism, attempting to study what becomes news and understand the factors that influence news prioritisation, Barclay (2024) examined the relevance of traditional news values and introduced taxonomies that are peculiar to the digital space and contemporary times.

Empirical data

Adapting this concept of values that determine news selection, this chapter answers the question: What makes sensational sexual crime stories? This study analyses the front pages of a popular Indian broadsheet daily to identify the essential ingredients and patterns that the top news stories of sexual violence feature—or they may be understood as the factors that have influenced their selection to and positioning on the front pages of the newspaper. A handful of studies have attempted to examine news values that affect editorial selection. Sex itself has been identified as a critical news value, but the levels of attention and emphasis accorded to assorted cases of sexual violence have been disparate. Barclay (2024) identified 18 news values. Of them, 10 are adapted for the present study: Progression, Threshold, Celebrity, Personalisation, Conflict, Unexpectedness, Visuality, Drama, Sensationalism and the Power Elite.

For this study, *The Times of India* is selected as it is the top-selling English newspaper in India with wide reach across the nation and the front pages of this newspaper (New Delhi edition) are sampled for the analysis during the window of examination: 1 June to 31 December 2023, covering seven months. The unit of analysis is a news article, published on the 307 front pages of the newspaper, including brief news and excluding teasers, standalone images, pointers and advertisements. From these 307 front pages published during the sampling period of 213 days, as many as 116 news articles that directly referenced sexual violence against women were chosen for analysis. A manual content analysis was performed for this study as it involves the interpretation of both manifest and latent meanings of news text.

The variables chosen for the study are Period (month of the publication of the article), Priority (weightage based on the positioning of the article on the front page [vertical and horizontal placement was considered, with more importance accorded to the article that is placed more up and left], headline font size [the bigger, the more important] and font style [the bolder, the more important] and space allocated [in terms of the number of columns provided to the news article]), Form, Nature of the Crime reported, Subtopics that it covers, News Values and the presentation of the Victims and Accused in the news report analysed. Categories of the variables chosen for the study, their descriptions and measurements are presented in Tables 1.1 and 1.2.

A pilot study was conducted on 50 front pages randomly selected from the study period to identify the variables and their categories. Form factors identified for the study are presented in Table 1.1. Based on a manual review and identification, they were coded as either present or absent. Similarly, the categories for the sexual crime reported, along with allied crimes, were chosen based on the literature

Table 1.1 Variables and measurement

Factor	*Description or categories*	*Measurement*
Period	The month of the publication of the article	June to December
Position	Article position on the front page (based on the position and headline size)	One indicates top priority, with increasing number indicating decreasing priority
Column	Number of columns given to the news article	Column count
Priority	Reversed Position * Column	Scale
Form	Headline, Subhead, Slug, Kicker, Photograph, Illustration, Infographics, Quote, Blurb, Info box Social media messages	Present or absent
Sexual crime	Gangarape, Rape, Molestation, Sexual harassment at the workplace, Disrobing, Stalking, Eve-teasing, Cybercrime, Recording of the crime, Transmission of the record, Partner violence, Disrobing and causing public humiliation, Mob sexual assault, Flashing, Lewd remarks or gestures	Present or absent
Allied crime	Abduction, Illegal detention, Torture, Extortion, Acid-attack, Verbal abuse, Blackmail, Destruction of property, Threatening, Robbery	Present or absent
Nature of physical assault	Not described or nil Minor as described in the news story Major as described in the news story Fatal as mentioned in the news story	Nominal
Region of the crime	Metros (Delhi, Mumbai, Chennai, Kolkata or Bangalore); Other state capitals; Other districts; Undisclosed	Nominal
State where the crime occurred	Indian state as mentioned in the news article	Nominal
Crime location	Private, undisclosed, secluded and public	Nominal
Subtopic	Crime, Public reaction, Legal action, Judicial action, Government action, Institutional action, Activism, Political statement, Punishment	Present or absent
News values	Progression, Threshold, The power elite, Celebrity, Personalisation, Conflict, Unexpectedness, Drama, Sensationalism, Political, Caste, Visual impact, Hyperdetail and Exclusive	Absent, Not Sure, Mildly present and Strongly present

review and the pilot study. Nature of physical assault, Region of the crime, State where the crime occurred and Location of the crime were also identified as factors that could possibly affect news prioritisation, based on literature review. Similarly, both the pilot study and past studies (Barclay, 2024) were helpful in identifying the subtopics and news values. After the identification, they were defined for the expert coders as follows:

Table 1.2 Characterisation of the accused and victims

Factor	*Categories*	*Measurement*
Victim		
Naming	Named, pseudo-named, unnamed	Nominal
Age group	Less than 10 years, 10–18 years, 19 to 30 years, above 30 years, information withheld or unavailable	Nominal
Education	Details disclosed, undisclosed, uneducated	Nominal
Profession	Details disclosed, undisclosed, unemployed	Nominal
Familial details	Disclosed, partially disclosed, undisclosed	Nominal
Marital status	Unmarried, undisclosed, married	Nominal
Social status	Well-known, not sure, unknown	Nominal
Background	Privileged, not sure, underprivileged	Nominal
Accused		
Naming	Named, pseudo-named, unnamed	Nominal
Age group	Less than 10 years, 10–18 years, 19 to 30 years, above 30 years, information withheld or unavailable	Nominal
Education	Details disclosed, undisclosed, uneducated	Nominal
Profession	Details disclosed, undisclosed, unemployed	Nominal
Familial details	Disclosed, partially disclosed, undisclosed	Nominal
Marital status	Unmarried, undisclosed, married	Nominal
Social status	Well-known, not sure, unknown	Nominal
Background	Privileged, not sure, underprivileged	Nominal
Acquaintance with the victim	Acquantained, information withheld, unacquainted	Nominal

Subtopics

Crime. News article describes sexual or allied crime

Public reaction. The news article reports a reaction to the crime

Legal action. News article reports on police action, including investigation and arrest

Judicial action. Refers to court proceedings or judicial comment

Government action. Refers to government action

Institutional action. Reports about established bodies, such as the commissions for women and STs

Activism. Reports actions of student bodies or civil society groups, such as protests or calls for justice

Political statement. Includes comments of political parties or leaders

Punishment. Discusses the punishment for the perpetrators of the crime

News values

Progression. Timely and developing news: Current news event that has just happened with imminent implications, unfolding or ongoing

Threshold. News exhibits superlativeness (large scope or scale of an event or issue) and impact (high significance of an event or issue in terms of its effects or consequences)

The power elite. Involves influential individuals, institutions, organisations and corporations

Celebrity. Involves an already famous person
Personalisation. News event is contextualised in personal terms, with a human-interest angle
Conflict. News is about conflicts and conflicting ideas
Unexpectedness. The news event reported is extraordinary, unexpected, rare, odd, shocking, extreme, severe or gruesome
Drama. The news story has an element of drama, such as escapes, accidents, searches, sieges, rescues, battles or court cases
Sensationalism. Is exposive, exaggerating, evaluative, extolling, schismatic, generalising, dehumanising or demonising
Political. Reports a political angle
Caste. Reports a caste angle
Visual impact. Features dramatic, emotive, explicit, gory or impactful imagery
Hyperdetail. News stories with micro details
Exclusive. Branded as a special or exclusive story

Factors related to the characterisation of the accused and victims, as presented in the news story analysed were identified and categorised as presented in Table 1.2.

Analysing the front pages from 213 days, as many as 116 news articles were found to be on the topic of sexual violence against women. A descriptive analysis is performed on the variables to understand the news trends and identify the editorial patterns. In essence, this analysis aims to understand how news on sexual violence against women was covered and presented on the front pages of the chosen newspaper. Table 1.3 presents the period-wise prevalence of news articles on sexual crimes against women on the front pages.

Analysis indicates that July (23) and August (21) were the months during which the frequency of articles on sexual violence against women was high, courtesy of the case of sexual violence reported against the backdrop of ethnic conflict from Manipur. During November and December, 8 to 10 stories were featured on the front pages, most of which were single-column stories or brief news. Even in July, on only three days, the lead story was about sexual violence against women, same as in June. In August, sexual crime occupied the prime slot twice.

Given the frequency of sexual crimes, including rape and gangrape, in India, the low prevalence of articles related to them on the front pages indicates desensitisation. Rape, gangrape and disrobing were found to be the most-featured sexual crime against women. Of the 28 cases of gangrape featured on the front pages, in nine cases, the victims were murdered, while of the 37 rape cases, in 11 cases, the victims were murdered and in nine, they were severely injured.

Statistical tests were also performed to identify the relationships among the sexual and allied crimes featured on the front pages and the results are presented in Table 1.4.

The cases of gangrapes presented on the front pages during the study period were mostly related to the Manipur incident that also included other sexual crimes such as disrobing and causing public humiliation and mob sexual assault and allied crimes such as extortion, verbal abuse and destruction of property.

On the front pages, the rape cases reported also included crimes such as blackmail and physical assault. Illegal detention, extortion, acid attack, verbal abuse and robbery

Table 1.3 Period-wise prevalences of sexual crime

Period	*1*	*2*	*3*	*4*	*5*	*6*	*7*	*Total*
Months	*June*	*July*	*Aug*	*Sept*	*Oct*	*Nov*	*Dec*	*June to Dec*
Pages analysed	35	45	48	49	42	47	41	307
Articles on sexual crimes against women identified	19	23	21	19	16	8	10	116
Average position	5.58	5.43	6.19	7.89	7.63	8.75	7	6.66
Average column	1.84	1.91	1.76	1.21	1.31	1	1.90	1.61
Average priority	27.74	29	25.95	14.16	16.75	10.25	24.20	22.41
Sexual crime								
Gangarape	1	10	10	5	1	0	1	28
Rape	0	4	10	4	4	7	8	37
Molestation	7	3	1	4	4	2	1	22
Sexual harassment at workplace	12	1	2	4	3	0	1	23
Disrobing	1	15	4	4	1	2	3	30
Stalking	2	0	0	0	3	0	2	7
Cybercrime	0	1	0	1	1	0	0	3
Recording of the crime	0	8	5	3	1	1	1	19
Transmission of the record	0	7	5	2	1	0	0	15
Partner violence	0	1	0	0	0	2	1	4
Disrobing and causing public humiliation	0	13	4	2	0	0	0	19
Mob sexual assault	0	12	6	0	0	0	0	18
Flashing	0	0	0	0	1	0	0	1
Sexual remarks or gesture	0	0	0	0	1	0	0	1

were found to be associated with molestation and sexual harassment at the workplace. While the sexual crime of disrobing was predominantly reported in the Manipur case, a case of mob violence in which the women were publicly humiliated and their ordeal was video recorded and transmitted online, allied crimes that were found to be co-occurring with such crimes in the front-page news stories were illegal detention, torture, extortion, acid attack, blackmail and destruction of property. Cybercrime was found to be associated with the recording of the crime, the transmission of the record and partner violence—which was associated with threatening and blackmail.

To understand the prevalence and patterns of the news values identified in the news articles on sexual violence against women published on the front pages, a factor analysis was performed and the results are presented in Table 1.5.

An examination of the Kaiser–Meyer–Olkin measure of sampling adequacy suggested that the sample was factorable (KMO = 0.734) and Bartlett's test of sphericity was significant ($\chi 2 = 378.981, p < .0005$). For this extraction, principal component analysis was employed, along with Varimax rotation with Kaiser normalisation (rotation was reported to have converged in six iterations). Three components were identified and their Eigenvalues were 3.101, 2.529 and 1.054. Thus, three patterns of news values were identified within the published top news stories.

In the first pattern of news stories identified that was prioritised the most on the front pages, sexual violence was politicised and conflicts were highlighted in

Table 1.4 Associations among the crimes

Sexual crime	*Associated sexual crime*	*Allied crime*
Gangrape	Disrobing and causing public humiliation, mob sexual assault	Extortion, Verbal abuse, Destruction of property.
Rape		Blackmail, Physical assault.
Molestation	Sexual harassment at the workplace	Illegal detention, Extortion, Acid attack, Verbal abuse, Robbery.
Disrobing	Recording of the crime, Transmission of the record, Disrobing and causing public humiliation, Mob sexual assault	Illegal detention, Torture, Extortion, Acid attack, Blackmail, Destruction of property
Stalking		
Cybercrime	Recording of the crime, Transmission of the record, Partner violence	
Recording of the crime	Disrobing, Cybercrime, Transmission of the record, Disrobing and causing public humiliation, Mob sexual assault	
Transmission of the record	Disrobing, Cybercrime, Recording of the crime, Disrobing and causing public humiliation, Mob sexual assault	
Partner violence	Cybercrime	Blackmail, Threatening
Disrobing and causing public humiliation	Gangrape, Disrobing, Recording of crime, Mob sexual assault	Destruction of property
Mob sexual assault	Gangrape, Disrobing, Recording of the crime, Transmission of the record, Disrobing and causing public humiliation	Verbal abuse, Destruction of property
Flashing	Sexual Remarks or gesture	

Table 1.5 Patterns of prevalences of news values

News values	*Pattern 1*	*Pattern 2*	*Pattern 3*
Progression			0.739
Threshold			0.773
The power elite	0.768		
Celebrity	0.716		
Personalisation		0.491	0.490
Conflict	0.718		
Unexpectedness		0.646	0.407
Drama		0.578	0.482
Sensationalism		0.725	
Political	0.861		
Hyperdetail		0.722	
Priority	**0.457**[**]	**0.234**[*]	**0.283**[**]

** Correlation is significant at the 0.01 level (2-tailed).
* Correlation is significant at the 0.05 level (2-tailed).

the news stories that also involved the power elite or celebrities. Another pattern featured dramatised human-interest stories that highlighted the unusualness of the events and were hyperdetailed. A third pattern of news articles on sexual violence that were prioritised on the front pages was majorly timely and developing stories that exhibited enormity. Those within this pattern were also personalised stories that were high on drama and presented as extraordinary news events.

Potential variables were related to position, column and priority to identify editorial priorities and the results are presented in Table 1.6.

Table 1.6 Editorial top priorities

Factor	*Frequency*	*Position*	*Column*	*Priority*
Gangrape	28	5.18	1.86	28.64
Rape	37	7.84	1.51	18.76
Molestation	22	7.05	1.77	25.50
Sexual harassment at workplace	23	5.65	1.65	24.52
Disrobing	30	4.97	2.17	33.70
Stalking	7	6	1.71	24.86
Cybercrime	3	10.67	1.67	19.67
Recording of the crime	19	4.47	2.21	35.42
Transmission of the record	15	4.13	2.40	39.13
Partner violence	4	11.75	1	7.25
... causing public humiliation	19	3.16	2.53	42.11
Mob sexual assault	18	3.22	2.50	41.67
Death	21	6.05	1.71	24.71
Subtopics				
Crime	109	6.80	1.61	22.34
Public reaction	13	4.92	2.08	32.85
Legal action	74	6.36	1.66	23.78
Judicial action	40	5.88	1.78	25.93
Government action	23	3	2.48	41.04
Institutional action	11	4.18	1.91	29.64
Activism	11	3.91	2.55	41.64
Political statement	16	3.38	2.75	44.38
Punishment	16	6.25	1.81	25.38
Extrajudicial action	7	3.57	2.43	40.86
Victim				
Named	5	4.60	2	31.60
19-30 years of age	18	8.17	1.72	22.78
Professional details divulged	19	5.74	1.79	26.68
Familial details divulged	8	3.13	2.63	44.38
Well-known	2	4	2	31
Underprivileged	11	6.55	1.36	18.72
Accused				
Named	37	6.05	1.84	26.38
Above 30 years of age	14	7.50	2	28
19 to 30 years of age	10	9.80	1.20	12.20
Well-known	21	4.52	1.86	28.14
Privileged	33	6.03	1.61	23.27
Acquainted with the victim	38	6.76	1.63	22.58

Among the sexual crimes reported, gangrape, disrobing, recording of the crime and transmission of the record were prioritised in the news reports. Of them, disrobing and causing public humiliation and mob sexual assault were highlighted the most.

Further, the analysis also revealed that the front pages prioritised stories that had a political angle to them, featured activism and focussed on public reaction, government and extrajudicial action as a response to the crime. Subtopics such as legal action, crime and punishment, though widely prevalent, were not the ones that were prioritised when such news became the leads. To test if the information (or the characterisation) of the victim and the accused as printed on the front pages were associated with prioritisation, a test was conducted and the study results indicated that the stories that had named the victims divulged their familial details or that had well-known personalities as the victims were prioritised more, while news that had underprivileged victims were largely single-column stories or brief news. On the other hand, the stories were multi-columned when the accused were named, above 30 years of age and well-known. Stories that had accused belonging to the age group of 19 to 30 years or who were acquainted with the victim were relatively downplayed.

When it came to the form of the stories, of the 116 analysed, 17 featured a subhead, 22 came with kickers, indicating branding of the news, 12 with photographs (in most cases, small ones, as the front pages were mostly halved with advertisements), 8 with infographics and 19 with quotes highlighted. Of the 116 analysed, a majority of the news articles were about crimes reported in New Delhi (28), Madhya Pradesh (five), Maharashtra (nine), Manipur (16), Rajasthan (13), Uttar Pradesh (20) and West Bengal (four).

Several crimes, including abduction, illegal detention, torture, extortion, threatening and blackmail, were found to accompany sexual violence against women.

Study findings that gangrape, disrobing in public, recording of the event and online transmission are prioritised on the front pages are in line with observations in past studies that severe forms of corporeal violence inflicted on female autonomy receive sensationalist media treatment (Fadnis, 2017; Sreedharan & Thorsen, 2021). As scholars have observed, the gendered structure (van Zoonen, 1994) of news production plays a role in providing "wilful neglect" to certain stories of sexual crime that do not "fit" the news agenda (Skidmore, 1998, p. 215). Aroustamian (2020) stated that media frames of sexual violence can influence public perceptions. Hence, these findings acquire significance as they help in understanding the editorial reporting pattern and news prioritisation with regard to sexual violence against women on the front pages of a popular Indian newspaper.

Study results also indicated that politicisation, conflict, involvement of the power elite or celebrities, over-detailing, dramatisation and human-interest influenced prioritisation and placement. Reflecting the observations of Serisier (2017) that media often covers sex crimes (rape and child abuse) with a distorted image of reality, focusing more on violent crimes committed by strangers, the poor or men of colour, this investigation also pointed to a preference for the privileged and certain age groups of the victims and accused.

In summary, violent-timely news stories that exhibit the enormity and extremity of the sexual crimes that have also caused public humiliation for the victims and drawn political and public reaction are the ones that are prioritised and garner prime space on the front pages.

References

Ahmad, A. (2019). Coverage of issues related to sexual violence: Comparative study of The Indian Express and The Times of India. *Asian Review of Social Sciences*, *8*(3), 42–46.

Aroustamian, C. (2020). Time's up: Recognising sexual violence as a public policy issue: A qualitative content analysis of sexual violence cases and the media. *Aggression and Violent Behavior*, *50*, 101341. https://doi.org/10.1016/j.avb.2019.101341

Barclay, F. P. (2024). What makes top stories: Rethinking news values in digital space. In: Dahiya, S. and Trehan, K. (Eds.), *Handbook of digital journalism: Perspectives from South Asia*. Springer, Singapore. https://doi.org/10.1007/978-981-99-6675-2_16.

Drache, D., & Velagic, J. (2014). Sexual violence journalism in four leading English language Indian publications before and after the Delhi rape. *Journal of Research in Gender Studies*, *4*(2), 11.

Fadnis, D. (2017). Uncovering rape culture: Patriarchal values guide Indian media's rape-related reporting. *Journalism Studies*, *19*(12), 1750–1766. https://doi.org/10.1080/1461670X.2017.1301781

Galtung, J., & Ruge, M. (1965). The structure of foreign news: The presentation of the Congo, Cuba and Cyprus crises in four Norwegian newspapers. *Journal of International Peace Research*, *2*, 64–90.

Gangopadhyay, S., Bandopadhyay, S., & Chatterjee, A. (2012). Depiction of violence against women in leading English newspapers of India: A study. *Mass Communicator: International Journal of Communication Studies*, *6*(1), 13–24.

Jolly, J. (2016, July 20). *Rape in India: Is the English-language press falling back on stereotypes?* Columbia Journalism Review. https://www.cjr.org/analysis/india_rape_journalism.php

Joy, J. (2022). Print media reports of sexual violence against women: A qualitative study. *International Journal of Indian Psychology*, *10*(2), 694–703.

Kundu, P. B. T. (2018, April 24). 99% cases of sexual assaults go unreported, govt data shows | *Mint*. Mint. https://www.livemint.com/Politics/AV3sIKoEBAGZozALMX8THK/99-cases-of-sexual-assaults-go-unreported-govt-data-shows.html

Langston, A. (2016, August 15). Sexual violence in India's headlines | Harvard Magazine. *Harvard Magazine*. https://www.harvardmagazine.com/2016/08/sexual-violence-in-india-headlines

NCRB. (2022). *Crime in India 2022 – Statistics* Vol 1. National Crime Records Bureau of India-Ministry of Home Affairs.

NCRB (2021). *Crime in India 2021: Statistics* Vol 1. National Crime Records Bureau of India-Ministry of Home Affairs. Retrieved May16, 2023, from https://ncrb.gov.in/sites/default/files/CII-2021/CII_2021Volume%201.pdf

Serisier, T. (2017). *Sex crimes and the media*. Oxford Research Encyclopedia of Criminology and Criminal Justice. https://doi.org/10.1093/acrefore/9780190264079.013.118

Sharma, N. (2023, December 4). Delhi leads in crimes against women, Rajasthan in rape cases in 2022: NCRB Report. *India Today*. https://www.indiatoday.in/law/story/delhi-leads-in-crimes-against-women-rajasthan-in-number-of-rape-cases-in-2022-ncrb-report-2471924-2023-12-04

Singh, A. (2020, October 30). *Media sensationalism and mob mentality in India: Which rapes cause outrage?* Women's Media Center. Retrieved June 10, 2024, from https://womensmediacenter.com/women-under-siege/media-sensationalism-and-mob-mentality-in-india-which-rapes-cause-outrage

Singh, I. (2022). Analysis of front page rape stories in local newspapers. *Communication Today*, 26, 71–82.

Skidmore, P. (1998). Gender and the Agenda: News reporting of child sexual abuse. In: Allan, S., Branston, G., & Carter, C. (Eds.). *News, gender and power* (1st ed., pp. 204–218). Routledge.

Sreedharan, C. & Thorsen, E. (2021). *Sexual violence and the news media: Issues, challenges, and guidelines for journalists in India.* UNESCO. ISBN: 978-81-89218-78-2, Retrieved, from https://eprints.bournemouth.ac.uk/35830/7/MAAR%20REPORT%20PDF%20Online%20.pdf

van Zoonen, L. (1994). *Feminist media studies*. SAGE Publications.

2 Predatory Journalism

Conceptualisation

What is conceptualised as "Predatory Journalism" in this chapter and accounted for in the subsequent parts of this book is not a phenomenal peculiarity hot off the press, but an editorial eyesore that has dotted and daunted the history of news. Even so, what had been perceived as a perimetric problem has now become mainstream—extensively explicit and extreme—warranting a receptive nomenclature and theoretical exposition that encompass the incitements and implications of an ultraist form of journalism prominent in the present times. Where does the concept of "sensationalism" fall short in sufficiently describing the destructive form of journalism perceptible in a section of the news media at a time when online social media hold sway? How can Predatory Journalism be conceptualised when the audience is overwhelmed with apparently unlimited news mediums and sources? What are the needs for such a conceptualisation? This chapter attempts to answer these critical and timely questions with a conceptual review of existing terms and a succinct spotlight on contemporary editorial eccentricities and anomalies.

Tracing the historical roots of unethical reporting, in the nineteenth century, penny papers (such as the *New York Sun* and *Herald*) were criticised for embracing a form of "sensational" and "aggressive" journalism, publishing "flippant" and "trivial" content to widen readership (Emery, 1962; Nordin, 1979; Udeze & Uzuegbunam, 2013; Sachsman & Bulla, 2017). Yet another prime time in the history of sensationalism that blurred the line between tabloid and traditional journalism was the era of yellow journalism (Jackson, 2005).

On the reemergence of unethical journalism, Udeze and Uzuegbunam (2013) write:

> Sensationalism epitomized by yellow journalism has been an issue of concern since the 20th century. It was during this period that the call for a socially responsible media became intense because the press was seen to be perpetuating a culture of irresponsibility in the face of the freedom they enjoyed when the libertarian philosophy of the press held sway. Yet, a century later, the media is seen to be reverting back to the same unacceptable, unethical practices.
>
> (Udeze & Uzuegbunam, 2013, p. 69)

Conceptually a close relative of Predatory Journalism, sensationalism was initially suspected to have seeped from tabloid into traditional journalism. More

DOI: 10.4324/9781003468042-4

recently, in the Indian subcontinent, when loud-shallow debates hogged the prime time of round-the-clock television reporting and promptitude became the hallmark of online journalism, traditional newspapers had to adapt and adopt, enduring the effects of inter-media agenda setting.

Reckless reporting in vogue in the present times is even discharged as "market-driven" journalism (Udeze & Uzuegbunam, 2013) based on search trends, website analytics and social-media feedback, sidelining value-based ethical news prioritisation—prompting the need to uncover the preying posture of rapacious reporting and brand it, critically.

Journalism has traditionally been viewed as a cultured and cultivated profession, tasked with the critical commitment of informing the public—prioritising people's needs and shining a light on the powerful, holding them accountable for their actions. In recent times, however, there has been a growing disturbing trend of Predatory Journalism and allied criticism. Predatory Journalism stands in stark contrast to responsible and ethical reporting, as it is exploitative and prioritises sensationalism over accuracy and integrity. In India, too, this phenomenon has become increasingly evident and extensive, attracting widespread attention from media watchdogs and concerned citizens alike. Still, sensationalism remains an elusive and underdeveloped concept, without consensus among scholars about its definition and requiring an update now and then—thanks to the incessant advancements in the mediascape and evolutions in readership.

On this conceptual conundrum, Brown et al. (2018) write:

> Sensational stories meant to grab readers' attention are nothing new… But the definition of sensationalism has evolved over time, leaving scholars in disagreement about its actual meaning and its implications. Its association with tabloids and subjects of violence and sex often renders sensational news as separate from traditional standards of journalism. Since the age of yellow journalism (Spencer, 2007), the concept and presentation of sensationalism has evolved, and so should its evaluation in the digital realm.
>
> (Brown et al., 2018, p. 1498)

Sensationalism has understandably been placed in a bipolar continuum that ranges between unethical or unwarranted and innate or essential. On one side, news sensationalism is viewed as an "appeal to emotion and human instinct" (Slattery & Hakanen, 1994) through "dramatisation" (Wang & Cohen, 2009) and "attention-grabbing elements" (Grabe, Zhou & Barnett, 2001) to stir "unwholesome emotional responses" (Mott, 1962) and "empathy" (Graber, 1994) and evoke "curiosity" (Haskins, 1984), justifying it when the readership is declining and the news media is facing fierce challenges from other sources of information such as the social media. Sensationalism has even been listed as a news value (Harcup & O'Neill, 2017). Stephens (2007) observed that sensationalism is unavoidable in the news as "humans are wired, probably for reasons of natural selection, to be alert to sensations, particularly those involving sex and violence". On the other hand, sensationalised news is also downcried as "stupid" and "unfit" content (Bernstein, 1992; Slattery & Hakanen, 1994) that evokes "morbid" curiosity (Haskins, 1984) and hence "undesirable". Similarly, while sensationalism is found to stimulate news viewing time and an efficient strategy to sell news (Hendriks Vettehen & Kleemans, 2018), the rise of sensationalist news is also presented as an explanation for the increasing distrust and aversion among the audience across the world (Kleemans et al., 2017).

Largely, sensationalism studies have been medium-specific and examining the form factor—mostly focusing on television journalism (Brown et al., 2018).

Calling for a reevaluation of sensationalism, Brown et al. (2018) write:

> ...with so many news sites–and not just tabloids–accused of sensationalizing news, an updated assessment of sensationalism and its potential implications for defining news becomes all the more important and timely.
>
> (Brown et al., 2018, p. 1498)

Examining news in the digital space, Brown et al. (2018) associate sensationalism with certain salient news values (such as human interest, conflict, controversy and unusualness), topics (such as sex, crime and lifestyle) and audience interaction (such as likes, shares and comments), operationalising sensationalism as a "stylistic treatment" that combines category and form in a "tabloid-like way" to trigger reader emotions. Brown et al. (2018) coded news articles that "intentionally evoked emotion at the beginning of the article, used extreme circumstances to grab attention, simplified and trivialised a complex topic, promoted shock value or were presented in a tabloid-like way" as sensational in their study. Similarly, Hendriks Vettehen and Kleemans (2018), while studying video news, also defined sensationalism as "content and form features" that elicited attention and aroused responses among the viewers. Hendriks Vettehen and Kleemans (2018) focussed on two categories of sensationalist news features: Negative content (negative topics such as disasters and crime, and negative imagery such as blood and gore that usually accompany such stories) and tabloid packaging (such as layout, headline sizes and pictorial material in the case of print media and salient production features such as multiple camera shots, sound effects and decorative editing for video news), citing several studies. Udeze and Uzuegbunam (2013) viewed sensationalism as a discursive practice, situating it within the theoretical frameworks of media framing and constructivism.

Grundlingh (2017, p. 117) noted that journalists often manoeuvre evident and subtle ways to expand the "entertainment value of a specific event or crime in order to grab and keep the attention of the readers". In this process, they heavily rely on sensationalism to influence the reader's opinion on the crime committed and the people involved in it. While objectivity that separates facts from fiction, balance and fairness are considered primary to news reporting (Maras, 2013, p. 8), Grundlingh (2017, p. 120) noted that there may be an intentional or unintentional reflection of the subjective "emotions" of the journalist in news reports, but evaluation of the degree of manipulation of the readers in the news reports was worth investigation. The "entertainment value" that Grundlingh (2017, p. 122) identified within sensationalist news reports borrowed from the Appraisal Theory.

This theory is concerned with attitudes and emotions expressed within the text that can elicit engagement, appreciation and judgement (Martin & Rose, 2003; Martin

& White, 2005). Observing that sensationalism has been a widely popular topic of "fiery discussions for centuries", Grabe, Zhou and Barnett (2001) pointed out that even scholars have failed to deal with the concept with precision. On this, they write:

> ...it appears that this topic is more often debated than systematically investigated. Indeed, the word, sensationalism, has become an easy name-calling device for those who are in the mood for criticising the mass media.
>
> (Grabe et al., 2001, p. 635)

Focusing on television news, Grabe et al. (2001) attempted to offer insights into the dimensions of sensationalism, examining their content and form.

Hendriks Vettehen (2015, p. 2) identified sensationalism as "a journalistic device" applied to grab mass attention and an "appropriate response to the evolutionarily developed human habit of attending to information that increases the chances of survival and reproduction".

Hendriks Vettehen (2015, p. 1) drew upon the psychological theories of information processing to explain sensationalist features, segregated as "arousing content, tabloid packaging and vivid storytelling". Hendriks Vettehen (2015) noted that the market-driven media industry was encashing on the basic human instinct such as the interest in stories about sex, violence, criminality, disasters or famines. Exemplifications in storytelling, using varied camera angles, swift transitions between camera shots, insertion of music, extraordinary font style and size usage in headlines and choice of brief comments from laypersons were identified as common features of sensationalism (Hendriks Vettehen, 2015).

Given the available advanced technological features and avenues for the presentation and dissemination of sensational news stories, exemplification has become a common trait to draw readers. Chermak (1994) posited that crime reports with a vivid description of crime popularised the news. Chermak (1994) further argued that news media select and produce stories keeping the basic human interest in focus. Chermak (1994, p. 570) stated:

> not all homicides are important news, and some never become stories because the news media recognize that not all have entertainment value... Bullets flying, police shooting, repeated incidents, twisted, weird. It's news. It's what people want to hear.

It is argued that a section of news organisations, to sensationalise and sell, presents gory details of crime in news stories (Chibnall, 1977; Grabosky & Wilson, 1989). Crime reportage has been resorting to sensationalism with vivid descriptions of "murder scenes, body bags, ambulances or grieving victims" (Chermak, 1994, p. 573).

Several recent studies have also examined allied issues such as politicisation (Van Scoy et al., 2021), misrepresentation and harmful recommendations (Dempster, Sutherland & Keogh, 2022), stigmatisation (Jones, Woods & Usher, 2020), victimisation (Wong & Harraway, 2020) and privacy (Bezanson, 1992; Smolla, 1999).

Reviewing and summarising past studies, sensationalism is largely viewed as a stylistic concept (paying attention to the form factor) in over-hyped and trivialised news content that is meant to grab the attention of the audience. While several studies have associated sensationalism with certain topics (such as crime and sex) and media (such as tabloids, television and websites), sensationalism is now found to pervade all forms of media and beats.

Paradoxically, sensationalism is both seen as an efficient selling strategy and the reason for distrust in journalism. There are also mixed opinions about it, with a section deeming it unwarranted. It is also evident that sensationalism, with a limited scope, fails to adequately describe the unethical trend of popular journalism in contemporary times, as it fails to look beyond topics and form to consider several other issues, such as privacy invasion and information distortion. It also fails to conduct an in-depth exploration into the exploitation of the actors involved in the news story and the audience—and its broader implications.

Predatory practices in India: A spotlight

In a 2020 commentary on "Backstory: Everything Wrong With the Media is Reflected in the Sushant Singh Rajput Coverage", *The Wire's* public editor Pamela Philipose outlined the discomforting aspects of contemporary journalism in India:

> Let me try and list them: hyper-personalisation; loud, sensationalism; rupturing the private-public separation with voyeuristic intent; the thrill of the chase to the extent that it becomes blood sport; the gossipy edge stained by deep shades of misogyny; the close nexus with powerful interests looking to influence content; the daily churning out of heroes and villains; the intense competition for circulation with rivals; the constant feeding of the insatiable appetite of readers for more; and, yes, the dressing up of fake content to make it appear authentic.
> (Philipose, 2020, September 12)

In the event of the death of Sushant Singh Rajput in 2020, several Indian news channels were accused of sensationalising the Bollywood actor's death, conducting parallel trials and promoting conspiracy theories without proper evidence (Scroll Staff, 2020, August 28). This led to public outrage and calls for media accountability, with several news channels facing legal action and criticism from industry bodies (PTI, 2020, September 15).

In a 2021 commentary on "What to Mourn More: Sushant's Death or Media's Depravity?", Ruben Banerjee lamented the media:

> Today, June 14, will mark a year of talented Bollywood actor Sushant Singh Rajput's death. The day will also mark the beginning of a media witch-hunt that began around the same time last year, sweeping up the nation on a voyeuristic ride cleverly disguised as a campaign for justice. That it scorched the life of a young lady in the process was only a small price to pay… Rhea Chakraborty became the victim of a media trial soon after Sushant's death last year. The lack of options for reining in a reckless media is the reason why she won't be the last.
> (Banerjee, 2021, July 12)

Banerjee (2021) terms the avid media coverage of the actor's death as a "*tamasha*" (joke or a nonsensical fuss) eyeing "TRP and better sales". On the media trial and victimisation of Sushant's girlfriend, Rhea Chakraborty, Banerjee further commented:

> Packaged and successfully sold as a campaign to secure justice for SSR, it zeroed in on Sushant's girlfriend, Rhea Chakraborty, as the prime suspect. Dubbed differently by disparate sections—from a gold digger to a drug peddler—she was doomed. Millions of Indians have been fed to believe that she is [the] devil incarnate. Besides being deprived of all dignity, I believe the media trial has robbed Rhea the prospect of public safety. Enough people have been brainwashed against her, and I do not believe she can venture out freely anymore without courting physical risks. I am ashamed that the profession that I belong to has brought things to such a pass.
>
> (Banerjee, 2021, July 12)

Banerjee was not alone in their criticism of the news media in this case. A string of media reports also deplored the trend of sensational media images and headlines (Singh, 2020) and irresponsible reporting (Chowdhury, 2020, June 14)—while some news reports outlined the method of Sushant's suicide, a few others published images of the actor lying dead in his bed. Rhea had to move the apex court to save her privacy from the media (Prakash, 2020, August 10).

Discussing the "slow death" of Indian journalism and offering a "wake-up call", Shetty (2015), in a media critique, commented:

> Today, the fundamental definition of journalism is under attack… [journalists] turn hunches into facts, gossip into evidence, and falsehoods into breaking news. We can all agree that nothing—nothing—is more important to a democracy than a well-informed electorate. But sadly, the agents of this information are today the creators of a polarisation that is slowly corrupting public opinion in our country. 'Journalists' are mocking the meaning of evidence, and major news outlets are making soap operas of news stories. Furthermore, opinionated anchors, selective coverage, and ideological loyalties are hurting the fundamental rule of journalism—to provide all the news to all the people with no distortion… the quality of coverage by our media is deteriorating to such an extent that (ironically) on World Press Freedom Day #GoHomeIndianMedia was trending on Twitter thanks to the dramatised coverage of the Nepal earthquake last month by our news channels. Journalists are today ridiculed as 'presstitutes'.
>
> (Shetty, 2015)

In a media commentary on "Distortions in news broadcasting", Bansal (2014, January 3) discussed the challenges facing India's news broadcasting industry, including financial vulnerability, the use of "Jimmy Jib journalism" to create sensationalised images, poor editorial quality and corporate ownership of media.

The author argued that these threats were jeopardising the credibility and quality of news reporting in India. Several other articles have also discussed the consequences of media distortions and the exaggeration of negative news (Khaliq, 2018, July 22; Pinker, 2018, February 19; ANI, 2022, September 29).

Sensationalised reporting is designed to attract readers or viewers at any cost and may rely on suggestive or biassed language to create a specific narrative or viewpoint. Several studies have critiqued generic sensationalism in Indian news media (Jaggi & Majumdar, 2009; Ghosh, 2014; Jain & Kumar, 2016; Aravindh, 2018), particularly while reporting incidents such as the Delhi gangrape (Rao, 2014; Thomas, 2018) and other sexual crimes (Sreedharan, Thorsen & Singh, 2020).

There have also been instances where a section of the Indian mainstream news media has been found to report distorted or fake news (2017's Top Fake News Stories Circulated by the Indian Media, Jawed, 2018, January 3). Regrettably, sensationalism has become the new(s) normal for a section of the Indian media landscape, with journalists often prioritising the presentation of news in an interesting or attention-grabbing way.

Conceptualising Predatory Journalism

In this book, Predatory Journalism is conceptualised as a discursive evolution and practice, accommodating sociological and psychological theories. In generic terms, it can refer to an aggregation of unethical practices that primarily aim to sell news content—sidelining other journalistic purposes such as the sharing of legitimate and useful information—often involving the exploitation of readers. But to deepen understanding and define Predatory Journalism in the context of reporting sexual crimes against women in India, we borrow from the theory of pragmatics and identify several key issues and dimensions that could be associated with such an unethical practice. Predatory Journalism is thus posited as a (generative, thematic or episodic) demand-driven news discourse that is insensitive (unempathetic) and stimulating (evoking emotive and erotic responses using over-descriptive text and explicit imagery) while prioritising certain topics with regional and other biases (selective exposure), using popular tropes (frames and devices) and presenting problematic illocutions (sensationalist, sexist, sexual and sectionalist) with dissonant composition (information and sources) from a discordant locus (obtrusive or obscure)—conclusively exhibiting a tendency of exploiting the actors involved in the story and the audience for sustenance (prompting reading [or viewing] and reaction). Predatory Journalism, as conceptualised, is presented in Figure 2.1.

Viewing Predatory Journalism as a multidisciplinary concept, we situate its schema at the intersection of pragmalinguistics and critical discourse, and thus, a preliminary framework is offered to study and position the vulturous trend in vogue in contemporary journalism, practised in a section of the media and confounding the profession of journalism in its entirety. Though discourse analysis is fairly frequent in media studies, pragmalinguistics is rare as a methodological approach while critically examining news discourse, even while media scholarship primarily aims to offer a socio-political and cultural criticism of factors that influence

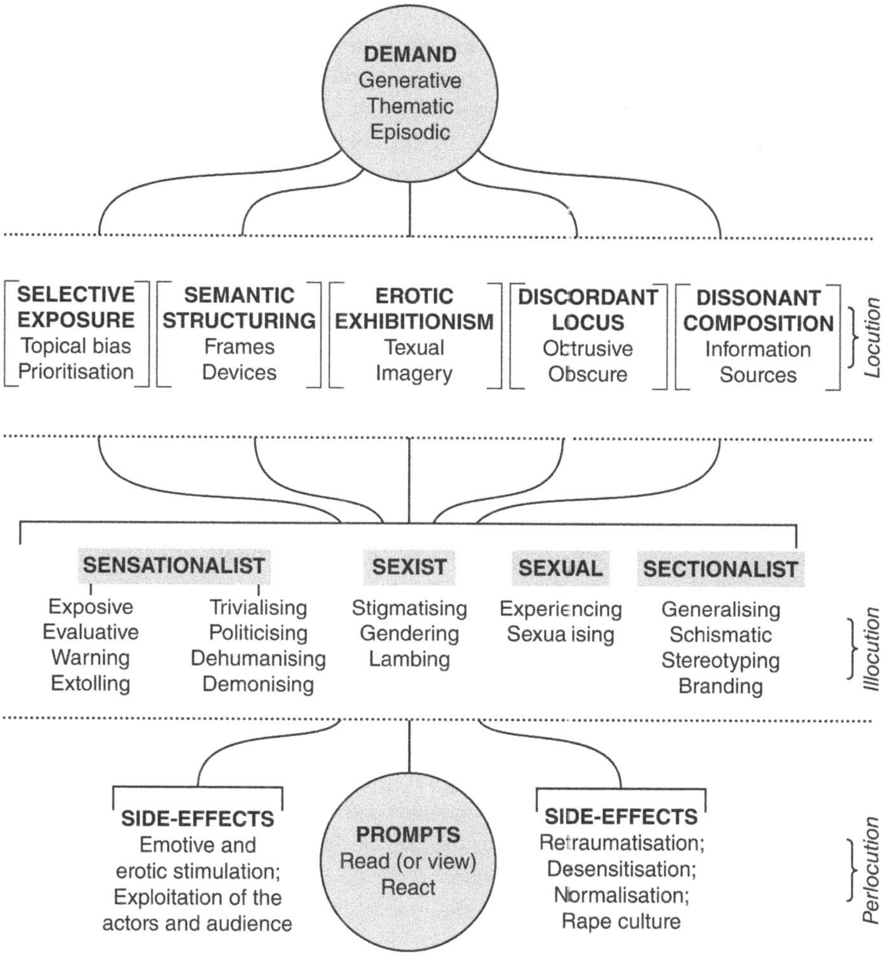

Figure 2.1 Predatory Journalism: A model

news production (Molek-Kozakowska, 2013). Molek-Kozakowska (2013, p. 177) observed that "some texts are powerful enough to attract and keep readers' attention, even to make them react in similar ways despite socio-cultural diversities... with textual patterns and pragmalinguistic devices that tend to prescribe certain cognitive responses, notably collecting attention". Mey (1979, p. 11), while explaining pragmalinguistics, noted that "the conditions for speaking and understanding, for 'production' and 'consumption' of language, cannot be divorced from the conditions of production and consumption in the society in general". Consequently, Bang and Door (2017, p. 23) related "use of language" with the "user" where the "actors performing speech acts are not just actors" but follow the "rules determined by the stage. The stage is conditioned by the specific politico-economic organisation of society".

Particularly, this chapter borrows the concepts of discourse (locutionary, illocutionary and perlocutionary) acts from the pragmalinguistic theory to conceptualise Predatory Journalism. Further, the critical perspective aims to expand the understanding of communication, analysing ideological biases and socio-political power plays that influence news production. In the context of reporting sexual crimes against women in India, the ideological biases underlying news text could perhaps be sexism and voyeurism. Media could also be exhibiting its power and authority as an independent and self-regulated social entity, overstepping its roles and responsibilities while reporting such crimes through sensationalism, baseless speculation, parallel investigation and media trial—which a critical exploration could expose.

Locutionary issues

In the conceptualisation of Predatory Journalism, *Locus* alludes to the distance from where (or the position from which) information is gathered for news stories. Locus could be problematic when the point of reporting becomes uncomfortably close (*obtrusive*)—perhaps, invading privacy—or when it is distant or isolated (*obscure,* as in the case of armchair reporting)—lacking an understanding of ground realities and event entanglements. To draw readers or viewers, often invasive journalism is employed—especially in the context of reporting sexual crimes against women—for exclusive and emotional content. If the story involves a celebrity, the level of privacy invasion becomes even more alarming with interviews of victims and their families.

A handful of studies have discussed privacy and its relationship to newsgathering (Bezanson, 1992; Smolla, 1999). Several recent cases, such as the sudden demise of young Indian actors Sushant Singh Rajput and Siddharth Shukla, witnessed obtrusive reporting, with the media channels surrounding the cremation ground and reporters even climbing walls for footage of the funeral pyre. Similarly, their friends and family members were hounded for emotional breakdowns. Predatory journalists published speculations on the mental health of the late Sushant Singh Rajput, interviewing the mental health practitioner whom he was consulting (Mantri, 2020). Unconfirmed, confidential and private details of the late actor's diagnosis and treatment were also published. Live and instant reports were published on the funeral and cremation of the actor, covering the visits of his friends and other celebrities who paid their last respects to the deceased, their attire and their emotional state of mind. Some of these privacy violations and hypercoverages were gendered: Rhea Chakraborty, in the case of Rajput's death, and Shahnaz Gill, for Shukla, were turned into the archetype of the vamp and the virtuous by predatory journalists. The privacy of the victims and their kin gets subdued under the right to gather news. In the case of victims of sexual crimes or those who are grieving, predatory journalists may exploit their vulnerability and pressurise them to share details that they may not be comfortable doing. Journalists might also publish identifying details about the victim, such as her name or location, without proper consent, which can compromise her safety.

Conducting a historical analysis, Kitzinger (2004) explains how sexual violence makes "good copy" and evidently becomes "perfect fodder" for the media outlets in "hot competition". Take, for instance, the Muzaffarpur shelter home sex abuse case (Singh, 2018, August 6; India Today Web Desk, 2018, August 6), where the Indian apex court—to draw an ethical *Laxman-Rekhaa* (line) for predatory journalists—had to warn against interviewing minor victims of sexual abuse, stating that it has a "serious mental impact" and issue guidelines for print, electronic and social media, against publishing pictures of sexual abuse victims, even if they are blurred or morphed (Press Trust of India, 2018, August 7). The Supreme Court of India also noted that the "victims of child sex abuse could only be interviewed by members of the National Commission for Protection of Child Rights (NCPCR) and State Commissions for Protection of Child Rights in the presence of counsellors" (Press Trust of India, 2018, August 7).

Apart from invasive reporting, predatory journalists also engage in armchair reporting or recycling content. Davies (2008, p. 62) stated that "greater numbers at greater speed and of much worse quality" are the result of recycling or *churnalism* of news in digital media. This practice makes *churnalism* deskbound without any possibilities of field investigations, fact-checking and verification of sources (Davies, 2008). Johnston and Forde (2017, p. 943) suggested that the internet had catapulted the "recycling and repurposing of news like never before" for digital platforms through "aggregation of information", often referred to as *churnalism*. Erroneous reports are constructed based on imagined conspiracy theories, or recycling of unverified claims and sources. To present the inside story as amazing and at great speed, predatory journalists end up recycling news, adding a new angle to the story. Within the context of reporting sexual crimes against women in India, the undue and extended news coverage accorded to certain popular sub-themes, crime types or tropes (*selective exposure*) has also become a locutionary issue as more critical and insightful subtopics are ignored.

Erotic Exhibitionism is another locutionary issue with *Textual* (involving over-detailed textual descriptions of the sexual crime) and *Imagery* (exhibiting actual or representational gory or explicit images) dimensions. For example, media coverage may focus excessively on the sexual aspect of the incident without considering other important factors such as consent, power dynamics and societal attitudes towards sex and sexuality. This can further stigmatise and shame the victims while reinforcing harmful stereotypes and attitudes towards sexuality. In addition, media coverage may glorify or celebrate the perpetrator of the sexual abuse or assault, which can contribute to a culture of impunity or disregard for ethical standards in journalism. Media watchers have highlighted several issues related to reporting sexual violence in the Indian media, such as the glorification of rape (TNN, 2012, October 15), inbred sexism (Bhandari, 2021), media trials and the promotion of rape culture (Lee, 2021, November 22).

In the event of covering tragedies or events where people are grieving, predatory journalists clamour for exclusive interviews with grieving family members or friends, even if they are not ready or willing to speak to the media. In some cases, insensitive journalists might also use manipulative tactics to elicit emotional outbursts from their subjects, which can be exploitative and harmful. Just a day after the 2019 Pulwama attack that killed about 40 Indian paramilitary soldiers, there was a slew of media reports based on interviews of family members of the victims and political outrage, embracing nationalistic rhetoric and fuelling war hysteria ("Punjab father loses only son in Pulwama attack" [Singh, 2019, February 15]; "Pulwama attack: Mandya jawan was keen to serve nation" [Kaggere, 2019, February 15]; "CRPF jawan spent five days with family, slain on return" [Press Trust of India, 2019a, February 15]; "Pulwama terror attack: Kangra braveheart leaves behind a 22-day-old son" [Thakur, 2019, February 15]; "Proud of my father, says killed CRPF soldier's daughter" [Mohanty, 2019, February 15]; "Brother of CRPF jawan killed in Pulwama attack recalls last conversation" [Press Trust of India, 2019b, February 15]; "Pulwama terror attack: He said he'll call in evening, but call was about his death" [Sharma, 2019, February 15]; "BJP tells MPs not to speak on Pulwama attack, but calls for 'vengeance' ring loud" [Kaushika, 2019, February 15]; "Pulwama attack: Ravish Kumar wants restraint, Aaj Tak wants badla, others bay for blood" [Choudhary, Sirur & Bajpai, 2019, February 15]). Gory images and videos circulated on online social media—mostly fake—and war-mongering headlines led to a nationwide emotional outpouring and brought the nuclear-armed neighbours (India and Pakistan) to the brink of a major war.

Dissonant Composition is another locutionary issue, where information-related problems (publishing digested [borrowed], deficient [malinformed], distorted [misinformed] and devised [fabricated] information) and source-related issues are highlighted. Predatory news reports can be segregated into four categories based on the kinds of sources referred to: *Devoid* (without sources), *Discordant* (inappropriate sources), *Delusive* (fake sources) and *Resourced* (using indirect sources). News *devoid* of sources is primarily based on the reporter's ideological biases and hunches or cooked-up stories that are not substantiated by reliable sources. Lecheler and Kruikemeier (2015) state that journalists resort to using online news sourcing in their everyday production process and struggle with verification. *Discordant* stories rely on unverified or inappropriate sources. In the coverage of Sushant Singh Rajput's suicide, sources such as mental health practitioners, Sushant's cook, his house help and social media posts were extensively used to spin special stories and fan conspiracy theories. Stories with *delusive* sources, on the other hand, use fabricated sources. With the speed of the internet, such stories get spun into exclusive and explosive narrations of an incident to titillate the target audience.

Lecheler and Kruikemeier (2015, p. 164) stated that "unsurprisingly, journalists often use search engines and online encyclopaedias such as Wikipedia to find online sources and information". Scholars such as Lih (2004), Messner and Distaso (2008) and Messner and South (2011) point out that most journalists treat Wikipedia and Google as accurate and credible sources of information, disregarding verification. Broersma and Graham (2013, p. 461) observed that for sensationalised news, "tweets seem to be taken at face value", eroding news integrity and sidelining the practice of verification in journalism. Resourced sources may be used in recycled or rehashed stories on trending topics. The trend of quick reporting with misinformation and without proper sources is detrimental to journalism.

In attempts to sensationalise news stories and when recycled content is rewritten to make it seem original, the facts get distorted. It may involve exaggerating and manipulating facts to fit a particular agenda or to create a more compelling narrative. These apart, predatory journalists may selectively quote sources, take statements out of context, use misleading statistics to support their claims or present fabricated information. When journalists sensationalise stories or distort facts, they pollute news with misinformation.

According to observers, 2019 was a year marked by a surge in misinformation and fake news, driven in part by events such as the Pulwama attack and its aftermath, the Indian Parliamentary elections, the scrapping of Article 370 and the protests against the Citizenship Amendment Act. Fact-checkers were on their toes to counter this trend as predators on the prowl sought to exploit these issues for their own gains (Chaturvedi, 2019, December 20).

Al-Zaman (2021) reviewed Indian fake news articles about COVID-19 and found that online media produced more fake news than mainstream media. A majority of those fake news was found to have international connections and be negative, posing a threat to public health.

In certain cases, journalists report sexual assaults as episodic events without contextualising them and cold-shouldering critical information, to present news in a certain frame. Deliberate or unintentional, such omissions can have serious consequences, as they can mislead readers and prevent them from thoroughly understanding the situation being reported on. This is particularly problematic when the omitted context is essential for comprehending the full scope and impact of the news story. Lack of diversity in newsrooms can contribute to Predatory Journalism, as a homogenous group may be more likely to share biases. This can result in certain voices or perspectives being marginalised, which can perpetuate existing power imbalances. Several media reports and research studies have highlighted the lack of diversity in the newsrooms (Balasubramaniam, 2011; Thadani, 2020; AP, 2021, October 14).

Perhaps, the news media may also be exhibiting selection bias, according priorities to certain types of sexual crimes (such as gruesome gangrape-murders) and highlighting certain subtopics (for instance, public outrage) using sensationalist-sexist frames and devices.

Demand

Predatory Journalism is demand-driven, mostly focusing on news topics, issues and events that are trending or have the attention of the audience and also concentrates on generating new demand by introducing new styles and topics. Such demand-driven journalism could focus on creating content on a particular topic that is known to have a continuing demand (*Thematic*) or on a topic or event with a temporary and sudden rise in demand garnering the attention and curiosity of the target audience (*Episodic*).

Predatory Journalism can be fuelled by the professional pressure to produce content quickly, especially in today's 24-hour news cycle. Such stress to produce half-baked news and keep up with the competition may force reporters to cut corners or engage in unethical practices. The generative demand involves media consumers directly, as they are ideologically conditioned to desire explosive, sensationalist and thrilling news stories. Exploiting the senses of the audience, journalists could introduce topical and stylistic innovations to create new news demands. The recent deterioration of journalism could be attributed to the shift in news focus from information to entertainment. Clickbaits, misleading images or videos and inflammatory language are used to generate engagement and interest in news stories. These reports predate on emotions, desires and other such basic human instincts of the readers.

Illocutionary issues

Drawing from the theory of pragmatism, the text is considered to imply discourse (or speech) acts. In the conceptualisation of Predatory Journalism, the sensationalist illocutions that can be identified are *Exposive* (announcing and condemning the sexual crime or allied issue or event), *Evaluative* (using evaluative language: Affect, judgement and appreciation [Appraisal Theory]), *Warning* (generating anxiety about an issue), *Extolling* (presenting an event as extraordinary or extreme), *Trivialising* (trivialisation of serious issues), *Politicising* (establishing the news event as political), *Dehumanising* (describing the crime as "horror" or inhuman) and *Demonising* (presenting the perpetrator as monstrous). Similarly, the sexist illocutions that can be identified are *Stigmatising* (describing or regarding something or somebody as worthy of disgrace or great disapproval), *Gendering* (establishing gender differentiations) and *Lambing* (presenting the victims as hapless, vulnerable and ideal). Illocutions that can be sexual are *Experiencing* (offering a voyeuristic narration of the news event for the audience to experience it) and *Sexualising* (viewing the event in sexual terms or making it sexually exciting). Illocutions that can be sectionalist are *Generalising* (extrapolating a trend out of an event or issue or passing a judgement about a whole group of people), *Schismatic* (presenting a biassed point of view about a social group such as sexist), *Stereotyping* (using or supporting a generalised belief about a particular category of people) and *Branding* (connecting the news event with a symbol). While examining sensationalism in news headlines, Molek-Kozakowska (2013) identified exposing, speculating, generalising, warning and extolling as sensationalist illocutions. Apart from misleading or hyped headlines, sensationalism can manifest in a plethora of forms inside the news stories as well, including hyperbolising and focusing on salacious or scandalous aspects of a story rather than its more substantive elements.

Perlocutionary effects

In Predatory Journalism, the central aim is to generate news views and audience reaction (such as likes, shares and comments; *Prompts*), ultimately to generate revenue and sidelining other important perlocutions such as informing the public. On the sides, such unethical editorial practices could cause *Exploitation* (of the actors involved in the news story and the audience) and *Stimulation* (emotional and erotic responses due to the explicit imagery and detailed descriptions of the crime and news sensationalism), among other side-effects such as desensitisation of the audience, normalisation of sexual violence, re-traumatisation of the victims and propagating a culture of rape. The *Emotive* instinct will be targeted by nudging reader emotions through coverage of issues that are highly traumatic to the readers or audience. Sensationalism engages to arouse the "human sensory system" as noted by Grabe et al. (2001, p. 637), but Predatory Journalism turns the extensive detailed description of the crime into an erotic episode. In cases of sexual abuse of minors, sex scandals and sexual assaults such as rape in India, Predatory Journalism can have particularly damaging consequences.

These issues are often highly sensitive and traumatic and require careful and sensitive reporting to minimise harm to the victims and their families.

Characterising Predatory Journalism, this chapter exposes the unethical and exploitative practices that a section of media organisations and journalists indulge in, revealing the devastating impact such reporting can have on victims and society. Not just the social media news channels that are popularly broadcasting and critiquing news events in a predatory fashion, even traditional media houses are often embracing unethical journalism to adapt to changing times. While the explicit cues are an unsympathetic attitude, exploitation of trauma, sensationalism and sexualisation, issues that are underlying and hidden are sexism, divisiveness, distortion of facts and privacy invasion—all for clicks, views and gain. Additionally, it may involve the use of unreliable sources, robbed paraphrases, fake quotes or the glorification of perpetrators at the expense of the interests of the victims.

In the long run, Predatory Journalism can threaten egalitarianism and emancipation, eroding public trust in traditional journalism and perpetuating harmful stereotypes.

Lack of responsibility and accountability is sometimes perceivable in contemporary journalism. In some cases, journalists may even actively seek to avoid accountability by hiding behind the guise of "freedom of the press" or other similar justifications.

Currently, there is a growing negative sentiment about news media being irresponsible at times and needing to be held more accountable. Media watchers have pointed out that it is important for the Indian media to reflect on these criticisms and work towards improving their standards of reporting (Katju, 2021, December 4). Lack of sensitivity and empathy can also be perceived in contemporary news reporting. Predatory Journalism may involve the invasion of privacy of individuals involved in a story, such as publishing their photographs and social or personal information without explicit and informed consent. This can contribute to a culture of non-consensual sharing of intimate information. It is important for journalists to protect the privacy and well-being of the individuals involved in the news. Predatory journalists can be exploitative and harm individuals or communities in pursuit of a story.

Through this book, we present a more comprehensive conceptualisation of this disturbing contemporary trend in Indian journalism. Predatory Journalism and media sensationalism may be related concepts, but they operate on different levels. Media sensationalism may refer to employing content and form factors to capture the attention of media audiences. It can be viewed (positively) as a tactic that media outlets use to sustain readership. It may not seem unethical or harmful. On the other hand, Predatory Journalism, with an expanded scope and encompassing quite a few unethical reporting practices, is presented as a specific type of journalism that involves exploitation of sources, subjects and the audience.

The rise of social media—especially YouTube—journalism may have created new opportunities for content creators to exploit users. Along with it, the affordability of online space has also lowered the barriers to entry for individuals to launch their own news channels or websites. While this can help independent journalists pursue stories that traditional media outlets may not cover, it has also led to an increase in Predatory Journalism, enticing the mainstream media to emulate its success story. Some individuals may use the affordability of creating news websites or YouTube channels to exploit issues and sell news that is sensational or misleading. Journalism is a powerful tool of information dissemination with socio-political benefits and journalists, whether working in traditional media or on social media, have a duty to uphold ethical standards. A review of recent cases, however, reveals that a section engages in predatory practices, as characterised in this chapter. In the following chapters, the facets of this contemporary trend will be dealt with in-depth.

References

Al-Zaman, Md. S. (2021). COVID-19-related social media fake news in India. *Journalism and Media*, *2*(1), 100–114. MDPI AG. http://dx.doi.org/10.3390/journalmedia2010007

ANI. (2022, September 29). Western media distorts India's global image by farcical coverage. *ANI News*. Retrieved April 21, 2023, from https://www.aninews.in/news/world/asia/western-media-distorts-indias-global-image-by-farcical-coverage20220929204453/

AP. (2021, October 14). *Efforts to track diversity in journalism are lagging*. Retrieved April 21, 2023, from https://www.thehindu.com/news/international/efforts-to-track-diversity-in-journalism-are-lagging/article36999808.ece

Aravindh, R. V. (2018). Sensationalism of news by dailies in Tamil Nadu. *WWJMRD*, *4*(3): 190–194.

Balasubramaniam, J. (2011). Dalits and a lack of diversity in the newsroom. *Economic and Political Weekly*, *46*(11): 21–23.

Banerjee, R. (2021, July 12). *What to mourn more: Sushant's death or media's depravity?* https://www.outlookindia.com/. Retrieved April 20, 2023, from https://www.outlookindia.com/website/story/opinion-what-to-mourn-more-sushants-death-or-medias-depravity/385071

Bang, J. C, & Door, J. (2017). Language, theory, and conditions for production. In Jacob L. Mey (Ed.). *Pragmalinguistics: Theory and practice* (Vol. 85). De Gruyter.

Bansal, S. (2014, January 3). Distortions in news broadcasting. *Mint*. Retrieved April 21, 2023, from https://www.livemint.com/Consumer/tfDXxC714XdpDO8pHtwDSM/Distortions-in-news-broadcasting.html

Bernstein, C. (1992). The idiot culture. *The New Republic*, *8*, 22–28. http://charlesrehn.com/thekingdomofgod/uptotheminutenews/categories/storiesbycategory/war/bernsteinidiot culture.pdf

Bezanson, R. P. (1992). The right to privacy revisited: Privacy, news, and social change, 1890–1990. *California Law Review*, *80*(5): 1133–1175.

Bhandari, A. (2021). *Indian media narratives in gang rape* [Master of Arts (MA), Thesis]. Sociology & Criminal Justice, Old Dominion University. http://dx.doi.org/10.25777/m39f-s864. https://digitalcommons.odu.edu/sociology_criminaljustice_etds/55

Broersma, M., & Graham, T. (2013). Twitter as a news source: How Dutch and British newspapers used tweets in their news coverage, 2007–2011. *Journalism Practice*, *7*(4), 446–464. https://doi.org/10.1080/17512786.2013.802481

Brown, D. K., Harlow, S., García-Perdomo, V., & Salaverría, R. (2018). A new sensation? An international exploration of sensationalism and social media recommendations in online news publications. *Journalism*, *19*(11), 1497–1516.

Chaturvedi, A. (2019, December 20). 2019 – The year of fake news. *The Economic Times*. Retrieved April 21, 2023, from https://economictimes.indiatimes.com/news/politics-and-nation/fake-news-still-a-menace-despite-government-crackdown-fact-checkers/articleshow/72895472.cms?from=mdr

Chermak, S. M. (1994) Body count news: How crime is presented in the news media, *Justice Quarterly*, *11*(4), 561–582. https://doi.org/10.1080/07418829400092431

Chibnall, S. (1977) *Law and order news*. Tavistock.

Choudhary, R., Sirur S., and Bajpai S. (2019). Pulwama attack: Ravish Kumar wants restraint, Aaj Tak wants badla, others bay for blood. *ThePrint*. https://theprint.in/plugged-in/pulwama-attack-ravish-kumar-wants-restraint-aaj-tak-wants-badla-others-bay-for-blood/193253/

Chowdhury, A. (2020, June 14). The irresponsible reporting of Sushant Singh Rajput's death. *BOOM*. Retrieved April 20, 2023, from https://www.boomlive.in/fact-file/the-irresponsible-reporting-of-sushant-singh-rajputs-death-8479

Davies, N. (2008). *Flat Earth news: An award-winning reporter exposes falsehood, distortion and propaganda in the global media*. Vintage

Dempster, G., Sutherland, G., & Keogh, L. (2022). Scientific research in news media: a case study of misrepresentation, sensationalism and harmful recommendations. *Journal of Science Communication*, *21*(1), A06.

Emery, E. (1962). *The press and America: An interpretative history of journalism* (2nd ed.). Prentice-Hall.

Ghosh, J. (2014). Ethics of Indian news media: Aberrations and future challenges. *Global Media Journal: Indian Edition*, *5*(2), 1–11.

Grabe, M. E., Zhou, S., & Barnett, B. (2001). Explicating sensationalism in television news: Content and the bells and whistles of form. *Journal of Broadcasting & Electronic Media*, *45*(4), 635–655.

Grabe, M.E., Zhou, S. Lang, A., & Bolls, P.D. (2000) Packaging television news: The effects of tabloid on information processing and evaluative responses. *Journal of Broadcasting & Electronic Media*, *44*(4), 581–598. http://dx.doi.org/10.1207/s15506878jobem4404_4

Graber, D.A. (1994). The infotainment quotient in routine television news: A director's perspective. *Discourse & Society*, *5*(4), 483–508. https://doi.org/10.1177/0957926594005004004

Grabosky, P., & Wilson, P. R. (1989). *Journalism and justice: How crime is reported* (p. 31). Pluto Press. https://www.ojp.gov/ncjrs/virtual-library/abstracts/journalism-and-justice-how-crime-reported

Grundlingh, L. (2017). Identifying markers of sensationalism in online news reports on crime. *Language Matters*, *48*(2), 117–136. https://doi.org/10.1080/10228195.2017.1341543

Harcup, T., & O'Neill, D. (2017) What is News? *Journalism Studies*, *18*(12), 1470–1488. https://doi.org/10.1080/1461670X.2016.1150193

Haskins, E. W. (1984). Black: Defiance, sensationalism and disaster. *ETC: A Review of General Semantics*, 398–401. https://www.jstor.org/stable/42576706

Hendriks Vettehen, P., & Kleemans, M. (2018). Proving the obvious? What sensationalism contributes to the time spent on news video. *Electronic News*, *12*(2), 113–127. https://doi.org/10.1177/1931243117739947

Hendriks Vettehen, P. (2015). Sensationalism. *The International Encyclopedia of Communication*. https://doi.org/10.1002/9781405186407.wbiecs030.pub2

India Today Web Desk. (2018, August 6). The girls returned crying: Child reveals details of abuse at UP shelter home. *India Today*. Retrieved April 20, 2023, from https://www.

indiatoday.in/india/story/the-girls-returned-crying-child-reveals-details-of-abuse-at-up-shelter-home-1306417-2018-08-06

Jackson, J. E. (2005). Sensationalism in the newsroom: Its yellow beginnings, the nineteenth century legal transformation, and the current seizure of the American press. *Notre Dame Journal of Law Ethics & Public Policy*, *19*(2), 789–816.

Jaggi, R., & Majumdar, P. (2009). Popularity vs. credibility: An analysis of public perception of sensationalism in Indian television news. *IMS Manthan*, *4*(2), 171–179.

Jain, N., & Kumar, S. (2016). Is suicide reporting in Indian newspapers responsible? A study from Rajasthan. *Asian Journal of Psychiatry*, *24*, 135–138.

Jawed, S. (2018, January 3). 2017's Top Fake News Stories Circulated by the Indian Media. *The Wire*. Retrieved April 21, 2023, from https://thewire.in/media/2017s-top-fake-news-stories-circulated-by-the-indian-media

Johnston, J., & Forde, S. (2017). Churnalism. *Digital Journalism*, *5*(8), 943–946. https://doi.org/10.1080/21670811.2017.1355026

Jones, R., Woods, C., & Usher, K. (2020). The impact of media sensationalism and crisis framing on stigma and negative attitudes towards methamphetamine users. *International Journal of Mental Health Nursing*, *29*, 319–321. https://doi.org/10.1111/inm.12708

Kaggere, N. (2019, February 15). Pulwama attack: Mandya jawan was keen to serve nation. *Deccan Herald*. Retrieved April 24, 2023, from https://www.deccanherald.com/state/mandya-jawan-was-keen-serve-718553.html

Katju, M. (2021, December 4). *Media and issues of responsibility*. Retrieved April 21, 2023, from https://www.thehindu.com/opinion/lead/Media-and-issues-of-responsibility/article13059658.ece

Kaushika, P. (2019, February 15). BJP tells MPs not to speak on Pulwama attack, but calls for "vengeance" ring loud. *The Print*. Retrieved April 1, 2023, from https://theprint.in/politics/bjp-tells-mps-not-to-speak-on-pulwama-attack-but-calls-for-vengeance-ring-loud/193371/.

Khaliq, A. (2018, July 22). A matter of untruth. *The Indian Express*. Retrieved April 21, 2023, from https://indianexpress.com/article/opinion/columns/fake-news-oxford-dictionary-word-of-the-year-216-post-truth-5270328/

Kitzinger, J. (2004). Media coverage of sexual violence against women and children. In: Karen Ross and Carolyn M. Byerly (Eds.), *Women and media: International perspectives, Blackwell Publishing* (pp. 13–38), https://doi.org/10.1002/9780470776421.ch2

Kleemans, M., Hendriks Vettehen, P. G. J., Beentjes, J. W. J., & Eisinga, R. (2017). The influence of sensationalist features in television news stories on perceived news quality and perceived sensationalism of viewers in different age groups. *Studies in Communication Sciences*, *17*(2), 183–194. https://doi.org/10.24434/j.scoms.2017.02.004

Lecheler, S., & Kruikemeier, S. (2015). Re-evaluating journalistic routines in a digital age: A review of research on the use of online sources. *New Media & Society*, *18*(1), 156–171. https://doi.org/10.1177/1461444815600412

Lee, H. (2021, November 22). Normalizing sexual violence through media fuels rape culture. *Saratoga Falcon*. Retrieved April 21, 2023, from https://saratogafalcon.org/content/normalizing-sexual-violence-through-media-fuels-rape-culture/

Lih, A. (2004). Wikipedia as participatory journalism: Reliable sources? metrics for evaluating collaborative media as a news resource. *Nature*, *3*(1), 1–31. https://citeseerx.ist.psu.edu/document?repid=rep1&type=pdf&doi=f5d4720f9b5ed36efb629409240c1f194e733316

Mantri, G. (2020, October 16). How the coverage of Sushant Singh's death was a disservice to mental health reportage. *The News Minute*. https://www.thenewsminute.com/article/how-coverage-sushant-singh-s-death-was-disservice-mental-health-reportage-135460

Maras, S. (2013). *Objectivity in journalism*. John Wiley & Sons.

Martin, J. R., & Rose, D. (2003). *Working with discourse: Meaning beyond the clause*. Continuum.

Martin, J. R., & White, P. R. R. (2005). *The language of evaluation*. Palgrave Macmillan.

Messner, M., & Distaso, M. W. (2008). The source cycle: How traditional media and weblogs use each other as sources. *Journalism Studies*, *9*(3), 447–463. https://doi.org/10.1080/14616700801999287

Messner, M., & South, J. (2011). Legitimizing Wikipedia: How US national newspapers frame and use the online encyclopedia in their coverage. *Journalism Practice*, *5*(2), 145–160. https://doi.org/10.1080/17512786.2010.506060

Mey, J. (1979). Introduction. In: Jacob L. Mey (ed.), *Pragmalinguistics: Theory and Practice*. Volume 1. Mouton Publishers, The Hague. pp. 9–20. ISBN: 9027977577

Mohanty, D. (2019, February 15). Proud of my father, says killed CRPF soldier's daughter. *Hindustan Times*. Retrieved April 1, 2023, from https://www.hindustantimes.com/india-news/proud-of-my-father-says-killed-crpf-soldier-s-daughter/story-KrcngxUQR3jHQ5kPnrcuRI.html

Molek-Kozakowska, K. (2013). Towards a pragma-linguistic framework for the study of sensationalism in news headlines. *Discourse & Communication*, *7*(2), 173–197.

Mott, F. L. (1962). *A history of American journalism*. Macmillan.

Nordin, K. D. (1979). The entertaining press: Sensationalism in eighteenth-century Boston newspapers. *Communication Research*, *6*(3), 295–320.

Philipose, P. (2020, September 12). Backstory: Everything wrong with the media is reflected in the Sushant Singh Rajput coverage. *The Wire*. Retrieved April 20, 2023, from https://thewire.in/media/back-story-indian-media-sushant-singh-rajput-coverage

Pinker, S. (2018, February 19). The media exaggerates negative news. This distortion has consequences. *The Guardian*. Retrieved April 21, 2023, from https://www.theguardian.com/commentisfree/2018/feb/17/steven-pinker-media-negative-news

Prakash, S. (2020, August 10). Sushant Rajput death: Rhea alleges 'media trial', urges SC to protect her right to privacy. *Tribune India*. Retrieved April 22, 2023, from https://www.tribuneindia.com/news/nation/sushant-rajput-death-rhea-alleges-media-trial-urges-sc-to-protect-her-right-to-privacy-124687

Press Trust of India. (2018, August 7). Don't publish pictures of victims of sexual abuse in any form: SC to print, electronic, social media. *Hindustan Times*. Retrieved April 20, 2023, from https://www.hindustantimes.com/india-news/don-t-publish-pictures-of-victims-of-sexual-abuse-in-any-form-sc-to-print-electronic-social-media/story-VCObgU5xMX4KVMQGwlTC2I.html

Press Trust of India. (2019a, February 15). CRPF Jawan spent five days with family, slain on return. *Deccan Herald*. Retrieved April 1, 2023, from https://www.deccanherald.com/national/pulwama-attack-crpf-jawan-vv-vasanth-kumar-spent-five-days-718594.html

Press Trust of India. (2019b, February 15). Brother of CRPF Jawan killed in Pulwama attack recalls last conversation. *Hindustan Times*. Retrieved April 1, 2023, from https://www.hindustantimes.com/india-news/brother-of-crpf-jawan-killed-in-pulwama-attack-recalls-last-conversation/story-6e69W5clYFhc9lWLd8d3pJ.html

PTI. (2020, September 15). *Third plea filed against media coverage of Sushant Singh Rajput's death*. Retrieved April 22, 2023, from https://www.thehindu.com/news/cities/mumbai/hc-notice-to-centre-on-plea-over-sushant-case-media-coverage/article32609307.ece

Rao, S. (2014). Covering rape in shame culture: Studying journalism ethics in India's new television news media. *Journal of Mass Media Ethics*, *29*(3), 153–167. https://doi.org/10.1080/08900523.2014.918497

Sachsman, D. B., & Bulla, D. W. (2017). *Sensationalism: Murder, mayhem, mudslinging, scandals, and disasters in 19th-century reporting*. Routledge.

Scroll Staff. (2020, August 28). Sushant Singh Rajput death: Media must not conduct parallel trial in case, says Press Council. *Scroll.in*. Retrieved April 22, 2023, from https://scroll.in/latest/971660/sushant-singh-rajput-death-media-must-not-conduct-parallel-trial-in-case-says-press-council#:~:text=%E2%80%9CThe%20media%20is%20advised%20not,key%20accused%20in%20Rajput's%20death.

Sharma, A. (2019, February 15). Pulwama terror attack: "He said he'll call in evening, but call was about his death": CRPF Jawan's family. *Hindustan Times*. Retrieved April 1,

2023, from https://www.hindustantimes.com/india-news/recently-promoted-crpf-soldier-from-punjab-among-those-killed-in-pulwama-attack/story-C3wVCizXDNjEAYVTNXj5XK.html

Shetty, S. (2015). The slow death of Indian journalism and why it is dangerous for India. *The Logical Indian*. https://thelogicalindian.com/opinion/the-slow-death-of-indian-journalism-and-why-it-is-dangerous-for-india/

Singh, B. (2019, February 15). Punjab father loses only son in Pulwama attack. *Hindustan Times*. Retrieved April 1, 2023, from https://www.hindustantimes.com/india-news/punjab-father-loses-only-son-in-pulwama-attack/story-Ccdy7xaPXvukwqMBBc9ByN.html

Singh, N. (2020). Sensational images, deplorable headlines: How news channels reported Sushant Singh Rajput's death. *The Logical Indian*. https://thelogicalindian.com/news/media-houses-sushant-singh-death-21700

Singh, S. (2018, August 6). Muzaffarpur shelter home abuse case: Six senior officers among 23 suspended. *The Indian Express*. Retrieved April 20, 2023, from https://indianexpress.com/article/india/muzaffarpur-shelter-home-abuse-case-six-senior-officers-among-23-suspended-5293043/

Slattery, K. L., & Hakanen, E. A. (1994). Trend: Sensationalism versus public affairs content of local TV news: Pennsylvania revisited. *Journal of Broadcasting & Electronic Media*, *38*(2), 205–216. https://doi.org/10.1080/08838159409364257

Smolla, R. A. (1999). Privacy and the first amendment right to gather news. *The George Washington Law Review*, *67*(5), 1097–1138.

Spencer, D. R. (2007). *The yellow journalism: The press and America's emergence as a world power*. Northwestern University Press.

Sreedharan, C., Thorsen, E., & Singh, A. (2020). *Hold your story: Reflections on the news of sexual violence in India*. https://eprints.bournemouth.ac.uk/34772/1/Hold%20Your%20Story-Print-Final.pdf

Stephens, M. (2007). *A history of news*. Oxford University Press.

Thadani, R. (2020). Why Indian media houses must fix their diversity problem. *Youth Ki Awaaz*. https://www.youthkiawaaz.com/2020/08/the-death-of-diversity/

Thakur, N. K. (2019, February 15). Pulwama terror attack: Kangra braveheart leaves behind a 22-day-old son. *Hindustan Times*. Retrieved April 1, 2023, from https://www.hindustantimes.com/india-news/pulwama-terror-attack-kangra-braveheart-leaves-behind-a-22-day-old-son/story-EcgQmFEWydJzivSaQMg9cJ.html

Thomas, R. (2018). The Nirbhaya effect and media sensationalism revisited. *Journal of Polity & Society*, *10*(1&2), 66–78.

TNN. (2012, October 15). Media seeks to glorify rape, Mamata Banerjee says. *The Times of India*. Retrieved April 21, 2023, from https://timesofindia.indiatimes.com/india/media-seeks-to-glorify-rape-mamata-banerjee-says/articleshow/16829775.cms

Udeze, S. E. & Uzuegbunam, C. E. (2013). Sensationalism in the media: The right to sell or the right to tell. *Journal of Communication and Media Research*, *5*(1), 69–78.

Van Scoy, L. J., Snyder, B., Miller, E. L., Toyobo, O., Grewel, A., Ha, G., … & Lennon, R. P. (2021). Public anxiety and distrust due to perceived politicization and media sensationalism during early COVID-19 media messaging. *Journal of Communication in Healthcare*, *14*(3), 193–205.

Wang, T. L., & Cohen, A. A. (2009). Factors affecting viewers' perceptions of sensationalism in television news: A survey study in Taiwan. *Issues & Studies*, *45*(2), 125–157. https://rb.gy/miys2

Wong, J. S., & Harraway, V. (2020). Media presentation of homicide: Examining characteristics of sensationalism and fear of victimization and their relation to newspaper article prominence. *Homicide Studies*, *24*(4), 333–352.

Part II

Unmasking the Predator

3 Headline Horrors

Losing Sense for Sexist Sensationalism

In 2020, the gangrape and murder of a young woman from Hathras in the Indian state of Uttar Pradesh once again brought media coverage of sexual crimes in India under critical scrutiny (Pal, 2019, June 15; Shinde, 2020, October 12). While the case was a heinous crime that deserved attention, several media outlets were criticised for their indifferent, sensationalist and insensitive coverage, playing the caste card and politicising the event. Headlines such as "Hathras Horror, India's Shame, Once again" (NDTV, 2020, September 29) and "Attempted strangulation, fracture in neck: Chilling details of Hathras rape victim's postmortem emerge" (Taneja, 2020, October 1) zoomed in on the graphic details and used language that dehumanised the crime and sensationalised the violence. Such news headlines not only perpetuate harmful stereotypes about sexual violence but also undermine the credibility of the media.

Reporting in a country like India with a diversified population in socio-economic and cultural terms needs to be shrewd and extra-judicious, also because research has pointed out the predominant presence of intermedia agenda setting (Barclay, 2015; Barclay, Pichandy & Venkat, 2015; Barclay, 2017; Barclay, 2019)—where traditional media views dominate the new media avenues and ideologies. In populous India, consumption is high in a diversified, connected and converged media climate. Social media is omnipresent and the millennials cloud most of these current online spaces. The editorial case of Hathras was just one example of the many instances that witnessed the loss of news sense and sensitivity while covering sexual violence. In recent years, the rise of online social media and the 24-hour news cycle has led to a proliferation of such sexist and sensationalist headline "horrors".

Sensationalism in contemporary times

Studies of sexual crime reporting on local television (Dowler, 2006) and online news portals (Grundlingh, 2017) have found that these stories often feature elements of sensationalism, such as the exhibition of brutality to instil a sense of fear and increase entertainment value. Such sensationalist reporting can influence public opinion and policy change, as seen in the case of prostitution reporting in the mid-twentieth century (Laite, 2014), but is it a healthy trend in contemporary times? What about the sociopolitical side-effects? Is sensationalism helpful in

DOI: 10.4324/9781003468042-6

abasing sexual crimes or is it being counterproductive, engendering and propagating it?

Scholars have noted that the use of sensational production techniques in news media houses has increased but not consistently across all indicators and newscasts.

Further, the impact of legislation on media reporting of serious sex offenders has been mixed. For instance, several indicators of sensationalism increased after the introduction of the Serious Sex Offender Monitoring Act 2005 in Victoria (Ducat, Thomas & Blood, 2009). Sensationalism in the news—characterised by overstatement, invasion of privacy, inaccuracy and lack of perspective (Lindstrom, 1956)—is viewed as a complex phenomenon that can be linguistically analysed through illocutions, semantic structures and narrative formulas (Molek-Kozakowska, 2013). This approach is particularly relevant in the digital age, where sensationalism is not limited to traditional categories but also drives audience engagement (Kilgo, 2021).

Grundlingh (2017) identified subtle and obvious markers of sensationalism in crime news intended to "increase the entertainment value" and "grab and keep the attention of the readers". Analysing sensationalist language, Grundlingh (2017) defined subtle sensationalism as any information that sparks the reader's interest but is unnecessary. She deemed sensationalism obvious when the "attitude of the journalist is clearly identifiable", offering examples and explanations about how they can trigger speculations about the crime and suspects.

Grundlingh viewed sensationalism as a stylistic pattern that "manipulate[s] readers to form opinions on either the crime being reported or the individuals involved. The presence of sensationalist language or other strategies means that a reporter is no longer a completely objective observer who is merely 'mirroring' the events taking place" (Grundlingh, 2017, p. 120). According to Grundlingh, sensationalism focuses more on "brutality", the "otherness" and "outside the norm" nature of the story, "adjusting the threshold to keep the story fresh… creating opposition and emphasising any celebrity component of a crime" (p. 133).

Offering a psychological perspective on sensationalism, Hendriks Vettehen, Nuijten and Beentjes (2005) defined it as stimuli that "elicit automatic attentive processes". Hendriks Vettehen et al. (2005, p. 285) placed the markers of sensationalism in media messages under four categories: Basic needs content, tabloid packaging, concreteness and proximity. Besides competition, technological innovation, journalistic routines and values were seen as the drivers of sensationalism (Hendriks Vettehen et al., 2005, p. 292). In a more recent study, Hendriks Vettehen (2015) noted that the market-driven media industry was exploiting human interest in sex, violence, criminality, disasters and famines. Exemplifications in storytelling, using varied camera angles, swift transitions between camera shots, insertion of music, extraordinary font style and size usage in headlines and choice of brief comments from laypersons were identified as common features of television sensationalism (Hendriks Vettehen, 2015).

Carter (1998), from her quantitative content analysis of 840 news accounts, explored the ways in which news media reports of sexual violence contribute to its "normalisation" in media discourse. Carter (1998, p. 219) noted that the "ideological shift in news coverage of sexual violence" pushes the ordinary everyday violence against women to go unreported, whereby the "extraordinary is normalised into the ordinary". Conducting linguistic analysis of a corpus of 543 articles from the most-read British national newspapers, Harper and Hogue (2015) found that sexual crime articles featured "angrier and more emotionally negative tones", offering the cognitive-experiential self-theory as a socio-psychological framework to understand the role of emotion in sexual crime reporting. Preferring an evolutionary perspective, Davis and McLeod (2003) found that the categories that emerged in sensational news correspond to major themes in evolutionary psychology, such as altruism, cheater detection, reputation and treatment of offspring. They proposed that "like gossip, sensational news stories may trigger an evolved tendency to attend to categories of information that increased reproductive fitness in the Environment of Evolutionary Adaptedness (EEA)".

Slattery and Hakanen (1994) observed that people harboured interest and moral responsibilities towards the well-being of communities and humanity, adding that certain news labelled as sensational appealed to that human-interest. Slattery and Hakanen (1994) suggested methods journalists can apply to cover stories traditionally deemed sensational responsibly.

Brown et al. (2018) identified sensationalism in the so-called "hard" news topics apart from the popular categories traditionally sensationalised. Employing a content analysis of 400 articles from online-native news organisations, Brown et al. (2018) evaluated the sensational treatment of news categories and news values, analysing the associated social media interaction numbers on Facebook and Twitter (now X) and comparing the use of sensationalism in online-native news organisations from different countries. Meanwhile, Arbaoui, De Swert and van der Brug (2020) observed that commercial channels deploy higher levels of sensationalism in more fragmented or competitive markets. Both audience fragmentation and the dependence on commercial revenue significantly affected sensational news coverage, while the public broadcasters served as counterbalancers (Arbaoui et al., 2020). Online media, in particular, tends to report gender-based violence or sexual crimes using sensational headlines. The competition for maximum clicks and page views often leads to exaggerating facts or titillating thumbnails. In the process, the privacy of sexual crime survivors or victims is violated for the benefit of exhibitionist media outlets. Sensational headlines of sexual crimes tend to present the case as a one-of-a-kind event rather than acknowledging its systemic nature. The emphasis is on the unusualness or novelty of the crime while drawing a monstrous image of the perpetrator (Ghosh, 2019).

The sensationalist construction of the monstrosity of perpetrators tends to be directed more towards men belonging to minority or distressed communities compared to other "respectable men" in society (Ghosh, 2019). Also, wherever possible, the headlines tend to incorporate communal references to use popular stereotypes and characterise the victims or accused. For instance, check this recent news headline that reads, "Dalit woman raped, set afire in Rajasthan dies" (PTI, 2023a, April 8). While the victim is identified as a Dalit woman, the accused is referred to as a Muslim man in the lead paragraph. Another headline from *the Times of India* reads,

"Unnao gang-rape: Accused set minor Dalit victim's house on fire; her infant son and sister fight for life" (PTI, 2023b, April 18). While case identities are becoming news values, it is appropriate to ask: What will be the long-term sociopolitical implications of communal references, especially in the news headlines? The Supreme Court of India has laid down directives on non-disclosure of the identity of victims of rape, both adult and children, to avoid "unnecessary ridicule, social ostracisation and harassment" (Indulia, 2018, December 12).

The same directive also bars the media from sensationalising sexual crimes and makes publishing anything that would identify the victim a criminal offence (Indulia, 2018, December 12). Although these directives restrict media outlets from directly naming the victim, the name of the village, caste, religion, age and family details are freely circulated in the news reports.

Apart from sensationalism, news reports of sexual violence against women could feature sexual, sectionalist and sexist (Charles, 2019; Layman, 2020; Lockyer & Savigny, 2020) undertones that could exploit reader emotions for clicks.

Headlines: The hotspot of sensationalism

Globalisation and market pressures have transformed Indian journalism into a marketable news production and dissemination industry. In India, the privatisation and deregulation of media in the 1990s led to a rapid expansion of commercial television channels (Rani, 2013). By the end of 1999, the number of channels had risen from two to more than 50 (Crawley & Page, 2001, p. 11), with massive investments leading to high demand for revenue and proliferation. This increase in content and options brought more competition among news channels, with Indian audiences now having to choose from a multitude of channels broadcasting 24 hours a day, compared to the limited broadcast of Doordarshan before 1991. News featuring crime, sex and violence has become a quick resource for grabbing maximum eyeballs. Headlines are the first thing a reader notices in a story and, in online reports, it is the headline that leads the reader to navigate to a webpage. As a result, online media heavily rely on intriguing headlines to capture reader attention. Traditionally, headlines were skilfully written to convey the essence of the news story. However, the basic economics of online media pushes news outlets to prioritise generating more clicks, traffic and revenue. This has led to the use of more attention-grabbing and sensational headlines, often erasing the line between sensationalism and misinformation. Using a case study, this Chapter has, hence, chosen to analyse news headlines to identify markers of sensationalism, sexism, sexuality and sectionalism and relate them to relevant factors.

Case study

Manipur is a northeastern state of India with a geographical area of 22,347 square kilometres and inhabited by ethnic communities with a total population of about 25.70 lakhs (Annexure 1, 2015). Of this population, 35.12% constitute

Schedule Tribe and 3.77% constitute Schedule Caste (Annexure 1, 2015). Most of the Meitei community resides in the valley, which accounts for about 10 percent of the geographical area of Manipur, while the other two ethnic communities, Kuki and Nagas, reside in the hills (Khamrang, 2023). In the last few decades, Manipur has been enduring frequent armed insurgents and violent ethnic clashes that the deep-rooted hill-valley divide and sociocultural differences fuel (Khamrang, 2023). On 27 March, the Manipur High Court passed an order directing the state government to recommend including Meitei in the Scheduled Tribe list, which led to protests by the Kuki-Zo community (Deka, 2023, May 5). These escalated into violent clashes on 3 May 2023, during a "Tribal Solidarity March" organised by the All Tribal Students' Union of Manipur (ATSUM) in the Torbung area of Churachandpur district (Deka, 2023, May 5). Violence quickly spread to the Meitei and Kuki-dominated areas, resulting in the burning down of churches, mob violence, arson, sexual assault and displacement of both community members (Kuthar, 2023, July 20), leading to the death of 219 people and the displacement of 60,000 (Scroll Staff, 2024, February 29).

Viral video and its aftermath

On 19 July 2023, a video of the public sexual assault of two Kuki-Zo women became a top news story in India and certain other parts of the world. The 26-second video showed a mob groping and sexually assaulting the victims, who were then dragged to a field (Baruah, 2023, August 2). On 19 July, the Manipur police tweeted on its X (formerly Twitter) account that the incident occurred on 4 May in the Thoubal district of Manipur (Ali, 2023, July 20; Lama, 2023, July 20). The video that went viral created a social media outrage, demanding the arrest of the perpetrators and stringent punishment (Chetry, 2023, July 20). Further, it led to offline protests and widespread condemnation (Aljazeera, 2023, July 24; Sharma & Choudhury, 2023, July 20) and forced the Manipur police to speed up the identification and arrest of the perpetrators (Chaurasia, 2023, July 24). It also resulted in a media frenzy, where online news portals and social media channels competed to report the event using exclusive interviews and news angles, partially-blurred images and video either embedded or used as thumbnails, hyperdetailed descriptions, conspiracy theories and dramatisation.

While several markers of sensationalism were evident from a critical reading of news articles—such as the unwarranted victim age-identification, divulgence of the gory details of the assaults through imagery and text, exhibition of brutality, politicisation of the assault and communal references—it warranted a systematic analysis to understand the sensationalism exhibited in these news reports empirically. To analyse sensationalism and other such issues, the pragma-linguistics theory is consulted as it provides a framework to investigate latent meaning comprehensible from the manifest content using concepts such as illocutions.

Pragmalinguistics and discourse acts

Velikova (2021) explored the pragmatic functions of news to characterise news actors and understand how perspectives are created for the readers (Velikova, 2021). According to Molek-Kozakowska (2013), sensationalism is instantiated through specific illocutions, semantic macrostructures, narrative formulas, evaluation parameters, and interpersonal and textual devices. Using a case study, Molek-Kozakowska (2013) demonstrated how sensationalism is manifested through specific linguistic and structural elements in news headlines.

Using pragmalinguistics, Haenko (2019) investigated the significant roles of language in manipulating ideology and controlling the behaviour of people. The analysis of modality in media discourse reflects the choices in language between polarities and their influence on the macro-level of social context (Haenko, 2019). Hence, modality becomes an important aspect of categorising evaluative language, including both positive and negative, implicit and explicit evaluation and involves a pragmatic-functional account (Haenko, 2019).

Within the broad schema of pragmatics—that studies linguistic behaviour—pragmalinguistics focuses on resources that language provides for conveying pragmatic (illocutionary and interpersonal) meaning (Marmaridou, 2011). Pragmalinguistics, hence, becomes the study of what is termed as speech acts, and in the present study, the linguistic forms and aspects of news discourse (news headlines) are analysed to identify the semantic functions (that could be sensationalist, sexual, sexist or sectionalist) they convey.

In linguistic terms, the speech act is viewed as an "utterance defined in terms of a speaker's intention and the effect it has on a listener" (Esenova, 2017). As in the present study, news is considered a discourse, it is termed discourse act or illocution. This frame of understanding helps analyse the news headlines on the Manipur sexual violence and identify the editorial intentions behind the language use. Speech (or discourse) acts can be analysed at three levels: locution, illocution and perlocution. In the framework and definitions of John L. Austin, who introduced the concept of illocutionary acts, locution is "what is said", illocution is "what is meant" and perlocution is "what happens as a result" (Austin, 1975; Esenova, 2017).

Austin also identifies locution as the "act of saying something", illocution as "what one does in saying it" and perlocution as "what one does by saying it" (Esenova, 2017).

While locution is explicit, illocution and perlocution may be implicit or inferential. This framework of pragmalinguistics, hence, becomes an ideal tool to unearth hidden semantics (such as sensationalism that, more often than not, is implicit) embedded within news headlines. For instance, a journalist may present an exaggeration (locution) in a news headline to sensationalise the crime story (illocution) and prompt the reader to read and react (perlocution).

Empirical data

As many as 254 news headlines published on the Manipur sexual violence case during 20–28 July 2023, were content analysed to identify the key Topics discussed, Grammatical structures and Literary devices employed, news Frames applied and

Table 3.1 Topics and grammatical structure

Factor	*Description*	*Measurement*
Topics		
Crime		
Physical assault	Referring to physical violence or murder	Absent or present
Sexual assault	Referring to the sexual violence, including disrobing, groping and public "parading"	
(Gang) Rape	Referring to the rape or gangrape of the victim	
Video	Referring to the video footage of the sexual assault that was circulated on social media	
Violence	Referring to the ethnic violence in Manipur	
Response		
Judicial action	Referring to the court proceedings or judicial comments	Absent or present
Public reaction	Referring to the response of the people to the crime or investigation	
Legal action	That includes the police case, investigation, police action and CBI intervention	
Institutional action	Involving established bodies, such as the Commissions for women and STs	
Governmental action	Involving the governments at the Centre or State	
Political statement	Includes comments of political parties or leaders	
Activism	Involving student bodies or civil society groups	
Punishment		
Punishment	Discussing the punishment for the perpetrators of the crime	Absent or present
Grammatical structure	Question, Quotation, Narration, Description, Call to Action, Speculation, Suggestion, Statement, Kicker, Slug, Voice (Active or Passive)	Absent or present

the Illocutions implied to identify key illocutionary discursive themes, using the pragmalinguistics theory. The factors used to analyse the headlines and their descriptions and measurements are detailed in Tables 3.1–3.4.

Popular topics and grammatical structures used in the Manipur headlines were identified using a pilot study. As many as 13 topics were identified and grouped under three broad themes: Crime, response and punishment. Articles were selected for the study using Google News search API and specific date ranges. The window of examination was chosen to be 20 to 28 July 2023, as the video footage of the sexual assault incident, which occurred on 4 May 2023, in the Kangpokpi district of Manipur, was widely circulated on 19 July 2023 and became an instant top news story at the national level (Raj, 2023, July 20; Sharma & Choudhury, 2023, July 20).

For the present study, news articles published on popular Indian news websites were prioritised, excluding editorials, standalone videos and pictures and social media messages.

An *a-priori* study design was used, where the variables and categories were predetermined using a pilot study of 50 news headlines. An inter-coder reliability of more than .80 (Cronbach's alpha) was found to be adequate for the present study.

As many as 20 news Frames and 13 literary-rhetorical devices were identified during the pilot study. A news frame refers to "aspects of a perceived reality"

Table 3.2 Frames and measurement

Frame	*Descriptions*	*Measurement*
Extreme violence	Framing the event as an act of extreme violence	Absent, Not Sure, Mildly present and Strongly present
Sexual violence	Mentioning and describing sexual violence	
Social impact	Discussing the social impact of the crime	
Psychological impact	Discussing the psychological impact of the crime	
Diagnostic	Identifying the problems that have caused the issue	
Prognostic	Offering solutions to the problems or discussing its history or origin	
Morality	Referring to social norms, morality, moral messages, God or religious tenets	
Socio-economic impact	Referring to damage to property or financial loss	
Identification	Identifying the stakeholders using personal or demographic information	
Celebrity	Involving a popular person	
Outrage	Emphasising public reactions, protests or demands for justice	
Communal reference	Referring to communal or religious identities	
Conflict	Referring to conflict or disagreement between individuals or groups; presenting conflicting views	
Blaming	Attribution of responsibility	
Detailing	Offering micro details about the news event	
Marginalisation	Highlighting regional or social marginalisation	
Police inaction	Referring to allegation of police inaction during the crime	
Police connivance	Allegation of police connivance in the crime	
Shame	Framing the sexual crime as a shame for the victims	
Institution	Involving a renowned or powerful institution or organisation	

Table 3.3 Devices and measurement

Device	*Description*	*Measurement*
Metalepsis	Using a word or a phrase from a figurative speech in a new context	Absent, Not Sure, Mildly present and Strongly present
Humour	Amusing or comic presentation	
Hyperbole	Exaggeration	
Alliteration	Repetition of the same letter at the beginning of words or syllables	
Sarcasm	Use of irony to mock or convey contempt	
Metaphor	Compares two things by stating one is the other	
Simile	Compares one thing with another thing of a different kind	
Understatement	Makes a person or idea seem less important	
Ridicule	Subjection of someone or something to contemptuous and dismissive language or behaviour	
Anaphora	Repetition of a word or phrase for emphasis	
Personification	Attribution of human characteristics to something not human	
Pleonasm	Use of more words than are necessary to convey meaning	
Oxymoron	Use of an apparent contradiction	

Table 3.4 Illocutions and measurement

Illocution	*Description*	*Measurement*
Exposive	Announcing and condemning the sexual crime or an allied issue or event	Absent, Not Sure, Mildly present and Strongly present
Evaluative	Using evaluative language: affect, judgement and appreciation [as described in the Appraisal Theory]	
Generalising	Extrapolating a trend out of an event or issue or passing a judgement about a whole group of people	
Warning	Generating anxiety about an issue	
Schismatic	Presenting a biassed point of view such as sexist	
Extolling	Presenting an event as extraordinary or extreme	
Trivialising	Trivialisation of serious issues	
Stereotyping	Using or supporting a generalised belief about a particular category of people	
Stigmatising	Describing or regarding something or somebody as worthy of disgrace or great disapproval	
Politicising	Establishing the news event as political	
Gendering	Establishing gender differentiations	
Dehumanising	Describing the crime as "horror" or inhuman	
Demonising	Presenting the perpetrator as monstrous	
Lambing	Presenting the victims as hapless, vulnerable and ideal	
Experiencing	Offering a voyeuristic narration of the news event for the audience to experience it	
Sexualising	Viewing the event in sexual terms or making it sexually exciting	
Branding	Connecting the news event with a symbol	

(Entman, 1993, p. 52) that a journalist presents in a news article to foreground the salience of certain aspects over others (Baden & Stalpouskaya, 2020). Table 3.2 presents the Frames identified for the present study and their descriptions. Further, Table 3.3 presents devices as a group of literary instruments that encapsulate symbolism and rhetorical choices in language (Ammanamanchi et al., 2023, p. 1).

For the present study, 17 illocutionary news discourse acts were identified and categorised under four broad themes: Sensationalist, sexist, sexual and sectionalist.

Here, illocutionary discourse acts refer to the implied latent meanings that the journalists or editors intend to convey through their lexical choices in the news headlines.

A headline was the unit of analysis for the present study.

The data collection period was divided into three: Period 1 (20–22 July), Period 2 (23–25 July) and Period 3 (26–28 July). After the headlines were coded using the chosen variables, descriptive analysis was performed on them, period-wise. Period-wise category frequencies for the variables topic and grammatical structures are presented in Table 3.5.

As many as 92 headlines published during 20–22 July were analysed under Period 1, while 82 headlines were analysed from Periods 2 and 3 each.

Under the topic of Crime, physical assault (discussed in 56 headlines) and the video of the assault that went viral (56) were the most covered during the first period. During the second period, the focus, however, shifted to sexual assault (28) and violence (27).

Table 3.5 Period-wise descriptives: Topics and grammatical structures

Factors	*Period 1*	*Period 2*	*Period 3*	*Total*
Description	20–22 July	23–25 July	26–28 July	20–28 July
Number of headlines analysed	92	81	81	254
Topics				
Crime				
Physical assault	56	8	17	81
Sexual assault	23	28	25	76
(Gang) Rape	1	5	6	12
Video	56	16	12	84
Violence	11	27	29	67
Response				
Judicial action	10	1	12	23
Legal action	16	14	22	52
Institutional action	15	9	21	45
Governmental action	5	13	21	39
Political statement	1	12	11	24
Public reaction	40	30	23	93
Activism	11	18	20	49
Punishment				
Punishment	4	1	2	7
Grammatical structures				
Question	5	4	4	13
Quotation	15	11	17	43
Narration	4	5	2	11
Description	48	22	16	86
Call to Action	8	13	21	42
Speculation	7	1	1	9
Suggestion	2	2	9	13
Statement	41	58	58	157
Kicker	50	37	29	116
Slug	8	2	1	11
Voice				
Active	59	53	52	164
Passive	33	28	29	90

A similar trend was reflected during the third period as well. Overall, the physical assault (81) and the viral video (84) were the most discussed topics under crime in the news headlines analysed. These findings need to be interpreted along with the word-phrase frequencies to understand the editorial patterns and word choices for the headlines (refer to Table 3.6).

During the study period, the high recurrence of the topics of physical assault and violence is reflected in the popular word choices of "violence" (recurring 89 times) and "assault" (43) in the headlines. "Sexual assault" was mentioned 39 times in the headlines.

Corroborating the manual analysis results, the frequency of "video" in the news headlines was found to be 61 and "internet" was mentioned seven times.

Table 3.6 Word-phrase frequencies

Word or phrase	*Frequency*	*Word or phrase*	*Frequency*
Places			
Manipur	246	India	32
Events and actions			
Violence	89	Incident	8
Manipur violence	57	Paraded	45
Horror	8	Naked	49
Raped	8	Paraded naked	43
Sexual	57	Says	19
Assault	43		
Sexual assault	39		
Sexual violence	13		
Protest	14	Probe	12
Arrested	13	Outrage	9
People and players			
Women	84	Police	19
Woman	10	CBI	17
Kuki	9		
Victims	9	Husband of	4
Kuki women	7		
State	17	Accused	14
Centre	16	Mob	12
Court	14	Govt/government	16
Modi	10	Amit Shah	6
Supreme court	11	DCW chief	5
		Swati Maliwal	5
Objects			
Video	61	Viral	15
Internet	7	Viral video	11
Assault video	7		

In the immediate aftermath of the release of the video footage that captured the sexual assault of the two women, public reactions hogged the media limelight, captured in 40 news headlines during the first period. It was also the most popular reaction to the sexual violence recorded in the news during the subsequent periods as well (with a frequency of 30 in the second period and 23 in the third). During these phases, news stories that highlighted activism were also popular (with a frequency of 18 during the second phase and 20 during the third). News stories started discussing the legal, institutional and government actions only during the third period. Reflecting similar trends, the word-phrase analysis also found the words protest and outrage recurring in the news headlines, along with the word "says" indicating quotation.

Statement and description were the most popular grammatical forms that the news headlines adopted. The crime was mostly described as "violence" (89), "sexual assault" (39) and "sexual violence" (13). Moreover, 116 of the 254 news headlines analysed used kickers and active voice. Manipur, sexual assault and video emerged as the most recurring in the kickers used. Analysing the period-wise

Table 3.7 Period-wise descriptives: Frames and devices

Factors	*Period 1*	*Period 2*	*Period 3*	*Total*
Description	20–22 July	23–25 July	26–28 July	20–28 July
Number of headlines analysed	92	81	81	254
Devices				
Metalepsis	2.87	1.4	1.36	1.92
Humour	1	1	1	1
Hyperbole	2.29	1.11	1.11	1.54
Alliteration	1.22	1.42	1.74	1.45
Sarcasm	1.15	1.17	1.25	1.19
Metaphor	1.03	1.14	1.15	1.1
Simile	1.03	1.01	1.04	1.03
Understatement	1.12	1.02	1.14	1.09
Ridicule	1.09	1.12	1.1	1.1
Anaphora	1.33	1.04	1	1.13
Personification	1.28	1.27	1.32	1.29
Pleonasm	1.79	1.12	1.09	1.35
Oxymoron	1.04	1.17	1.07	1.09
Frames				
Extreme violence	3.14	2.1	1.52	2.29
Sexual violence	2.93	1.86	1.64	2.18
Social impact	2.2	1.75	1.65	1.88
Psychological impact	2.02	1.54	1.31	1.64
Socio-economic impact	1.41	1.12	1.2	1.25
Prognostic	2.58	1.56	1.73	1.98
Diagnostic	2.28	1.64	1.77	1.91
Celebrity	1.13	1.48	1.46	1.35
Conflict	1.77	1.96	1.64	1.79
Communal reference	1.36	1.42	1.32	1.37
Marginalisation	1.99	1.19	1.23	1.49
Blaming	2.09	1.6	1.49	1.74
Morality	1.1	1.48	1.21	1.26
Outrage	1.85	1.73	1.95	1.84
Identification	2.29	1.57	1.3	1.74
Detailing	2.5	1.33	1.26	1.73
Police inaction	1.42	1.19	1.1	1.24
Police connivance	1.24	1	1.07	1.11
Shame	1.14	1.05	1.07	1.09
Institution	1.8	2.28	2.91	2.31

recurrence of the literary and rhetorical devices used in the headlines, metalepsis is found to be the most frequent (refer to Table 3.7).

Metalepsis was understood and operationalised as the use of words and phrases in new contexts. In the Manipur news headlines analysed, the act of sexual violence was described using the words "paraded" (45), "paraded naked" (43), "strip" (nine), "stripped" (five), "raped" (two) and "naked" (49). The words "paraded" (military) and "stripped" (as in strip clubs or a voluntary sexual act) are popularly used in contexts other than crime.

Table 3.8 Period-wise descriptives: Illocutions

Illocutions	*Period 1*	*Period 2*	*Period 3*	*Total*
Sensationalist				
Exposive	2.89	2.25	1.84	2.35
Evaluative	3.08	1.67	1.8	2.22
Warning	2.73	1.41	1.46	1.9
Extolling	2.88	1.57	1.25	1.94
Trivialising	2.02	1.04	1.11	1.42
Politicising	1.65	1.7	2	1.78
Dehumanising	2.45	1.09	1.11	1.59
Demonising	1.85	1.14	1.06	1.37
Sexist				
Stigmatising	1.24	1.06	1.14	1.15
Gendering	1.67	1.16	1.36	1.41
Lambing	2.05	1.21	1.22	1.52
Sexual				
Experiencing	2.29	1.15	1.11	1.55
Sexualising	2.48	1.28	1.17	1.68
Sectionalist				
Generalising	1.97	1.4	1.4	1.6
Schismatic	1.65	1.07	1.07	1.28
Stereotyping	1.42	1.09	1.09	1.21
Branding	2.88	2.68	2.79	2.79

Similarly, extreme violence, sexual violence and institutions were the popular semantic microstructures used to frame the Manipur sexual assault (Table 3.8). With regard to elite institutions, the State, Centre, Supreme Court, government and DCW were mostly mentioned. Kuki (18), Meitei (5) and Manipuri (2) were the communities identified in the news headlines.

Further, the illocutionary themes of Sensationalist, Sexist, Sexual and Sectionalist were associated with the variables of Grammatical structures, Topics, Frames and Devices to characterise them. Sensationalist illocutions were found to use quotations, descriptions and speculations, avoiding statements, mostly when reporting the physical assault and sexual assault video and recording public reaction. Such headlines were also found to use Extreme violence, Sexual violence and Marginalisation to frame the issues, with the devices of Detailing, Metalepsis, Hyperbole and Pleonasm. Meanwhile, when the headlines attempted to be sexist, they were mostly speculative, discussing the viral video and physical assault.

Such headlines used the frames of Sexual violence, Identification and Marginalisation and the devices of Metalepsis, Hyperbole and Pleonasm.

Sexual and sectionalist illocutions mostly relied on description and speculation (refer to Table 3.9) while discussing public reaction, viral video and physical assault. For all of these illocutions, the devices of metalepsis, hyperbole and pleonasm were used.

While the sexual illocutions were associated with the frames of Extreme violence, Sexual violence, Marginalisation and Detailing, the sectionalist illocutions were related to Marginalisation, Social impact and Psychological impact.

Table 3.9 Characterising the illocutions

Illocution	*Sensationalist*	*Sexist*	*Sexual*	*Sectionalist*
Grammatical structures (*P. Corr.* scores, significant at the 0.05 level)	Quotation (0.181) Description (0.164)	Speculation (0.248)	Description (0.287) Speculation (0.126)	Speculation (0.3) Kicker (0.326)
	Speculation (0.23) Slug (0.178) Avoided Statement (-0.253)	Avoided Statement (-0.188)	Avoided Statement (-0.255)	
Topics (*P. Corr.* scores, significant at the 0.05 level)	Public reaction (0.212)	Video (0.173)	Public reaction (0.144)	Video (0.174)
	Video (0.357) Phy. assault (0.547)	Physical assault (0.532)	Video (0.417) Physical assault (0.369)	Physical assault (0.344)
Frames (*P. Corr.* scores, significant at the 0.05 level)	Extreme violence (0.556)	Sexual violence (0.474)	Extreme violence (0.568)	Marginalisation (0.474)
	Sexual violence (0.566) Marginalisation (0.546) Detailing (0.641)	Identification (0.424) Marginalisation (0.474)	Sexual violence (0.681) Marginalisation (0.514) Detailing (0.667)	Social impact (0.326) Psy. impact (0.327) Hyperbole (0.488)
Devices	Metalepsis (0.574)	Metalepsis (0.429)	Metalepsis (0.673)	Pleonasm (0.464)
(*P. Corr.* scores, significant at the 0.05 level)	Hyperbole (0.77)	Hyperbole (0.59)	Hyperbole (0.71)	
	Pleonasm (0.629)	Pleonasm (0.605)	Pleonasm (0.639)	

Study results have indicated that the news headlines analysed were largely centred on the video of the sexual assault that went viral (with 84 headlines discussing it and 61 headlines carrying the word "video"), even ignoring or paying low attention to the gangrape of one of the victims. Further, the headlines also highlighted the public reaction to the crime, with 93 of the 254 headlines related to it and recording protests, expressions of "outrage" and calls for justice.

Another predominant aspect of the headlines analysed is the overuse of kickers carrying the words Manipur, paraded naked, video and sexual assault, which branded the news event using the location and the sexual violence. Metalepsis was the prominent device used, where the sexual assault was described using phrases such as "paraded naked" and "stripped naked", which may be construed as inappropriate. Further, the news headlines were presented using the frames of violence and institution, raking in the governments, apex court and top political leaders.

Study results also indicated that the news headlines analysed tended to be sensational, sexist, sexual and sectionalist, trying to be evaluative (expressing emotions), extolling (presenting the event as extraordinary or extreme), dehumanising (at times describing the assault as "horror"), lambing (presenting the survivors as hapless victims) and branding (with kickers).

For instance, these headlines "Women paraded naked in Manipur: Key accused arrested" (Chetry, 2023, July 20), "Manipur violence: Police confirm Kuki women paraded naked, gangraped by mob" (Lama, 2023, July 20), "Woman stripped and raped in Manipur speaks: Police were with the mob, they left us with those men" (Baruah, 2023, August 2), "Taken To Hilly Area…": Manipur Woman Narrates Gang-Rape Horror" (NDTV, 2023, July 25) and "In Manipur Horror, 2 Women Paraded Naked On Camera, Allegedly Gang-Raped" (Sharma & Choudhury, 2023, July 20) sexualise and dehumanise the sexual violence.

India's apex court has issued directives on ethical reporting of sexual crimes. However, the nature in which journalists approach victims post-complaint is often predatory, as media outlets seek to disseminate exclusive details of the crime to attract maximum readership.

Pragmalinguistics offered an ideal analytical framework that was helpful in identifying sexist and sensationalist illocutions in the headlines analysed. While it may appear to serve the interests of the victims, garnering public support, hypercoverage of sexual violence and sensationalism could be counterproductive, desensitising the readers, normalising the crime, re-victimising the survivors and intimidating their families. Such reporting trends could also propagate a rape culture and inhibit survivors of sexual violence from reporting the crime.

References

Ali, Y. (2023, July 20). "Manipur police were present, but didn't help us": Women in harrowing video tell "The Wire." *The Wire*. https://thewire.in/rights/manipur-police-women-video-paraded-naked

Aljazeera. (2023, July 24). US condemns 'brutal' sexual assault video from India's Manipur. *Al Jazeera*. https://www.aljazeera.com/news/2023/7/24/us-condemns-brutal-sexual-assault-video-from-indias-manipur

Ammanamanchi, S. L., Ahamed Meeran, J., Dharmapuri, K. & Sharma, N. (2023). *Basic concepts of literary devices in English literature*. Academic Guru Publishing House.

Annexure 1. (2015). Comprehensive details about Manipur State and its environmental & social sensitivities. Retrieved from https://manipur.gov.in/wp-content/uploads/2015/03/annexure-01-manipur-comprehensive.pdf

Arbaoui, B., De Swert, K., & van der Brug, W. (2020). Sensationalism in news coverage: A comparative study in 14 television systems. *Communication Research*, *47*(2), 299–320. https://doi.org/10.1177/0093650216663364

Austin, J. L. (1975). *How to do things with words*. Harvard University Press.

Baden, C., & Stalpouskaya, K. (2020). Maintenance of news frames: How US, British and Russian news made sense of unfolding events in the Syrian chemical weapons crisis. *Journalism Studies*, *21*(16), 2305–2325. https://doi.org/10.1080/1461670X.2020.1843066

Barclay, F. P. (2015). Inter-media interaction and effects in an integrated model of political communication: India 2014. *Global Media Journal*, *13*(25), 1–39.

Barclay, F. P. (2017). Media effect on media: Progression of political news and tweets during India 2014. *Journal of Media and Communication*, *1*(1), 1–28.

Barclay, F. P. (2019). Using cross-correlations to analyse inter-media political agenda setting, *SAGE research methods cases: Politics & international relations*. https://dx.doi.org/10.4135/9781526494658

Barclay, F. P., Pichandy, C., & Venkat, A. (2015). India elections 2014: Time-lagged correlation between media bias and Facebook trend. *Global Journal of Human-Social Science, 15*(2), 29–41.

Baruah, S. (2023, August 2). Woman stripped and raped in Manipur speaks: Police were with the mob, they left us with those men. *The Indian Express*. https://indianexpress.com/article/india/manipur-sexual-assault-mob-video-women-police-8849995/

Brown, D. K., Harlow, S., García-Perdomo, V., & Salaverría, R. (2018). A new sensation? An international exploration of sensationalism and social media recommendations in online news publications. *Journalism, 19*(11), 1497–1516. https://doi.org/10.1177/1464884916683549

Carter, C. (1998). When the 'extraordinary' becomes 'ordinary': everyday news of sexual violence gender and the agenda. In: Allan, S., Branston, G., & Carter, C. (Eds.). *News, gender and power* (1st ed., pp. 219–232), Routledge.

Charles, J. H. (2019). Coverage of Violence against Women in Print Media: Sexism and Victim Blaming in Headlines. BA (Journalism) thesis.

Chaurasia, A. (2023, July 24). Manipur violence: Another accused apprehended in Manipur viral video case; seven held so far, say Police. *India Today NE*. https://www.indiatodayne.in/manipur/story/manipur-violence-another-accused-apprehended-in-manipur-viral-video-case-seven-held-so-far-say-police-620078-2023-07-24

Chetry, B. (2023, July 20). Women paraded naked in Manipur: Key accused arrested. *India Today NE*. https://www.indiatodayne.in/manipur/story/women-paraded-naked-in-manipur-key-accused-arrested-617635-2023-07-20

Crawley, W., & Page, D. (2001). *Satellites over South Asia: Broadcasting culture and public interest*. Sage

Davis, H., & McLeod, S. L. (2003). Why humans value sensational news: An evolutionary perspective. *Evolution and Human Behavior, 24*(3), 208–216. https://doi.org/10.1016/S1090-5138(03)00012-6

Deka, K. (2023, May 5). Drugs, land rights, tribal identity and illegal immigration-Why Manipur is burning. *India Today NE*. https://www.indiatodayne.in/manipur/story/drugs-land-rights-tribal-identity-and-illegal-immigration-why-manipur-is-burning-553788-2023-05-05

Dowler, K. (2006). Sex, lies, and videotape: The presentation of sex crime in local television news. *Journal of Criminal Justice*, 34(4), 383–392. https://doi.org/10.1016/j.jcrimjus.2006.05.004

Ducat, L., Thomas, S., & Blood, W. (2009). Sensationalising sex offenders and sexual recidivism: Impact of the Serious Sex Offender Monitoring Act 2005 on media reportage. *Australian Psychologist, 44*(3), 156–165. https://doi.org/10.1080/00050060903127499

Entman, R. M. (1993). Framing: Toward clarification of a fractured paradigm. *Journal of Communication, 43*(4), 51–58.

Esenova, K. (2017). Pragmalinguistic studies in linguistics. *Editions du JIPTO/Academie Internationale CONCORDE.*

Ghosh, A. (2019, October 31). Why are sensationalist headlines of GBV cases A problem? | #GBVinMedia. *Feminism in India*. Retrieved from https://feminisminindia.com/2019/10/31/sensationalist-headlines-media/

Grundlingh, L. (2017). Identifying markers of sensationalism in online news reports on crime. *Language Matters, 48*(2), 117–136.

Haenko, V. (2019). Pragmatic essence of linguistic modality in media discourse. *Anglistics and Americanistics*, 16, 54–59. https://doi.org/10.15421/381906

Harper, C. A., & Hogue, T. E. (2015). The emotional representation of sexual crime in the national British press. *Journal of Language and Social Psychology, 34*(1), 3–24. https://doi.org/10.1177/0261927X14544474

Hendriks Vettehen, P. (2015). Sensationalism. In: Donsbach, W. (Ed.). *The international encyclopedia of communication* (1st ed.) John Wiley & Sons https://doi.org/10.1002/9781405186407.wbiecs030.pub2
Hendriks Vettehen, P., & Kleemans, M. (2018). Proving the obvious? What sensationalism contributes to the time spent on news video. *Electronic News*, *12*(2), 113–127. https://doi.org/10.1177/1931243117739947
Hendriks Vettehen, P. G. J., Nuijten C. M., & Beentjes J. W. J. (2005). News in an age of competition: Sensationalism in Dutch television news 1995–2001. *Journal of Broadcasting & Electronic Media*, *49*, 282–295. https://doi.org/10.1207/s15506878jobem4903_2
Indulia, B. (2018, December 12). SC issues directions for protection of identity of victims of rape and sexual offences; need for victim friendly trial stressed upon. *ssconline.com*. Retrieved from <https://www.scconline.com/blog/post/2018/12/12/sc-issues-directions-for-protection-of-identity-of-victims-of-rape-and-sexual-offences-need-for-victim-friendly-trial-stressed-upon/>
Khamrang, L. (2023). Manipur mayhem: A latent enmity, generalized violence and state's apathy. *Journal of Management and Public Policy*, *15*(1), 4–15. https://doi.org/10.47914/jmpp.2023.v15i1.001
Kilgo, D. K. (2021). When is the "Racist" designation truly applicable? News media's contribution to the debatability of racism. *Television and New Media*, *22*(2), 186–204. https://doi.org/10.1177/1527476420982229
Kuthar, G. (2023, July 20). Outrage in India over video of Manipur women paraded naked, raped. *Al Jazeera*. https://www.aljazeera.com/news/2023/7/20/outrage-in-india-over-video-of-manipur-women-paraded-naked-raped
Laite, J. (2014). Justifiable sensationalism: Newspapers, public opinion and official policy about commercial sex in mid-twentieth-century Britain. *Media History*, *20*(2), 126–145. https://doi.org/10.1080/13688804.2014.898896
Lama, P. (2023, July 20). Manipur violence: Police confirm Kuki women paraded naked, gangraped by mob. *Hindustan Times*. https://www.hindustantimes.com/india-news/manipur-violence-latest-updates-fir-claims-women-paraded-naked-gangraped-by-mob-101689788178688.html
Layman, K. E. (2020). The representation of rape and sexual assault within news media.
Lindstrom, C. E. (1956). Sensationalism in the News. *Journalism Quarterly*, *33*(1), 9–14. https://doi.org/10.1177/107769905603300102
Lockyer, S., & Savigny, H. (2020). Rape jokes aren't funny: The mainstreaming of rape jokes in contemporary newspaper discourse. *Feminist Media Studies*, *20*(3), 434–449.
Marmaridou, S. (2011). Pragmalinguistics and sociopragmatics. In: Bublitz, W., & Norrick, N. (Eds.) Foundations of pragmatics (pp. 77–106), De Gruyter Mouton. https://doi.org/10.1515/9783110214260.77
Mathur, M. (2020, October 16). Horror Haunts Hathras. *Tehelka*. Retrieved April 25, 2023, from http://tehelka.com/horror-haunts-hathras/
Molek-Kozakowska, K. (2013). Towards a pragma-linguistic framework for the study of sensationalism in news headlines. *Discourse & Communication*, *7*(2), 173–197. https://doi.org/10.1177/1750481312471668
NDTV. (2020, September 29). Hathras horror, India's shame, once again [Video]. *YouTube*. https://www.youtube.com/watch?v=TcJ4kaI1zl4
NDTV. (2023, July 25). "Taken To Hilly Area…": Manipur woman narrates gang-rape horror. *NDTV*. https://www.ndtv.com/video/taken-to-hilly-area-manipur-woman-narrates-gang-rape-horror-713590
Pal, S. (2019, June 15). Linguistics of blame: Rape reporting remains sensationalist. *NewsClick*. Retrieved April 25, 2023, from https://www.newsclick.in/linguistics-blame-rape-reporting-remains-sensationalist
PTI. (2023a, April 8). Dalit woman raped, set afire in Rajasthan dies. *The Times of India*. Retrieved from <https://timesofindia.indiatimes.com/city/jodhpur/dalit-woman-raped-set-afire-in-rajasthan-dies/articleshow/99339814.cms>

PTI. (2023b, April 18). Unnao gang-rape: Accused set minor Dalit victim's house on fire; her infant son and sister fight for life. *The Times of India*. Retrieved from <https://timesofindia.indiatimes.com/city/lucknow/unnao-gang-rape-accused-set-minor-dalit-victims-house-on-fire-her-infant-son-and-sister-fight-for-life/articleshow/99587387.cms>

Raj, Suhasini. (2023, July 20). Video of sexual assault goes viral in India, Renewing attention on ethnic conflict. *The New York Times*. Retrieved from https://www.nytimes.com/2023/07/20/world/asia/india-manipur-video-woman.html

Rani, P. (2013). Privatisation, convergence and broadcasting regulations: A case study of the Indian television industry. In the Asian conference on media and mass communication. Retrieved from https://papers.iafor.org/wp-content/uploads/papers/mediasia2013/MediAsia2013_0139.pdf

Scroll Staff. (2024, February 29). Manipur: 219 killed in ethnic violence since May, 10,000 FIRs registered, says governor. *Scroll.in*. https://scroll.in/latest/1064482/manipur-219-killed-in-ethnic-violence-since-may-10000-firs-registered-says-governor

Sharma, N., & Choudhury, R. (2023, July 20). In Manipur horror, 2 women paraded naked on camera, allegedly Gang-Raped. *NDTV.com*. https://www.ndtv.com/india-news/in-manipur-horror-2-women-paraded-naked-on-camera-allegedly-gang-raped-4223105

Shinde, R. (2020, October 12). From indifference to victim-blaming: Why the mainstream media's coverage of Hathras is unsurprising. *Newslaundry*. Retrieved April 25, 2023, from https://www.newslaundry.com/2020/10/12/from-indifference-to-victim-blaming-why-the-mainstream-medias-coverage-of-hathras-is-unsurprising

Slattery, K. L., & Hakanen, E. A. (1994). Trend: Sensationalism versus public affairs content of local TV news: Pennsylvania revisited. *Journal of Broadcasting & Electronic Media*, *38*(2), 205–216. https://doi.org/10.1080/08838159409364257

Taneja, N. (2020, October 1). Attempted strangulation, fracture in neck: Chilling details of Hathras rape victim's postmortem emerge. https://www.indiatvnews.com. Retrieved April 25, 2023, from https://www.indiatvnews.com/news/india/hathras-rape-dalit-girl-postmortem-report-neck-broken-killed-horrific-details-emerge-653530

Velikova, S. (2021). The pragmatics of news actor labelling in media discourse: A case study. *Research Result Theoretical And Applied Linguistics*, *7*(4), 31–43, http://dspace.bsu.edu.ru/bitstream/123456789/60122/1/Velikova_Pragmatics_News.pdf

4 Prejudicial Reporting and Media Trials

Case Studies

Is public perception pivotal? Ideally and reasonably, what news channels broadcast and media audiences think should not predispose or conclude culpability. In (certain) popular criminal (and "sensational" sexual violence) cases reported in India, nevertheless, prejudicial reporting and popular public opinion seem to have altered the legal and judicial courses of action. Now, yet another critical question arises: Is it for the good or bad?

Taking cognisance of this conundrum, the Supreme Court of India, in September 2023, took "strong exception to media trials", referring to "biassed reporting (that) gives rise to public suspicion the person has committed an offence" and sought the Government of India to prepare guidelines for police to follow during press briefings in relation to criminal cases (Bhargava, 2023, September 13; BS Web Team, 2023, September 13). The apex court also stressed that the news media should not usurp the jurisdiction of the courts while drawing limitations on its role in proclaiming a person guilty or innocent (Khan & Ahsan, 2023, November 14).

One overarching observation is that media trails hurt the accused. Reflecting this sentiment, in a commentary posted on Bar and Bench, Khan and Ahsan (2023) write:

> In the recent past, the Indian mainstream media has not exactly covered itself in glory when it comes to reporting on cases that attract the public eye. TRP-driven narratives often cause prejudice against the accused, deeming them guilty before the courts have their say. Another allied concern, as highlighted by the apex court, is the leaking of information by the police to the media.

Reviewing recent cases that "garnered over-the-top coverage" and quoting several legal luminaries to frame the issue, the commentary underscored that in several cases, the media have gone to "great lengths and breadths to cover all angles" and "prime-time debates turned into jury trials even before the investigation was complete". It observed that several recent instances of "prejudging under the garb of reporting" have drawn criticism and even litigations.

DOI: 10.4324/9781003468042-7

Hearing one such litigation against media trial, the Bombay High Court observed that:

> These TV channels took upon themselves the role of the investigator, the prosecutor as well as the Judge and delivered the verdict as if, during the pandemic, except they all organs of the State were in slumber.
>
> (The Print Team, 2021, January 19)

Khan and Ahsan (2023) noted that besides self-regulation, news channels need to follow the Programme Code under the Cable Television Networks (Regulation) Act which prohibits television channels from broadcasting programmes that contain anything "defamatory, deliberate, false and suggestive innuendos and half truths".

In several instances, the courts have recognised and restricted media trials, especially while covering celebrity suicides (Joshi, 2020, October 23) and sexual violence (Kanth, 2023, December 22). Recently, the Kerala High Court laid down guidelines for the media to not reveal the identity of suspects to avoid a media trial (Kanth, 2023, December 22). It observed that prejudicial reporting can compromise the dignity and privacy of both the accused and the victim and also interfere with fair trial (Kanth, 2023, December 22).

In another case, the Delhi High Court observed that free speech does not mean the "right to publish just any kind of report concerning a matter before the court" or "carry out sting operations" on matters under trial (Tankha, 2020, September 30).

Another concern is that media trials and prejudicial reporting will also hurt the victims. Several recent studies have critically discussed the fairness of media trials (Armstrong et al., 2018; Gupta, Mawandiya & Gupta, 2021; Jain, 2021).

Jaffe (1965) saw the issue of prejudicial news reporting arise at the intersection of three conflicting concepts: the freedom of the press, the right to a free-fair trial and the administration of criminal justice. If the media coverage of sexual violence, in a way, could alter legal and judicial courses of action, either depriving the accused of an impartial trial or hampering the prosection's administering of criminal justice, it could be termed prejudicial reporting or media trial. In the context of the US, Jaffe (1965, p. 1) notes that prejudicial publicity can "expose jury members to information which is not eventually admitted in evidence at the trial. By thus enabling the jury to consider incompetent material, publicity can be prejudicial to the defendant, with the result that he is unable effectively to exercise his right to a fair trial".

Shaikh (2020) observed that media trials have the potential to influence judicial actions and hamper the "fundamental and constitutional rights of both the accused and the victim".

Even while appreciating the activist role of news media as a facilitator and expediter in "many matters including those affecting the collective conscience", Singh and Kumar (2014, December 1) deem media trials as a cause for concern, especially in cases of sexual violence against women, as sensationalism and hyperdetailing impinge upon the "victim's right to privacy or unfair denunciation of an alleged assailant". Singh and Kumar (2014, December 1) identify the facets of media trials: prematurely labelling the accused as guilty before the judgement is passed, conception of bias based on inadmissible evidence and interfering in the judicial process by impacting the sentencing process. Echoing similar views and exploring the associations among the media, judiciary and public opinion, Thomas (2023) notes that while media coverage can foster transparency and accountability, sensationalist and biassed media trials can create a prejudiced environment and skew public opinion, influencing court decisions and judgments.

Analysing two recent cases of sexual crimes against women in India (the 2019 Hyderabad gangrape-murder and the 2017 Kerala actress abduction-molestation case involving a popular actor) and their television coverage, this chapter reviews the gimmicky news media tendency to engage in prejudicial reporting and conduct media trials—overstepping their role as a watchdog and defender of democracy through information dissemination. Using a critical discourse analysis, this chapter identifies cues of prejudicial reporting that could potentially hinder legal action or influence judicial evaluation and biassed media trials that could skew public opinion and create an emotional outpour that may be misinformed or misdirected. This CDA approach also offers the scope to discuss power struggles (or the misuse of power) and inherent sexism.

Empirical data

Using a socio-cognitive CDA framework, this study analyses a sample of eight video YouTube posts from news outlets. Verbal and visual cues are analysed to identify key news frames and categorise them under distinctive discursive themes.

Case studies: On 27 November 2019, a veterinarian (in her 20s) was reportedly raped and murdered in Hyderabad (India) and four accused were arrested in the case on 29 November (Deshpande, 2021, November 28). On the same day of their arrest, their names, photographs and micro-details of the crime were reported in the news (Pavan, 2019, November 29). According to news reports, on 6 December 2019, all four accused were killed in a "fake" police encounter (Express Web Desk, 2022, May 20; PTI, 2019, December 6).

On 17 February 2017, a popular South Indian actor was reportedly abducted and sexually assaulted in a moving car near Kochi in the Indian state of Kerala (Oommen, 2022, January 12). Her assault was stated to be recorded. While three were reportedly arrested within two days in connection with the case, the prime accused, along with another, surrendered before a magistrate on 23 February 2017. Visual evidence of the assault was also handed over to a magistrate. In July 2017, a popular actor was arrested in the case and was alleged to have conspired the sexual assault that involved at least seven men (PTI, 2020, January 6).

In 2024, the trial of this controversial case was stated to be nearing conclusion (Express News Service, 2024, February 21; Varma, 2023, August 4).

Eight video news items related to these cases were purposively selected employing the search API of YouTube using relevant search terms.

A qualitative discourse analysis was performed on the video news items, analysing verbal and visual elements, and News Frames (or abstractions of the news messages) were identified by applying an inductive-manual analysis approach. The

Table 4.1 News frames and discursive themes

Discourse and Frames	*Description*	*Prevalence*
Convictive Discourse		
Establishment frame	Establishing the crime without (proper) evidence and terming the accused as guilty (before conviction)	Videos [1], [2] and [8]
Evidence frame	Presenting unverified or incomplete evidence establishing the crime or framing the accused	Video [8]
Emotional frame	Presenting public, political and familial sentiments against the accused	Videos [1], [2] and [3]
Punishment frame	Discussing or prescribing punishments for the accused	Videos [1], [2], [3] and [4]
Instigation frame	Prescribing legal and judicial courses of action	Videos [1] and [2]
Sensationalism frame	Using language that sensationalises the crime, potentially triggering emotional outpour in favour of the victim or altering the legal and judicial actions against the accused in the case	Videos [1] and [2]
Exonerative Discourse		
Victim-blaming frame	Suggesting that the victim was the cause of the crime	Videos [6]
Speculative frame	Raising doubts or presenting speculations (or conspiracy theories) that exonerate the accused	Videos [3] and [5]
Decriminalisation frame	Suggesting that the act of crime was not a criminal offence	Videos [3], [4] and [7]
Character assassination frame	Critically evaluating the victim or assassinating her character using cues such as lifestyle choices	Video [6]
Emotional frame	Presenting public, political and familial sentiments in favour of the accused in the case	Videos [3], [5], [6] and [7]
Evaluation frame	Evaluating investigation or evidence	Video [7]

identified frames were then categorised under broader discursive themes and presented in Table 4.1.

Identified news frames were categorised under two distinctive discourses: Convictive and exonerative. While the former is described as a multimodal discourse that uses language and symbols to establish the crime (sans evidence that proves it beyond reasonable doubt) and suggests that the accused is guilty (before a court verdict), potentially impeding the scope of an impartial trial, the latter is defined as a news discourse that uses language or symbols to suggest the exoneration of the accused. Under these discursive themes, the identified frames are described (refer to Table 4.1). In the discourse analysis of the news videos sampled for the study and presented below, the frames are identified from the news text and described.

News item [1] **(Republic World, 2019, November 30)**

Posted by Republic World on 30 November 2019 with 17,896 views (as of 13 June 2024), this news video is titled "Hyderabad Horror: 4 Accused In The Vicious Gangrape-Murder Sent To Judicial Custody For 14 Days". This title applies sensationalist stereotypes with the use of words such as "horror" (that dehumanises the crime) and "vicious" (for emphasis on violence and cruelty). With an animated background, the news video starts with the announcement that:

> and we have this breaking news coming in right now that the four accused have been sent to judicial custody, will be remanded to 14 days of judicial custody.

As the animated background changes to accommodate video footage of the four accused whose faces are covered, the news anchor reads:

> In fact, what we are getting to know is that the magistrate himself went to the jail premises and passed the very orders as the police couldn't move out the accused out of the jail as the roads were blocked as there were… continuous protests taking place outside the police station.

Meanwhile, in the background, altering headers are presented:

INDIA RISES IN ANGER

PARLIAMENTARIANS STILL SILENT

.

#ParliamentRaiseHyderabad

WON'T PARL DEBATE HYDERABAD?

.

#ParliamentRaiseHyderabad

'HANG RAPISTS' DEMAND

.

INDIA RISES IN ANGER

PROTESTS ACROSS INDIA

.

#ParliamentRaiseHyderabad

ANGER OVER HYDERABAD HORROR

As the animated background presents these headers, the voiceover shifts to another news anchor named Krishnamurti, who comes "live from" ground zero and is asked to divulge “details you’re picking up”. Krishnamurti informs about a public road blockade, a “lot of anger against them [the accused]” and a demand for “mob justice”.

While the news anchor terms the four people arrested as “accused”, the headers post a “hang rapists” demand, indirectly suggesting them as guilty. Here, this news video uses the Establishment frame, where the news media terms the accused as guilty (before conviction).

Further, using the header space, the news video features an Emotional frame (where it presents public sentiments through the headers “PROTESTS ACROSS INDIA” and “ANGER OVER HYDERABAD HORROR”). It also uses the Punishment frame, discussing (or prescribing) punishment using the header “‘HANG RAPISTS’ DEMAND”, and the Instigation frame (prescribing legal and judicial courses of action) with the headers “PARLIAMENTARIANS STILL SILENT”, “#ParliamentRaiseHyderabad” and “WON’T PARL DEBATE HYDERABAD?” This video news uses a language of generalisation (India rises in anger), exaggeration (Protests across India) and sensationalisation (terming the event as a horror), demands a Parliamentary debate through the tactful use of hashtag and question and suggests capital punishment for the “rapists” through single quotation that is also backed by public emotion. It is also to be noted that the sources of the generalised information and opinions presented in this news video are undisclosed, raising doubts about their veracity.

***News item [2]* (Republic World, 2019, December 2)**

Posted as a sequel to News item [1] by Republic World on 2 December 2019 with 19,893 views (as of 13 June 2024), this news video is titled “Big Statement By VP Venkaiah Naidu On Horrific Hyderabad Gangrape-Murder Case”. This news video presents a live feed from Rajya Sabha on the left and footage titled as “NATIONWIDE ANGER” on the right using a split screen. It carries the header “JAYA: LYNCH THE RAPISTS”, while the footer brands the news as “R. HAPPENING NOW” along with a statement that reads “OPPN RAISES HYD GANGRAPE IN PARLIAMENT”. Then, interchanging headers and footers read that:

> LYNCHING’ CALL BY RS MP
>
> MASSIVE UPROAR IN PARLIAMENT
>
> .
>
> PARL FORCED TO RAISE HYDERABAD
>
> OPPN RAISES HYD GANGRAPE IN PARLIAMENT
>
> .
>
> MPs FORCED TO BREAK SILENCE
>
> .
>
> IMPACT: MPs RAISE HYDERABAD
>
> .
>
> CALL FOR ACTION IN RAJYA SABHA

Meanwhile, the live feed from Rajya Sabha shows Rajya Sabha Chairman M. Venkaiah Naidu making statements such as "These men do not deserve mercy. Why should they be given appeal by state and central government?" and "What is required is not a new bill. What is required is political will, administrative skill, change of mindset and then go for [the] kill of the social evil". Using the headers, this news video sensationalises the parliamentary remarks as a "massive uproar" that calls for the "lynching" of the accused. It also frames the Rajya Sabha remarks as "forced" and "impact". Indirectly, this news report suggests extrajudicial execution as the punishment. It uses the Emotional, Instigative and Punishment frames.

***News item [3]* (WION, 2019, December 6)**

Posted by WION on 6 December 2019 with 6,205 views (as on 13 June 2024), this news video is titled "Hyderabad rape and murder case: Huge crowd gather at encounter site".

This news feature starts with a statement from the anchor that brands it as "a big story" who then begins the news with stress on "all four accused in the rape and murder of the 26 years old veterinary doctor in the Indian city of Hyderabad have been killed in a police encounter". The footer brands the news further with a Slug "HYDERABAD RAPE AND MURDER CASE" with an interchanging footer that reads:

ALL FOUR ACCUSED KILLED IN AN ENCOUNTER

ACCUSED WERE TAKEN TO CRIME SCENE FOR A RECREATION

.

ALL FOUR ACCUSED KILLED IN AN ENCOUNTER

ALL FOUR ACCUSED TRIED TO ESCAPE FROM THE SCENE

.

ACCUSED SHOT DEAD BY TELANGANA POLICE

ACCUSED ENCOUNTERED AT HH 44 HIGHWAY

.

LAST WEEK 26-YR-OLD RAPED, SET ABLAZE

POLICE: ALL 4 KILLED IN AN ENCOUNTER

.

ALL FOUR ACCUSED KILLED IN AN ENCOUNTER

AT LEAST 2 POLICEMEN ALSO INJURED IN THE INCIDENT

The news feature employs a Speculation frame to present that the "4 men were trying to escape from the scene and that is when the police had to resort to shooting them dead" and that the "accused tried to snatch weapons from the police", blaming the accused for their extrajudicial killings. It also hails the police action of arresting the victims in less than "twenty-four hours after the crime". The news video also employs an Emotional frame when they provide reactions from the family members of the victim stating "the family of the victim reacted to the encounter". The faces of the family members are blurred and changing footers are presented:

VICTIM'S FAMILY

.

ITS BEEN 10 DAYS SINCE MY DAUGHTER HAS PASSED AWAY AND WITHIN 10 DAYS THE ACCUSED HAVE BEEN KILLED

.

VICTIM'S FAMILY

.

I CONGRATULATE THE TELANGANA GOVERNMENT, POLICE AND EVERYONE WHO STOOD BY US

.

VICTIM'S FAMILY

.

MY DAUGHTER'S SOUL SHALL REST IN PEACE NOW

The news story claims that "the people of Hyderabad wanted a vandal styled justice" presenting the news frames of Emotion and Punishment.

It describes the crime as "brutal" while giving glimpses of the crime using words such as "punctured the tire", "gangraped at a deserted spot", "strangulated" and "burnt alive". It also shows crowds of protesting people, framing that "this incident has sent shockwaves across the country" and referring to the 2012 Delhi gangrape case. It also congratulates the police for the killings, which, in 2022, were deemed to be fake encounters.

News item [4] **(News9 Live. (2019, December 6)**

Posted by News9 Live on 6 December 2019 with 418 views (as on 13 June 2024), this news video titled "Nation salutes Hyderabad police" starts with a statement running in the background that reads that "RAPE ACCUSED KILLED". The video starts with a semi-blurred image of the four dead accused along with the header that reads:

JUSTICE SERVED

.

PRAISES POUR IN FOR ENCOUNTER

The screen is then split with videos of celebrities praising the encounter on the right and statements flashing on the left. Statements justify and frame the encounter as "justice": "Police delivered justice. People who commit such acts and terrorists should be treated this way".

Here, it uses voices to support the police (and their extrajudicial action) after sensational coverage of the crime and a series of calls for "lynching" of the "rapists". Evidently, here, the news media is engaged in a (extrajudicial) trial exonerating the police, terming the untried accused as "demons" who "were served justice at the same spot, at the same time and with same terror". Most of these are presented through the headers "JUSTICE HAS BEEN SERVED!! #Encounter", recurrently branding the #encounter as legitimate: "justice served", "delivered justice" and "justice is served… god's always watching".

Using the frame of Decriminalisation, the news item justifies the encounter as an action wanted, terming the police as "heroes": "SANDALWOOD SALUTES POLICE OFFICIAL".

To sum it up, in this extrajudicial trial of the media, those responsible for the extrajudicial encounters are exonerated (or celebrated), with comments such as "fair verdict", "justice" and "satisfactory answer". It bases its trial on media-informed public opinion and, in the end, indicates that this trial (or hearing) will continue: "the debate over the encounter is sure to carry on for some more time but as of now the majority seems to be in favour of it", showing a semi-blurred video of the four dead accused lying on the ground.

***News item [5]* (Times Now, 2017, July 14)**

Posted by Times Now on 14 July 2017, with 3,849 views (as of 15 June 2024), this news video is titled "Malayalam Actress Molestation Case: Support Pours In For Actor Dileep". It brands the news items as "BREAKING NOW" and "AFTER ACTOR DILEEP'S ARREST".

Changing headers, then, uses the Speculation frame to exonerate the accused:

SUPPORT POURS IN FOR ACTOR DILEEP

.

NOW, HIS MANAGER ABSCONDING

.

'ACTOR DILEEP MADE A SCAPEGOAT'

.

MANAGER LINKED TO MOLESTATION CASE

.

POSTERS SUPPORTING ACTOR ERECTED

.

MANAGER IN THE PURVIEW OF PROBE

-

SUPPORT POURS IN FOR ACTOR DILEEP

-

HELD ON CHARGES OF ABDUCTION

Using a conspiracy theory (Speculation frame), this news item attempts to divert the case (to the manager) and exonerate the popular actor ("scapegoat") involved. It also uses the Emotional frame in support of the accused ("support pours in" and "posters erected").

News item [6] **(Reporter Live, 2017, June 27)**

Posted by Reporter Live on 27 June 2017 with 16,209 views (as of 15 June 2024), this news video is titled "DILEEP'S REMARKS AGAINST ATTACKED ACTRESS | Reporter Live".

In this news item, which presents an exclusive telephonic interview with the news channel, the popular actor accused of conspiring and instigating the sexual assault comments on the "past relationship" between the survivor of the sexual assault and the main accused, implicitly engaging in character assassination and victim-blaming, while exonerating himself.

This video news item starts with the actor's statement:

> *Nammal eppozhum chindikanam. Nammal aaroke aayitu kootu koodanam ennu ellavarum chindikanam.* (We need to think always. Everyone needs to think with whom we group with)

To which the news anchor comments "*Manasilayilla*" (can't understand) and the actor engaged in the interview replies:

> *Nammal... Nammde koot.* (We… our gang)

Then, he goes on to comment that:

> *Ivaru ellavarum orumich nadanna aalkkar alle...*
> *athoke police anweshikate…* (Aren't all of them people who were together… let the police investigate that…)

When the news anchor interrupts to ask "Who all?", actor Dileep adds:

> *Nikesh* [addressing the anchor] *ipo paranja aalkar oke onnichu nadanna aalkar alle? athoke avar anweshichitundo ennu ariyilallo...* (Nikesh, weren't all the people you mentioned now the people who walked together? All that, don't know whether they [the police] investigated)

-

Further, the actor tries to feign innocence in the interview:

Ivar oke orumich work cheythirunna aalkar alle? Njan kanditilla ivare onnum. Ennodu lalettan paranjitullathaanu.

Aa ellarum orumich Goa yil oke orumich work cheyyunna artists aayirunnu. Avar bayankara friends aayirunnu. Ennoke ennod paranjath alle. (Weren't all of them people who worked together? I haven't seen them. Brother [director] Lal told me. All of them were artists who worked together in Goa together. They were very close friends. That way I was told)

After these comments, the news anchor asks:

Athanu abakadathinu vazhi vechathu ennanu thangal viswasikkunnath? (So you believe that this has paved the way for the trouble?)

And the popular actor's (and accused's) reply was:

aa... Apo athaa... athe... Athinte karayngal oororutharu nokkande? Njan aaru aayitu kootu koodanam? Njan endayalaum ee vaka aalkaru onnumaayit kootu koodan thayyarumalla. Njan athil valare sradhichu nadakana aalumaanu. (Yes… then yes… yes… Don't each one [of us] need to look into its matters? Whatever happens, I won't join these types of men. I am a man who treads with extra caution about it)

***News item [7]* (Reporter Live, 2017, July 13)**

Posted by Reporter Live on 13 July 2017 with 570,943 views (as of 15 June 2024), this news video is titled "DILEEP IS COMPLETELY INNOCENT SAYS BROTHER ANOOP | Reporter Live". In this news, the brother of the actor-accused claims the innocence of his brother (employing an Emotional frame) stating that the evidence against the actor was fabricated (Evaluation frame) and terming the events a scripted drama that surpasses cinema (Decriminalisation frame). The news interview text of the actor's brother reflects familial sentiments, terming it a fake case and exonerating his brother (the accused):

Ithu bayankara naadakeeyamaanu ee cheyth kondirikkunne... Varum... Thirich verum (This what is being done is over dramatic… will come… will come around [implying that the truth will eventually be revealed]).

When asked if the letter was given to him, the actor's brother says:

"İlla... illa." (No… no) *"Ithonnum sathyam alla. Ithellam chamach kond irikukayaanu."* (This is not true. All of this is being fabricated)

Cinemaye vellunna script aanu nadannu kond irikkunne... Ithu thirich varum... Theliyikkum... Sathyam, daivam oke undekil varum... Nammal varum.

> (What is happening is a script that surpasses cinema… It will come around… will prove… If at all truth and God exist, will come… we will come)

***News item [8]* (The News Minute, 2022, April 10)**

Posted by The News Minute on 10 April 2022 with 111,321 views (as of 15 June 2024), this news video is titled "I surrendered after realising truth in Dileep case was different: Sai Shankar".

In this news item, a "hacker" who was tasked with destroying incriminating data (documents and pictures) in Dileep's phone as claimed by him, is interviewed telephonically. According to the hacker, initially, associates from Dileep's legal council contacted and gave him the job but later the actor himself was also directly involved in seeking technical help.

After understanding the criminality involved in this technical job and to avoid unnecessary trouble for his family, the hacker says, he surrendered to the police. This news item uses the Evidence frame (presenting unverified evidence) to establish or raise suspicion that the actor accused of instigating the sexual assault was, indeed, guilty.

In television reporting, reviewing the video news items, it is perceivable that there is a clear lack of proper attribution to sources from whom the information broadcast was acquired.

An analysis identified two overarching news discourses in the videos sampled: the Convictive (that explicitly or implicitly presents the accused as guilty of the crime before court conviction beyond reasonable doubt) and the Exonerative (diverting the case in favour of the accused). News frames identified from the news text and described under these discourses allude to prejudicial reporting and conducting media trials—that could be considered acts of misuse of media power and press freedom and reflections of inherent sexism, especially when the victim is blamed for the crime. In the case of the Hyderabad rape-murder, the news media reported a "nationwide emotional outpour" and political "calls for lynching" (possibly caused due to the hyper-sensational news coverage of the crime: describing the "heinous" crime in detail, naming the accused and circulating their photographs) that could have prompted the police to resort to extrajudicial measures of murdering the accused before they were produced in court.

A section termed these killings as "justice" served on time, which the "nation celebrated". Do the (judicial or extrajudicial) capital punishments delivered to the rapists in cases that the news media chooses to sensationalise deter sexual assaults?

In a media commentary (Singh, 2020, October 30), Flavia Agnes, a women's rights lawyer and co-founder of Majlis, points out that the "realities of rape are ignored when cases stir public sentiment and pressure". In the commentary, Agnes is quoted as saying:

> For us to say that the success of a case is only when the judge gives maximum sentencing [or] the death penalty is to give in to a demand made out of ignorance. Sensational demands are met with sensational solutions.

Agnes opines that "celebrating a death penalty only deters the majority of victims from reporting their cases" (Singh, 2020, October 30).

Indications are that the mass media still wields power. It is also a democratic device for positive social change. In several cases of violent (and fatal) sexual assaults against women, the news media has been instrumental in drawing public attention, standing by and supporting the cause of the victims, protecting them, forcing timely remedial measures, curtailing scopes for corruption-power abuse, holding the powerful accountable and leading to legal and judicial reforms. But there is always a more perilous threat lurking behind the mass media movements, partisan prejudicial publicity and media trials that may perhaps upset the equitable and tedious-but-lawful judicial processes: What if the news media is misdirected based on misinformation? When, with the help of online social media that dominates communication, messages can go viral in an instant and objective facts are less influential in shaping public opinion than appeals to emotion and personal belief (pointing to the phenomenon of post-truth), the news media need to be more aware of their limitations and judicial interference.

Prakash (n.d.) views the issue as a conflict between two parties engaged in the same task of discovering the "truth", upholding "democratic values" and dealing with "social problems". An intrusion happens creating friction between these pillars of democracy, when the media, with the onus of informing the public about crime and criminals, impedes impartial trials with an obvious lack of competence or attention to jurisprudence (Prakash, n.d.).

Several studies (Howitt, 1982; Imrich, Mullin & Linz, 1995; Oehmer, 2021) suggest that prejudicial reporting could hamper fair trials. Oehmer (2021) further questions the role of legal constraints in the reporting of trials, referring to the situation in Great Britain. Oehmer (2021) observes that the law on Contempt of Court has been used to control media activity in this area. However, much of this is built upon assumptions about the nature of the juror, which may not be well-founded (Oehmer, 2021). Research evidence is reviewed and it is suggested that the fairness of the juror and an ability to react in an unbiassed manner to evidence after being exposed to 'prejudicial' publicity are more accurate interpretations (Oehmer, 2021). It is suggested that there are alternatives to legalistic controls over the media and that abandoning some legal control might not have the undesirable consequences sometimes imagined. Imrich, Mullin and Linz (1995) and Dixon and Linz (2002) both provide empirical evidence of the prevalence of prejudicial reporting, with Imrich, Mullin and Linz finding that over a quarter of suspects in American newspapers were portrayed as problematic and Dixon and Linz (2002) revealing a higher likelihood of prejudicial information being associated with Black and Latino defendants on Los Angeles television news. These studies underscore the need for ethical and legal considerations in reporting criminal cases.

Dixon and Linz (2002) posit that 19 percent of defendants in crime stories had potentially prejudicial information associated with them. Phillipson (2008) noted that media sensationalism was influencing public perceptions and impacting judicial processes. It also goes against the criminal jurisprudence that an "accused (irrespective of the crime committed) is entitled to fair trial" and "is innocent till proven guilty beyond any reasonable doubt".

Media trial is now a familiar word, with the mainstream media drawing critical flak now and then when they overstep their legal and moral perimeters and venture into predatory practices to capitalise on sensitive and controversial cases that have gained public attention.

Freedom of the press is equated with the freedom of the people. And the power of the news media rests in the people, its abilities to control and present their perceptions (attitude, emotion, and eventually, behaviour), its access to information, its opportunity to choose and filter that information (sometimes, manipulating it) and wide reach to the masses. For instance, in the news item [1] analysed, Republic World was found instigating the Parliament to discuss "Hyderabad", reasoning that the "nation rises in anger" (personifying India) over the "Hyderabad horror" (dehumanising the crime). It also sets the agenda for Parliament, stating that there is a "hang rapists" demand. Here, the media can be perceived as tactfully trying to control the powerful using the power of the people (demand, quote and protest). In an illusive consequence to this news report, the same channel live streams footage from the Rajya Sabha discussion on the rape-murder case (news item [2]), which conceivably called for the "kill" (or "lynch" the "rapists") that the channel branded as "impact" (of its reporting?). Eventually, the accused are killed in an extrajudicial police encounter and the nation "celebrates" it. In the case of the Hyderabad "horror", the powerplay of the news media is identifiable: how it feeds the curiosities of the audience in certain cases, fuels an emotional outpour and uses that rage (indeed, which, most of us must have experienced when cases like the Hyderabad were reported) to "impact" the powerhouses. Or it seems so on the surface. Underneath, there is also a risk of the news media having a hidden agenda or it being used as a tool for diversion. Some could also use the mass media as a means to control public opinion and channel cases in desired directions.

When people, generally, still perceive the news media as a source of credible information, such media trials, presented as the people's court, could be seen as an abuse of (people's) power. In several recent instances, Indian courts, using their influence, have attempted to curb this abuse of media power in cases where the media went overboard, alluding to a power struggle.

Empirical studies that can identify cues and facets of prejudicial reporting that are at times not explicit in a converging and advancing digital media environment are needed to sensitise the stakeholders on this issue and frame policies for the curtailment of this conundrum.

References

Armstrong, G., Vijayakumar, L., Niederkrotenthaler, T., Jayaseelan, M., Kannan, R., Pirkis, J., & Jorm, A. F. (2018). Assessing the quality of media reporting of suicide news in India against World Health Organization guidelines: A content analysis study of nine major newspapers in Tamil Nadu. *Australian & New Zealand Journal of Psychiatry*, *52*(9), 856–863.

Bhargava, A. K. (2023, September 13). Supreme Court cracks down on 'Media trials', wants guidelines in 3 months. *NDTV.com*. Retrieved June 12, 2024, from https://www.ndtv.com/india-news/supreme-court-media-trials-police-guidelines-supreme-court-cracks-down-on-media-trials-wants-guidelines-in-3-months-4385927

BS Web Team. (2023, September 13). Supreme Court calls for guidelines on media reporting in criminal cases. www.business-standard.com. https://www.business-standard.com/india-news/supreme-court-calls-for-guidelines-on-media-reporting-in-criminal-cases-123091300856_1.html

Deshpande, A. (2021, November 28). Hyderabad veterinarian case: Rape, rage, and an exchange of fire. *The Hindu*. https://www.thehindu.com/news/national/telangana/rape-rage-and-an-exchange-of-fire/article61606028.ece

Dixon, T. L., & Linz, D. (2002). Television news, prejudicial pretrial publicity, and the depiction of race. *Journal of Broadcasting & Electronic Media*, *46*(1), 112–136. https://doi.org/10.1207/s15506878jobem4601_7

Express News Service. (2024, February 21). 2017 Actor sexual abuse case: Kerala HC orders sessions judge to give memory card 'leak' probe report to survivor. *The Indian Express*. https://indianexpress.com/article/india/dileep-sexual-abuse-case-kerala-hc-orders-sessions-judge-to-give-memory-card-leak-probe-report-to-survivor-9173802/

Express Web Desk. (2022, May 20). Recap: How 2019 Hyderabad gangrape accused were 'deliberately' shot dead by police. *The Indian Express*. https://indianexpress.com/article/cities/hyderabad/hyderabad-fake-encounter-recap-7927828/

Gupta, N. K., Mawandiya, S. K., & Gupta, P. (2021). Human rights, fair trial, media and criminal contempt in India: Critical analysis. *Turkish Online Journal of Qualitative Inquiry*, *12*(7), 2634–2653.

Howitt, D. (1982). *Pre-trial publicity: The case for reform. Current Psychological Reviews*, *2*(3), 311–322.

Imrich, D. J., Mullin, C., & Linz, D. (1995). Measuring the extent of prejudicial pretrial publicity in major American newspapers: a content analysis, *Journal of Communication*, *45*(3), 94–118. https://doi.org/10.1111/j.1460-2466.1995.tb00745.x

Jaffe, C. (1965). The press and the oppressed. A study of prejudicial news reporting in criminal cases. Part I: The problem, existing solutions and remaining doubts. *The Journal of Criminal Law, Criminology, and Police Science*, *56*(1), 1–17.

Jain, I. (2021). Media trial in India fair or not? *Nyaayshastra Law Review*, *2*(1), 1–11.

Joshi, N. (2020, October 23). [SSR Media Trial case] We are dealing with something unprecedented, so we have to lay down guidelines: Bombay High Court. *Bar And Bench - Indian Legal News*. https://www.barandbench.com/news/litigation/media-trial-case-have-to-lay-down-guidelines-bombay-high-court

Kanth, A. (2023, December 22). Media will no longer have free rein revealing accused in rape cases. *Open Digest*. https://opendigest.in/media-will-no-longer-have-free-rein-revealing-accused-in-rape-cases/

Khan, A. & Ahsan, S. (2023, November 14). Media trial conundrum: Experts say sensationalism generates good TRPs, not good outcomes. *Bar And Bench - Indian Legal News*. https://www.barandbench.com/columns/media-trial-conundrum-experts-say-sensationalism-generates-good-trps-not-good-outcomes

News9 Live. (2019, December 6). Nation salutes Hyderabad police [Video]. *YouTube*. Retrieved June 13, 2024, from https://youtu.be/PNCQq7ucm6g?feature=shared

Oehmer, F. (2021). Prejudgment of the accused (Justice and Crime Coverage). DOCA-Database of Variables for Content Analysis. file:///C:/Users/Kaifia%20Ancer/Downloads/2826-Article%20Text-4731-1-10-20210620%20(2).pdf

Oommen, R. (2022, January 12). Timeline of events in Kerala actor assault case as survivor reveals her identity. *India Today*. https://www.indiatoday.in/india/story/kerala-actor-assault-case-dileep-timeline-events-1899110-2022-01-12

Pavan, P. (2019, November 29). Hyderabad veterinary doctor gang rape, murder case: All four arrested accused are in 20s. *Mumbai Mirror*. https://mumbaimirror.indiatimes.com/news/india/hyderabad-veterinary-doctor-gang-rape-murder-case-all-four-arrested-accused-are-in-20s/articleshow/72298557.cms

Phillipson, G. (2008). Trial by media: The betrayal of the first amendment's purpose. *Law and Contemporary Problems*, *71*(4), 15–29. http://www.jstor.org/stable/27654682

Prakash, B. (n.d.). Trial by media - a threat to our judicial system? Retrieved June 14, 2024, from https://www.legalserviceindia.com/legal/article-4292-trial-by-media-a-threat-to-our-judicial-system-.html

PTI. (2019, December 6). All 4 accused in Hyderabad rape-murder case killed in encounter: Telangana police. *The Economic Times*. https://economictimes.indiatimes.com/news/politics-and-nation/all-4-accused-in-hyderabad-gang-rape-murder-shot-dead/articleshow/72393178.cms?from=mdr

PTI. (2020, January 6). Kerala actress abduction case: Charges framed against actor Dileep, nine other accused. *The Economic Times*. https://economictimes.indiatimes.com/magazines/panache/kerala-actress-abduction-case-charges-framed-against-actor-dileep-nine-other-accused/articleshow/73121894.cms?from=mdr

Reporter Live. (2017, July 13). Dileep is completely innocent says brother Anoop [Video]. YouTube. Retrieved June 13, 2024, from https://youtu.be/wbwKGorK2gQ?si=kL9zcMv4_Ub-wQoT

Reporter Live. (2017, June 27). Dileep's remarks against attacked actress [Video]. Retrieved June 14, 2024, from https://youtu.be/_fwj6uk5eOk?si=2xkBZ4Eu1XWzD-g5

Republic World. (2019, December 2). Big statement by VP Venkaiah Naidu on horrific Hyderabad gangrape-murder case [Video]. *YouTube*. Retrieved June 13, 2024, from https://youtu.be/J2I0TTvzy58?feature=shared

Republic World. (2019, November 30). Hyderabad horror: 4 accused in the vicious gangrape-murder sent to judicial custody for 14 days [Video]. *YouTube*. Retrieved June 13, 2024, from https://youtu.be/RQo1Uy4BsxQ?feature=shared

Shaikh, S. (2020). Law and media trial in India. *Journal of National Law University Delhi*, *7*(1-2), 76–93. https://doi.org/10.1177/22774017221096889

Singh, A. (2020, October 30). Media sensationalism and mob mentality in India: Which rapes cause outrage? *Women's Media Center*. https://womensmediacenter.com/women-under-siege/media-sensationalism-and-mob-mentality-in-india-which-rapes-cause-outrage

Singh, A., & Kumar, A. (2014, December 1). Media trials in India. Available at SSRN: https://ssrn.com/abstract=2552426 or http://dx.doi.org/10.2139/ssrn.2552426

Tankha, R. (2020, September 30). Where does press freedom end and trial by media begin? (n.d.). *The Wire*. https://thewire.in/media/press-freedom-trial-by-media-supreme-courthttps://theprint.in/judiciary/media-played-investigator-prosecutor-judge-in-rajput-case-full-text-of-bombay-hc-order/588471/

The News Minute. (2022, Apr 10). I surrendered after realising truth in Dileep case was different: Sai Shankar [Video]. *YouTube*. Retrieved June 13, 2024, from https://youtu.be/GZdUFKGzELI?si=tQl8Fg8ySXHm-k6l

The Print Team. (2021, January 19). Media played 'investigator, prosecutor & judge' in Rajput case—full text of Bombay HC order. *The Print*. https://theprint.in/judiciary/media-played-investigator-prosecutor-judge-in-rajput-case-full-text-of-bombay-hc-order/588471/

Thomas, C. R. (2023). The power and pitfalls of media trials: The effect on Indian judiciary. *International Journal of Law Management & Humanities*, *6*, 3348.

Times Now. (2017, July 14). Malayalam Actress Molestation Case: Support Pours In For Actor Dileep, YouTube. https://youtu.be/6MZy8hU6DsQ?si=b3jmlAArZ4MldvWE

Varma, V. (2023, August 4). SC extends time to complete trial in Kerala actress sexual assault case. *Hindustan Times*. https://www.hindustantimes.com/india-news/supreme-court-extends-time-for-trial-in-actress-abduction-case-completion-date-set-for-march-31-2024-101691176857787.html

Wion. (2019, December 6). Hyderabad rape and murder case: Huge crowd gather at encounter site [Video]. *YouTube*. Retrieved June 13, 2024, from https://youtu.be/vzXy2-G04Ok?si=oEv5qZ_Ru3568JiX

5 Eroticism and Exhibition

Editorial Exploits in Rape Reporting

Eroticism and sexualisation—through hyperdetailed news narratives—and exhibition—in terms of explicit imagery—while reporting extreme sexual violence against women such as rape continue to remain understudied issues. Several studies have performed content and discourse analysis of news on sexual crimes to analyse issues such as the gender difference in rape reporting (Pino & Meier, 1999), rape myths (Sacks, Ackerman & Shlosberg, 2018), characterisation of the perpetrators and victims in the news narratives (Breen et al., 2017; Skaff, 2022) and victim-blaming (Gravelin, Biernat & Kerl, 2016; Cabrera, 2018; Schwark & Bohner, 2019). A handful of studies have, however, pointed to a lack of empathy for the survivors (Baum & Schwarz, 2018). Still, the sexual and sexist aspects of such news reporting are yet to garner widespread scholarly attention and critical pondering.

Post the 2012 Delhi gangrape, sexual crimes against women, although with the essential news ingredients of prominence or extremities, have been hogging editorial limelight in India. In fact, convergent journalism has carved a niche area for such sexual crimes, allocating prime space and creating a reporting culture. As minute detailing, construction of engaging narratives, using headline shockers, offbeat news lead styles, anecdotal starts and literary devices and impactful imagery become the cornerstones of first-rate reporting in contemporary times, this beat takes a beating. Disturbing crimes such as the Delhi gangrape have received extensive coverage, detailing the violations and presenting gory imagery.

Hyperdetailing

When does it become too much when it comes to reporting sexual violence against women? In a multilingual national study of the news reporting of sexual violence in India and that UNESCO published, Sreedharan and Thorsen (2021) underscore through interviews how a section of journalists believe over-detailing is important while reporting such sexual violence.

According to the report, several journalists suggested that "highlighting details about the crime served to create an impact on the audience and jolted them out of indifference". News reports on crimes against women are deliberately over-detailed

DOI: 10.4324/9781003468042-8

so that "the reader feels for the victim and is angered by the perpetrator" (Sreedharan & Thorsen, 2021, p. 62). During interviews, a section of the news reporters presents a belief that over-detailing in such news reports is essential and in the best interests of the victims and against the crime. In their own words, "highlighting brutality was always a priority, but not just to grab eyeballs" (Sreedharan & Thorsen, 2021, p. 62). The same reporter was quoted as saying, "It's our job to hold a mirror to society. The charge has been levelled a lot of times that we get into titillating details, but I never agree with that because until we get into the nitty-gritty of what actually happened[,] the enormity does not come across" (Sreedharan & Thorsen, 2021, p. 62).

Over-detailing could be problematic while reporting sexual violence when:

1 There is an excessive focus on graphic or lurid details (unwarranted information about the crime that can re-traumatise the victim)
2 Such detailing is in some way gratuitous or exploitative, eroticising or sexualising the crime (through direct descriptions of the sexual acts and avoiding euphemisms)
3 There is a tendency to narrate the crime (presenting it as a first-person account [or witness] while it is not the case)

Eunbi et al. (2014), in a comparative study of news coverage of sexual crimes in major Korean and American newspapers, used the news framing approach to analyse 1,708 news articles and the nature of sensationalism. Study results identified that the Korean newspapers used more sensational headlines and images than informative ones compared to their American counterparts. While the Korean newspapers featured quotes and interviews of police or experts, often presenting over-detailed accounts as if the journalists were eyewitnesses to the sexual crime, the American newspapers used indirect quotes of the police. Further, the framing analysis showed that Korean newspapers typically detailed the process of the sexual crime, described the criminals and disclosed the personal information of the victims (Eunbi et al., 2014).

Stewart et al. (2023) identified the traumatisation of reporting as one of the main reasons why most victim-survivors never report their abuse or sexual violence. While this pertains to a lack of faith in the criminal justice system, when their case becomes a talking point in the press, the re-traumatisation that they suffer is manifold, especially in conservative settings.

Pande (2021, p. 403) argued that rape news in India often exploits the victims, sometimes revealing their identity or geographical location and providing "grisly details" of the crime.

Pande (2021) argued that Indian journalists provoked public reaction by providing gruesome details of the case and asserted that such hyper detailing might propagate a normalised culture of rape through desensitisation of the male readers.

Explicit imagery

While there is a generic editorial tendency to present news articles with imagery in contemporary times, perhaps for credibility and visual appeal, news stories about sexual violence, too, tend to feature explicit imagery in the form of blurred photographs and videos, gory representative images and illustrations. Along with hyperdetailed and titillating textual news content, this culture propagates a thirst for details and imagery, which is often followed by a social media search when sexual violence is presented as sensational breaking news.

Dodge (2016) observed that the ways in which photographs of sexual violence are recorded and digitally disseminated have long-term effects on the survivors and their lives. Documenting visual images of sexual crimes online could also normalise sexual violence (Dodge, 2016) and "the ubiquity and permanence of digital photographs create new concerns for victims of sexual violence". On three cases of sexual assaults that were recorded and disseminated over the online social media, Dodge (2016) writes that:

> In each of these cases, these girls were left not only to deal with the effects of being sexually assaulted, but were also left to grapple with the humiliation of their assaults being shared over and over again on social media networks and the resulting bullying and cyberbullying of peers who echoed sentiments that the girls were 'sluts' and therefore deserved this treatment.
>
> (Dodge, 2016, p. 66)

When the images of sexual violence, victims and gore feature in the news, they widen their reach and perpetuate a rape culture (Dodge, 2016). When people share, consume and comment on those images of sexual assault, they become more than mere evidence of sexual assaults. Dodge (2016, p. 66) also observed that young consumers drew gratification from the images of violated bodies. Similarly, when sexual assault videos are viewed and shared, excitement may disregard the fact that they are "morally disturbing" (Dodge, 2016, p. 72).

Taking the cases of the 2023 Manipur sexual violence, the 2020 Hathras gangrape-murder, the 2018 Kathua rape case and the 2017 Unnao rape and conducting a multimodal analysis of text and imagery, this chapter implicates the digital news media that encompasses social media channels of overt exhibitionism while reporting sexual crimes against women. This chapter pays attention to overdetailing in the textual descriptions of sexual crimes and explicitness in the gory news imagery to explain how contemporary news reporting tactics are trained to send shockwaves. Further, this chapter also discusses how this trend and discourse exploits and could stimulate the readers, evoking emotional and erotic responses.

Case studies

The 2023 Manipur sexual violence

In May 2023, two women were physically and sexually assaulted by a mob in the Indian state of Manipur when conflict and violence erupted between two communities of people in the state. Video footage of this atrocious sexual offence surfaced a month later and went viral, garnering international media attention and "drawing massive condemnation and calls for action" (Sharma & Choudhury,

2023, July 20). About a year later, the Central Bureau of Investigation filed a chargesheet against the perpetrators and six police personnel for the sexual assault (Livemint, 2024, May 1). While a slew of news articles with images and footage reported the crime, most of them described the event as the "Manipur horror" where two women were "stripped and paraded naked" with one of them "gangraped" in a "paddy field".

Even till May 2024, several online news articles from popular mainstream media still featured blurred images of the sexual assault, while a few others still carried illustrations of this crime. For instance, an India Today article (Deka, 2023, July 20) featured semi-blurred screengrabs from the sexual assault video that was circulated online. Another report, covered by The Wire Staff (2023, July 20), also features a semi-blurred screengrab from the viral video with details of the incident. The article uses words like "apparently Meiteis" indicating the communal identity of the perpetrators, "led into some fields" describing the location of the crime. Vivid terms were used in the article (The Wire Staff, 2023) to describe the crime: "some of the men groping the women", "forced all the women to strip" and "one woman, in her 20s, was gang-raped". Similarly, there was a string of hyperdetailed articles on the sexual assault.

For instance, an India Today article on "Manipur naked parade: Left to die in paddy field, how two women ran for life and justice" (Hauzel, 2023, July 23) uses phrases such as "naked parade" and "stripped naked" to describe the sexual violence meted out against the women.

This news report describes the village of the victims in detail:

> B Phainom is a nondescript village deep inside Manipur in Kangpokpi district. Had it not been for the leaked video of the two lady residents of the village who were paraded naked (one of them raped), this village would be just another sleepy village forgotten on the wayside just like many other adjoining villages that's now reduced to ashes. The 'B' in the name of village stands for "Buite" representing a clan of Vaiphei community who were the early settlers of this village which has about 40 houses.

Though the names of the two survivors are "withheld to protect the privacy of the survivors", the article provides detailed demographics of their families, including the ages and educational backgrounds of the victims. While one victim's brother is named, another victim's husband is named in the article. The younger victim is characterised as follows: "Those who know 'Miss Y' talk of her beauty and simplicity. 'She is quiet and reserved'."

Sexualised language is used to offer a witness-like narration of their ordeal:

> Stripped naked and walked the street with men following and forgetting they have their mothers, daughters and sisters at home. What is even more chilling is their tale of escape after they were subjected to the most heinous crime. The two ladies who were left to die in the paddy field rose like phoenixes to pick up their clothes. They ran many kilometres for their lives. They live to tell their stories.

A narrative style with lurid details and figurative language is employed to romanticise the crime and this is evident in the following excerpts of the news article:

> That's when the ladies were forced to strip or be killed... The two ladies were left to die in the paddy field. Perhaps, it was their spirit of resilience and inner strength that enabled them to picked themselves up after all that was done to them. They ran back towards their own village B. Phainom under the darkening sky. By then, it was deserted and all the houses were burnt... The villagers there had already fled and it wore a haunted look... The kind hospitality of the villagers was a much-needed balm. Yet the ladies did not speak a word about their ordeal while they died a thousand deaths inside...

This hyperdetailed article with gratuitous and voyeuristic descriptions does not mention its sources; instead, it is mostly presented like a first-person account.

At the end, it also, ironically, states:

> They are reeling under extreme shock and trauma. Media must report but not necessarily by asking them questions. To take them back to the trauma by asking very obvious questions might do more harm though the intention might be noble. That's where the role of responsible media comes in... At the back of my mind, an uneasy question haunts me. What if the video never went viral? Would we have ever allowed 'Miss Y' and 'Mrs. X' to live with their trauma and fight with the demon alone? Also, what about the many unreported cases of women who met the most wretched end from the day the violence erupted in May 3rd? Perhaps that's another story for another day!"

Extensive background information about the village, its inhabitants and personal details of the victims and their families seem unnecessary for the core reporting of the assault. Such levels of divulgence could be termed hyper detailing. The descriptive language used to depict the assault, such as "stripped naked and walked the street" and "left to die in the paddy field", while impactful, may cross a line into being overly graphic or voyeuristic. The article also spends a significant amount of time establishing the victims as virtuous, educated and innocent.

The key issue is finding the right balance between reporting the critical facts of the case and respecting the privacy and dignity of the victims. Excessive detailing could be exploitative.

2017 Unnao rape case

Popularly referred to as the Unnao rape case, it involved a group sexual assault of a female minor on 4 June 2017, in the Unnao district in the Indian state of Uttar Pradesh (The Tribune,9, December 20; Hindustan Times, 2018, April 10). The death of the victim's father in judicial custody and her attempt at self-immolation further drew media attention to the sexual assault, leading to protests and demand for arrests of the accused (Express Web Desk, 2018, April 14). Kuldeep Sengar, the prime accused of the sexual assault and who was also a Member of the Legislative Assembly of the ruling party, was arrested and sentenced to life imprisonment on 20 December 2019 (Achom, 2018, April 13; Pandey, 2018, April 13). He was convicted of the sexual assault as well as the death of the victim's father in judicial custody on 16 April 2019 (Hindustan Times, 2018, April 10; Khan, 2019, December 16).

A Hindustan Times article featured a pixelated image of the Unnao Rape survivor (Hindustan Times, 2018, April 10).

The rape of the minor and police inaction garnered media attention when her father died in judicial custody. Several media outlets published event timelines and ground reports (Express Web Desk, 2018, April 14; Hindustan Times, 2018, April 10; The Tribune, 2019, December 20; Sharma, 2018, April 12). A Delhi court in 2019 directed the media to abstain from reporting the names and addresses of the rape survivor, her family and witnesses (PTI, 2019, August 7). In a commentary on editorial insensitivity, Dutta (2018, May 1) writes:

> Do you see the paradigm here? We have been desensitised and dehumanised to an extent that we do not acknowledge rape for what it is, anymore. We acknowledge it for its associations and repercussions. Why was there so much outrage regarding the Kathua and Unnao cases? They had political connections and communal reasons. What we cannot ignore is the insensitivity by the press. Rape cannot be made a tool for propagation of political agenda. Yes, we should point out the communal or political aspects of the crime, but we point them out as aspects of the issue, and not the issue in itself.

Further, on media sensationalism of sexual violence, the writer observes:

> It is unbelievable that rape does not become a sensitive, widely spoken issue by itself. Instead, we have to produce elements for sensationalism, in order to acknowledge what has been done. We sensationalise, we don't speak, or empathise, or understand.
>
> (Dutta, 2018, May 1)

2018 Kathua rape case

Seven people were reportedly involved in the abduction, gangrape and murder case of an eight-year-old girl at Kathua in Jammu and Kashmir in early 2018. Six of them, including three police personnel, were convicted in 2019 for the gangrape and murder (Ohri, 2019, June 11). Pande (2021) noted that when the Kathua and Unnao rapes were reported, the identities of the victims were revealed, along with other minute details of the crime. Certain news outlets even published photographs of the dead victims.

While the Kathua rape victim was a child, the Unnao victim was a minor, and hence, the identity revelation led to stigmatisation and ostracisation of her family in the neighbourhood (Dua & Malhotra, 2018, April 14). On the coverage of the Kathua case, Pande (2021) observes:

> In the Kathua case, several media organizations revealed the girl's identity; when public protests began and coverage of the incident gradually grew, many media outlets published the girl's photograph along with her name. As the coverage continued, even pictures of her dead body were printed. Consequently, the Delhi High Court imposed fines on several media organizations for violating the privacy act of India.
>
> (Pande, 2021, p. 404)

Meanwhile, ANI (2018, April 18) reported that the Delhi High Court slapped a fine of Rs.10 lakh on each media house that revealed the identity of the Kathua rape victim and further warned that "anyone disclosing [the] rape victim's identity can be imprisoned for six months".

In a news report published by an online news portal, The Quint (2018, April 12), gory details of the Kathua rape case and murder were laid bare for the readers. The lead paragraph begins by dehumanising the victim by identifying the event as "the rape and killing of the Bakherwal girl" and the article offers voyeuristic narratives, such as the victim "was kept sedated so that she could be sexually assaulted once again before she was bludgeoned to death" (The Quint, 2018, April 12). For instance, the news report quotes the chargesheet but certain other statements, such as "Jangotra reached Rassana from Meerut after his cousin's call and raped the sedated girl along with the juvenile and Mannu. Ram and his nephew performed their usual daily rituals at the Devasthan to avoid suspicion", which are not attributed to any sources (The Quint, 2018, April 12). This chapter also offers other lurid details of the crime:

> Khajuria also reached the spot and told them to wait as 'he wanted to rape her before she is killed'. The chargesheet said the girl was once again gangraped and later killed by the juvenile. 'The juvenile hit the girl twice with a stone on her head and later dumped her body in the forest after their plan to throw the body in a canal could not materialise due to failure to arrange a vehicle'.
>
> (The Quint, 2018, April 12)

Hyperdetailing and exhibitionism in these cases could also propagate sexist stereotypes (Nwabueze & Oduah, 2015). Newton and Duncan (2021, p. 347) describe this journalistic culture of publishing explicit details about the dead as the "vulture" mode that could feed the sexual and sexist standpoints and propagate a rape culture, desensitising sexual violence.

2020 Hatras rape case

On 14 September 2020, a 19-year-old girl from Hathras in the Indian state of Uttar Pradesh was critically injured and admitted to the hospital (Ara, 2020, October 28;

Dongare & Pandey, 2020). Just before her death on 22 September, she testified that four men sexually assaulted her (Ara, 2020, October 28). Soon, the incident attracted a media frenzy (PTI, 2020a, October 2; PTI 2020b, December 21; Sharma, 2020; The New Indian Express, 2020;). It was also a case of rape where the press published chilling imagery and details of the sexual and physical assaults.

A Wire report (Ara, 2020, October 28) detailed the incident as follows:

> The mother, about 100 meters away from the daughter, heard her screaming and rushed to find her. When she found her, she saw her lying on the ground covered in blood, with her tongue cut off. She immediately covered the victim's body and called her son, who reached the spot on his bike. They then took the victim to the nearest police station – Chandpa police station.
>
> (Ara, 2020, October 28)

NDTV presented a narrative account of the brother of the victim:

> Four-five people came from behind, threw my sister's dupatta around her neck and dragged her inside the bajra field… My mother covered her up and we went to the police and lay her down there. Three bones on her neck were broken. She had difficulty breathing… She needed oxygen right from the beginning.
>
> (Dongare & Pandey, 2020, September 29).

This NDTV report further offered unattributed details of the crime: "when the family searched, they found her in the fields, naked and bleeding, with horrific injuries".

Thanks to the sensationalist reporting of the Kathua case, along with the divulgence of critical details, the victim's name became "the most searched item on a popular pornographic website" (Roy, 2018; Pande, 2021, April 16).

On the editorial eroticisation of this case, Roy (2018, April 16) writes:

> The death of a child is just another misery that can be consumed to satiate perversion. Out to relish any last videographic material on the victim, porn enthusiasts have searched multiple websites to find some sort of a clip… Porn enthusiasts have now created tags with the name of the rape victim, to which video are being added that are mostly clickbaits. The creation of tags on porn websites is like a marker for any future porn content that will be uploaded.

Such a trend stresses the importance of cautious and contextual reporting of cases of sexual violence. When such cases arise, there are debates about divulgence of critical details in media reports and there are divergent views about this ethical issue (Rao, 2014).

It was not the first or last time a rape victim's name topped the search trends on a porn website (Desk, 2019, December 2). In fact, it has been the case when news about sexual violence breaks out and imagery of the assault gets leaked.

A section of scholars also believe that the recent surge in rape cases in India and pornography addiction may be linked (Math et al., 2014; Vinnakota, Arafat & Kar, 2021). On the sides, reports have informed that sales of brutal rape and gangrape videos were on the rise in the Indian state of Uttar Pradesh (Ashraf, 2016, November 1; Roy, 2018, April 16). Amid this widespread perversion and rape culture, what kinds of meanings and messages do sensational, hyperdetailed (including identification details and vivid crime description) and imagery-loaded rape reporting send across? Are the news outlets also in a way propagating the rape culture, drawing the general audience through insensitive reporting? These become critical questions to ask in contemporary times and a converged media environment, when and where journalists need to exercise extra caution while reporting sensitive topics such as sexual assaults.

Analysis of these cases indicates the prevalence of a romanticised news discourse that is characterised by hyperdetailing, divulging unwarranted and critical information about the crime and victims, and accompanied by exhibitionist imagery that could potentially evoke erotic and emotional responses and propagate sexual and sexist standpoints during news consumption. This book views such a trend as a part of the predatory culture of news reporting of sexual violence in India.

References

Achom, D. (2018, April 13), Rape-accused BJP Lawmaker Kuldeep Singh Sengar taken in for questioning by CBI. *NDTV.com*. https://www.ndtv.com/india-news/rape-accused-bjp-lawmaker-kuldeep-singh-sengar-taken-in-for-questioning-by-cbi-1836914

ANI (2018, April 18). Kathua case: Delhi HC slaps Rs 10 Lakh fine on media houses for revealing victim's identity. *Business Standard.* Retrieved from https://www.business-standard.com/article/news-ani/kathua-case-delhi-hc-slaps-rs-10-lakh-fine-on-media-houses-for-revealing-victim-s-identity-118041800350_1.html

Ara, I. (2020, October 28). Hathras gang-rape and murder case: A timeline. *The Wire*. Retrieved from https://thewire.in/women/hathras-gang-rape-and-murder-case-a-timeline

Ashraf, A. (2016, November 1). A dark trade: Rape videos for sale in India. *Al Jazeera*. https://www.aljazeera.com/features/2016/10/31/a-dark-trade-rape-videos-for-sale-in-india

Baum, M.A., & Schwarz, S. (2018). (Sex) Crime and punishment: How legally irrelevant details influence crime reporting and sanctioning decisions.

Bieneck, S., & Krahé, B. (2011). Blaming the victim and exonerating the perpetrator in cases of rape and robbery: Is there a double standard? *Journal of Interpersonal Violence*, *26*(9), 1785–1797. https://doi.org/10.1177/0886260510372945

Breen, M. D., Easteal, P., Holland, K., Sutherland, G., & Vaughan, C. (2017). Exploring Australian journalism discursive practices in reporting rape: The pitiful predator and the silent victim. *Discourse & Communication*, *11*(3), 241–258.

Cabrera, A. (2018). "Boys will be boys and she was asking for it" How the media perpetuates victim blaming and the rape myth in rape cases. *Alpenglow: Binghamton University Undergraduate J Res Creative Activity*, *4*(1), 7.

Deka, K. (2023, July 20). The politics of keeping Manipur sexual assault video under wraps for 75 days. *India Today*. https://www.indiatoday.in/india-today-insight/story/the-politics-of-keeping-manipur-sexual-assault-video-under-wraps-for-75-days-2409463-2023-07-20

Desk, I. T. W. (2019, December 2). Perverse: Telangana rape-murder victim's name becomes top trend on porn website. *India Today*. https://www.indiatoday.in/india/story/telangana-rape-murder-victim-name-top-trend-1624373-2019-12-02

Dodge, A. (2016). Digitizing rape culture: Online sexual violence and the power of the digital photograph. *Crime, Media, Culture*, *12*(1), 65–82. https://doi.org/10.1177/1741659015601173

Dongare, A. K., & Pandey, A. (2020, September 29). UP Woman, gang-raped and tortured 2 weeks ago, dies in Delhi hospital. *NDTV.com*. Retrieved from https://www.ndtv.com/india-news/woman-gang-raped-and-assaulted-in-ups-hathras-two-weeks-ago-dies-in-delhi-hospital-2302445

Dua, R., & Malhotra, A. (2018, April 14). Unnao rape case: 'Fear forced me to hide in Delhi all this while.' *The Times of India*. https://timesofindia.indiatimes.com/india/unnao-rape-case-fear-forced-me-to-hide-in-delhi-all-this-while/articleshow/63754632.cms

Dutta, A. (2018, May 1). The dialogue on rape cases is taking a very unhealthy turn. *Feminism in India*. https://feminisminindia.com/2018/05/02/media-dialogues-rape-cases/

Express Web Desk. (2018, April 14). Unnao rape case: Here's everything you need to know. *The Indian Express*. Retrieved from https://indianexpress.com/article/india/unnao-rape-case-bjp-mla-kuldeep-singh-sengar-arrested-5137445/

Express Web Desk. (2018, April 14). Unnao rape case: Here's everything you need to know. *Indian Express*, Retrieved from https://indianexpress.com/article/india/unnao-rape-case-bjp-mla-kuldeep-singh-sengar-arrested-5137445/

Gravelin, C. R., Biernat, M., & Kerl, E. (2016). Assessing the impact of media on blaming the victim of acquaintance rape. *Psychology of Women Quarterly*, 48 (2), 209–231.

Hauzel, H. (2023, July 23). Manipur naked parade: Left to die in paddy field, how two women ran for life and justice. *India Today NE*. https://www.indiatodayne.in/opinion/story/manipur-naked-parade-left-to-die-in-paddy-field-how-two-women-ran-for-life-and-justice-619232-2023-07-23

Hindustan Times (2018, April 10) All that has happened in Unnao rape case, a timeline. *The Hindustan Times*. Retrieved from https://www.hindustantimes.com/india-news/all-that-has-happened-in-unnao-rape-case-a-timeline/story-mawXOV70RXnt74VNdiJ02I.html

HT. (2018, April 10). All that has happened in Unnao rape case, a timeline. *Hindustan Times*. Retrieved from https://www.hindustantimes.com/india-news/all-that-has-happened-in-unnao-rape-case-a-timeline/story-mawXOV70RXnt74VNdiJ02I.html

Khan, A. (2019, December 16), MLA Kuldeep Sengar held guilty of Unnao minor's rape. *Times of India* http://timesofindia.indiatimes.com/articleshow/72750747.cms?utm_source=contentofinterest&utm_medium=text&utm_campaign=cppst

Lee E., Hongsik Y., & Minjeong S. (2014). A comparative study on the reporting of sexual violence crimes in major Korean and American daily newspapers. *Journal of Media and Performing Arts*, *9*(1), 105–140.

Livemint. (2024, May 1). Manipur sexual assault case: Kuki women were driven to mob by cops, stripped naked, paraded, says CBI chargesheet | Today News. *Mint*. https://www.livemint.com/news/india/manipur-sexual-assault-case-kuki-women-stripped-naked-paraded-were-driven-to-mob-by-cops-says-cbi-chargesheet-11714524458591.html

Math, S. B., Viswanath, B., Maroky, A. S., Kumar, N. C., Cherian, A. V., & Nirmala, M.C. (2014). Sexual crime in India: Is it influenced by pornography? *Indian Journal Of Psychological Medicine*, *36*(2), 147–152. https://doi.org/10.4103/0253-7176.130976

Newton, J., & Duncan, S. (2021). Ethical approaches to reporting death and trauma affecting ordinary people. In L. T. Price, K. Sanders & W.N. Wyatt (Eds.). *The Routledge companion to journalism ethics* (pp. 201–209). Routledge. https://doi.org/10.4324/9780429262708

Nwabueze, C., & Oduah, F. (2015). Media re-victimization of rape victims in a shame culture? Exploring the framing and representation of rape cases in Nigerian dailies. *Global Media Journal*, *13*(24), 1–20.

Ohri, R. (2019, June 11). Six convicted, one acquitted in Kathua rape case; sentencing shortly. *The Economic Times*. https://economictimes.indiatimes.com/news/politics-and-nation/kathua-rape-case-verdict/articleshow/69720996.cms?from=mdr

Pande, S. (2021). The ethics of reporting rape in India: A case study. In L. T. Price, K. Sanders & W.N. Wyatt (Eds.). *The Routledge companion to journalism ethics* (pp. 237–244). Routledge. https://doi.org/10.4324/9780429262708

Pandey, A. (2018, April 13). Arrest BJP's Kuldeep Sengar, Says High Court, Raps Yogi Adityanath Government. *NDTV.com*. https://www.ndtv.com/india-news/allahabad-high-court-orders-arrest-of-bjp-lawmaker-kuldeep-singh-sengar-1837187

Pino, N. W., & Meier, R. F. (1999). Gender differences in rape reporting. *Sex Roles*, *40*(11), 979–990.

PTI. (2019, August 7). Court abstains media from reporting names, addresses of Unnao rape survivor, family & witnesses. *The Times of India*. http://timesofindia.indiatimes.com/articleshow/70573438.cms?utm_source=contentofinterest&utm_medium=text&utm_campaign=cppst

PTI. (2020a, October 2). Hathras gang-rape case a 'small issue', victim was not raped, says UP Minister Ajeet Singh Pal. *The Economic Times*. Retrieved from https://economictimes.indiatimes.com/news/politics-and-nation/hathras-gang-rape-case-a-small-issue-victim-was-not-raped-says-up-minister-ajeet-singh-pal/articleshow/78449504.cms?utm_source=contentofinterest&utm_medium=text&utm_campaign=cppst

PTI. (2020b, December 21). Lies of BJP govt in UP 'exposed' in Hathras rape case: Akhilesh Yadav. *The Business Standard*. Retrieved from https://www.business-standard.com/article/politics/lies-of-bjp-govt-in-up-exposed-in-hathras-rape-case-akhilesh-yadav-120122100341_1.html

Rao, S. (2014). Covering rape in shame culture: Studying journalism ethics in India's New Television News Media, *Journal Mass Media Ethics*, *29*(3), 153–167. https://doi.org/10.1080/08900523.2014.918497

Roy, K. (2018, April 16). *How perverted is India? Kathua victim's name becomes top trending search on porn websites*. Outlook India.

Sacks, M., Ackerman, A. R., & Shlosberg, A. (2018). Rape myths in the media: A content analysis of local newspaper reporting in the United States. *Deviant Behavior*, *39*(9), 1237–1246.

Schwark, S., & Bohner, G. (2019). Sexual violence—"victim" or "survivor": News images affect explicit and implicit judgments of blame. *Violence Against Women*, *25*(12), 1491–1509.

Sharma, A. (2020, October 9). New political turn in Hathras gangrape case. *The Economic Times*. Retrieved from https://economictimes.indiatimes.com/news/politics-and-nation/new-political-turn-in-hathras-gangrape-case/articleshow/78579978.cms?from=mdr

Sharma, N., & Choudhury, R. (2023, July 20). In Manipur horror, 2 women paraded naked on camera, allegedly Gang-Raped. *NDTV.com*. Retrieved 1 June 2024, from https://www.ndtv.com/india-news/in-manipur-horror-2-women-paraded-naked-on-camera-allegedly-gang-raped-4223105

Sharma, S. (2018, April 12). Unnao rape case ground report: MLA Kuldeep Singh Sengar's supporters protest against SIT probe. *Firstpost*. https://www.firstpost.com/india/unnao-rape-case-ground-report-mla-kuldeep-singh-sengars-supporters-protest-against-sit-probe-4428231.html

Skaff, P. (2022). The pussy as prey: Discourses of predation and human sexual violence.

Sreedharan, C., & Thorsen, E. (2021). *Sexual violence and the news media: Issues, challenges, and guidelines for journalists in India* (pp. 1–96). UNESCO.

Stewart, S., Willmott, D., Murphy, A., & Phillips, C. (2023). "I thought I'm better off just trying to put this behind me"–a contemporary approach to understanding why women decide not to report sexual violence. *The Journal of Forensic Psychiatry & Psychology*, *35*(1), 85–101.

The New Indian Express. (2020, October 3). Hathras rape case: Mayawati playing politics, has no right to demand Yogi's resignation, says Ahawale. *The New Indian Express*. Retrieved from https://www.newindianexpress.com/nation/2020/Oct/03/hathras-rape-case-mayawati-playing-politics-has-no-right-to-demand-yogisresignation-says-ahawal-2205318.html

The Quint. (2018, April 12). Drugged, raped, bashed to death: Chargesheet reveals Kathua horror. *The Quint*. Retrieved from https://www.thequint.com/news/india/lawyers-prevent-chargesheet-in-kathua-rape-and-murder-case#read-more

The Tribune. (2019, December 20). Chronology of events in Unnao rape case. *The Tribune.* Retrieved from https://www.tribuneindia.com/news/nation/chronology-of-events-in-unnao-rape-case-14641

The Wire Staff. (2023, July 20). Manipur: Shocking video shows two Kuki women paraded naked; one was allegedly. *The Wire*. Retrieved from https://thewire.in/communalism/manipur-video-two-kuki-women-paraded-naked-gang-raped

Vinnakota, D, Arafat S. M. Y., Kar S. K., et al. (2021). Pornography and sexual violence against women in India: A scoping review. *Journal of Psychosexual Health*, *3*(3), 216–221. https://doi.org/10.1177/26318318211023935

6 Churnalism

How "Spiced-up" Sexual Crime News Stories Are Cooked Up in Minutes

There's no smoke sans fire! If the current cries about sensationalism and churnalism going hand-in-hand—especially, on a vast section of online news platforms and concerning trending topics—aren't fake alarms, then hot (spiced-up) stories are cooked up with the flames (of churnalism) in a section of new media houses.

Thanks to the Internet that offers access to a wide array of news sources and online tools, including OpenAI-based text applications that aid in editing and rewriting, news stories can be churned in minutes. On the other hand, a seasoned journalist may want to add some masala (extra spice) to give curated content or the already trending story an authentic spin and make it more mouthwatering. When such desk-bound churnalism overshadows traditional journalism, it becomes a distasteful recipe for self-destruction. As much as it has been a scholarly concern, disheartened journalists have also been imprecating this perjurious issue for some time now.

In a recent media commentary on "Stifled Voices, Sensationalized Stories: Churnalism's Toxic Touch", Ayoob (2024, January 13) observed that:

> As a journalist genuinely invested in upholding truth and transparency, the current state of my profession is disheartening. Journalism, once revered as the voice of the people, has devolved into a disconcerting phenomenon I can only describe as a twisted joke. In an era where information reigns supreme, the proliferation of churnalism has cast a long, dark shadow over the integrity of news reporting.

Ayoob noted that churnalism—which he defines as the practice of "regurgitating" news content rather than "investing the time and resources required for original reporting"—was undermining the "valiant efforts of ethical journalists" who risk their lives to uncover truths. Delving on his mission, Ayoob (2024, January 13) further observes that:

> Their commendable work is increasingly overshadowed by the growing prevalence of churnalism within news outlets. This disturbing trend not only compromises the quality of news but undermines the very foundations of journalism. Newsrooms, once dedicated to investigative reporting and in-depth analysis, now succumb to the pressures of producing quick, attention-grabbing pieces that prioritize sensationalism over substance.

DOI: 10.4324/9781003468042-9

Several media commentaries have elaborated on the nuances of churnalism and fake news (Hussain, 2024, March 10). Ponsford and Davis (2022, August 11) analysed the first 100 stories published on the UK's six most-popular commercial news websites, to find out that four of these six leading websites featured less than 50 per cent of original content (involving some kind of "journalistic endeavour") posted, mostly and merely lifting, assembling and repeating content from social media websites such as Instagram, Twitter and TikTok. Originality in the two websites at the bottom of this list of six was stated to be dismally low (*The Independent* [24 per cent] and *The Sun* [21 per cent]). Round-the-clock demand for news, the rise of online social media and professional compulsions (or issues such as being understaffed) are cited as reasons for the snowballing culture of desk-bound journalism, which favours speed over accuracy, undermines news credibility and makes news outlets a source of more fiction than facts.

Saridou, Spyridou and Veglis (2017, p. 8) identified "churnalism" abounding in the Greek media landscape as well, recycling reams of pre-owned content. According to Saridou et al. (2017, p. 15), news production had fallen victim to the "production of large amounts of cheap and recycled news stories", normalising and establishing itself as a preferable alternative to expensive and time-consuming "good journalism". Echoing these notions, Klikauer (2022, May 31) notes:

> As such, work in journalism has become like work in a car factory with an assembly line producing articles, reports, and news items. Simply put, it is like churning out news in mass news manufacturing… specialist sports or finance reporters can remain stationary in their office. They can do their job miles away from the nearest sports field or boardroom.

A handful of research has studied churnalism as a practice of relying on and reusing wire copies or public relations (PR) material (Johnston & Forde, 2017).

Tony Harcup (2004, pp. 3–4) came up with the term "churnalists" and "churnalism" (Harcup, 2007, p. 92), the rise of which has been attributed mostly to the Internet and market forces that push journalism to "insidiously feed off itself and swallows up rivals". In essence, according to Johnston and Forde (2017, p. 943), media outlets are consuming and regurgitating their own content. This culture of churnalism could create clouds of similar and stereotypical content surrounding news issues. Despite the role of technological and economic factors, PR practitioners also play a significant role in churnalism, often providing tailored news copy to journalists (Jackson & Moloney, 2016). Further, churned-sensationalist content attracts new-age readers (Johnston & Forde, 2017, p. 943).

Miró-Llinares and Aguerri (2023, p. 367) observed that misinformation percolates news when journalists fail to follow "the traditional verification processes". Rich and Zaragoza (2020) cited the race for reporting as a reason for misinformation in the news. Moore (2011) observed that content churned out of existing news stories may not be of direct harm to the readers but termed them "manufactured" content that cannot be passed as news. Misinformation comes from unverified sources and can, in a way, be equated with churned stories (Moore, 2011). Further, Moore (2011) pointed to a lack of transparency in churned news reports. Another factor that has catapulted the rise in misinformation is a reduction in the engagement of specialised reporters in newsrooms and delegation to assignment staffers, with shorter deadlines that reduce the scope of verification of the accuracy of information before publication (Weiss, 2017, October 27).

This connected—or crossbred—practice of producing churned and concocted (or manipulated) news needs to be contextualised and better understood for the current chapter and the book before means are invented to appropriately underscore its high prevalence in reporting sexual crimes against women and investigate how this phenomenon is deep-seated in the synoptic practice of Predatory Journalism. In a view, churnalism is desk-bound journalism where news content is misappropriated and re-used, with diminished scope for fact-checking and understanding ground realities. To make it appear original, churnalists may add to, edit or exaggerate available content (creating misinformation or sensationalising the news). In these churned reports, the sources of information are mostly mal-mentioned (clouded or absent).

Yet another style of reporting, where information is collected remotely (telephonically) or using untrustable avenues (such as online social media platforms), also poses similar issues: The lack of first-hand experience and verification of information.

In essence, four issues emerge underscoring this phenomenon: The issue of being desk-bound (locus), indications of problematic sources, the circulation of non-original content and manipulation (or the eventual distortion) of information when the latter happens. Though several seminal studies have identified sex as a critical news value and sexual violence against women is establishing itself as a news genre, courtesy of recent popular cases of violent crimes and the readership that they have garnered, scholarship on churnalism and misinformation in the area of sexual violence against women is not substantial.

Two of the several concepts used to characterise the phenomenon of Predatory Journalism (refer to Figure 2.1)—Discordant Locus and Dissonant Composition—cover the concepts discussed here: Churnalism, misinformation and sham sources.

Locus alludes to the distance from where (or the position from which) information is gathered for news stories, which could be problematic when it is obtrusive or obscure. An obtrusive locus is when the point of reporting becomes uncomfortably close, invading privacy. An obscure locus is when the news story is reported from a location that is different from where the crime (or the event being discussed) has occurred, symptomatic of armchair reporting or churnalism, where news stories are amalgamated or misappropriated from other news sources.

In this chapter, information and source-related issues are identified under Dissonant Composition—another locutionary issue identified in the model of Predatory Journalism. Categories and their descriptions for factors under these two concepts are presented in Table 6.1.

Table 6.1 Discordant locus and dissonant composition

Factors	*Categories*	*Description*
Discordant locus	Obscure	When the news story is reported from a location that is different from where the crime (or the event being discussed) has occurred
	Obtrusive	When the point of reporting becomes uncomfortably close, invading privacy
Dissonant composition		
Information	Digested	Using borrowed content
	Deficient	Malinformation
	Distorted	Misinformation (exaggerated, generalised, rewritten, sensationalised or misrepresented)
	Devised	Fabricated
Source	Devoid	Sans sources
	Discordant	Inappropriate sources
	Delusive	Fake sources sans name, location, designation or demography
	Resourced	Indirect (poached) sources

Empirical data

Predatory Journalism and, apparently, churnalism are demand-driven. Such demand-driven journalism could focus on creating content on a particular topic that is known to have a continuing demand (*Thematic*) or on a topic or event with a temporary and sudden rise in demand garnering the attention and curiosity of the target audience (*Episodic*). Such an episodic outburst of demand, however, needs to follow a generative phase, where demand for readership is created around a news event that has the potential to interest the media audiences.

Sexual violence (especially, against women) could be considered to have a thematic demand, thanks to popular cases (that have occasionally become top stories on the front pages) that have generated interest in this area. This apart, when an extreme, extraordinary or violent event is reported, an episodic upsurge in demand may be witnessed, adding to the underlying thematic interest. To identify recent cases of sexual violence in India that have sparked episodic demand, Google News search trends are tracked for several terms related to sexual violence and the data acquired using the Google Trends application is presented in Figure 6.1.

The search terms were determined based on the Chapter 1 analysis which identified popular subcategories of sexual violence reported (refer to Table 1.3).

Reviewing the related queries sections for these topics and search terms, the key events or terms that have caused the episodic surges in search demands are identified to be the Manipur sexual assault case (where women were sexually assaulted in public in 2023 and video footage of this violence was circulated online in 2023), Jharkhand rape case of March 2024 that involved a foreign biker couple, the Ujjain rape case where a minor was raped in September 2023 and news about politician Prajwal Revanna, who in 2024 was entangled in a sexual abuse case. For this study, the rape cases of Ujjain and Jharkhand and the sexual assault case of Manipur that

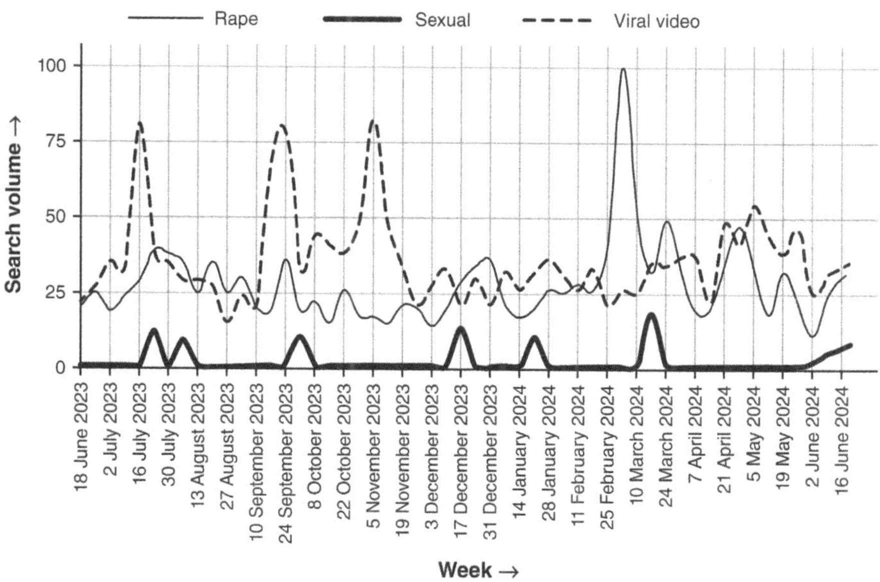

Figure 6.1 Google News search trends for 12 months

created episodic news demand are chosen to examine how certain news sources churned (recycled) news stories from an obscure locus, distorting information, or invaded privacy from an obtrusive locus, apparently, to sensationalise the issue and sell.

All of these three cases were sensationalised in the media, notably, had visual content to present and sparked what the news media termed "nationwide outrage".

In the case of the Ujjain rape, a minor girl (with a section of the media calling her to be a 12-year-old and the others claiming her to be 15) was reportedly raped in the early hours of 25 September 2023 in Ujjain, an ancient religious city and pilgrimage destination in the Indian state of Madhya Pradesh (Sikdar, 2023, September 28). On the next day, news about the assault surfaced, along with video footage of the girl walking on the street "after the sexual assault" and "seeking help" in vain (Jagran, 2023, September 26; Mishra, 2023, September 26; Mohan, 2023, September 27). Soon this news became a talking point and a multitude of media outlets started picking up this story. On September 28, two auto-rickshaw drivers were arrested in connection with the case, one "for the sexual assault" and the other for "failing to report the crime" (Sikdar, 2023, September 28). Apart from reporting the developments in this case, the news media explored the other popular avenues for generating stories, such as public response to the crime (mostly from the political elite or celebrities), political blame game and police (in)action.

In the case of Jharkhand, a foreign woman (again, reported to have multiple ages [Mukesh, 2024, March 2; Angad, 2024, March 3] showing signs of lack of fact-checking), who was in India on a global bike expedition along with her husband, was reportedly gangraped on 1 March 2024 (HT Correspondent, 2024, March 3;

Panda, 2024, March 5) in Dumka (Jharkhand). In this case, too, several issues were discussed and developments reported, including celebrity response to the crime (NDTV News Desk, 2024, March 3; Web Desk, 2024, March 3) and a media debate concerning a "viral trend" online on "What's wrong with India?" (India News Desk, 2024, March 13; Hindustan Times, 2024, March 13) involving social media users from across the globe.

About two months after three women were publicly and sexually assaulted in the Indian state of Manipur, against the backdrop of communal violence, video footage (showing the assault of two of the three) and news about it (NDTV, 2023, July 19; Singh, 2023, July 19; Baruah, 2023, July 19) surfaced on 19 July 2023, drawing political criticism (IANS, 2023, July 19; NDTV News Desk, 2023, July 19; The Quint, 2023, July 19) and prompting news interview of one of the victims (Saikia, 2023, July 19) giving away minute and salacious details of the assault on the same day. It also elicited judicial action the next day, where a "deeply disturbed" Supreme Court took *suo motu* cognisance of the "viral video" and ordered the Central government to "bring the perpetrators to book or step aside for it to take action" (Rajagopal, 2023, July 20).

News production on a specific event and audience interest in that news event can be reciprocative. That is, press publicity could trigger reader interest (generative) and reader interest in a specific topic could also prompt the churning of news stories concerning that topic.

To understand the web of relationships between search interest and news production in the cases (Ujjain, Jharkhand and Manipur) that have been chosen for the study, Google Search trends were associated with article counts estimated using the Google News search API.

Date-wise article counts of these three cases were plotted against Google Web Search trends for a corresponding period of 15 days after these cases were first reported (26 September to 10 October 2023, for the Ujjain case; 1 March to15 March 2024, for the Jharkhand case and 19 July to 2 August 2023, for the Manipur incident) and three plots are presented in Figure 6.2 to visually analyse their relationships. Furthermore, cross-correlation tests were performed to check if the press publicity triggered public interest in the case (creating generative demand) or if public interest prompted press coverage (based on an episodic demand) and estimate the time lags.

In the case of the Ujjain rape, the cross-correlation test (Figure 6.3) indicates that search trends and press publicity were associated with the strongest of positive correlations at lag zero (0.830) and lag −1 (0.871), indicating a trend where news publication on the case has generated public interest that waned as news reports on the case dwindled in less than two weeks.

Similarly, tests were performed to understand the trend in the Jharkhand rape case and the cross-correlation test indicated that immediate public interest was created when the news was reported with the strongest positive correlation (0.961) witnessed at lag zero and showing strong signs of both generative and episodic demands (0.730 at lag −1 and 0.731 at lag 1). That is, as the news about the rape of the foreigner was reported, immediate and long-term public interest was generated, propelling Web searches, which, in turn, sustained reporting in this case.

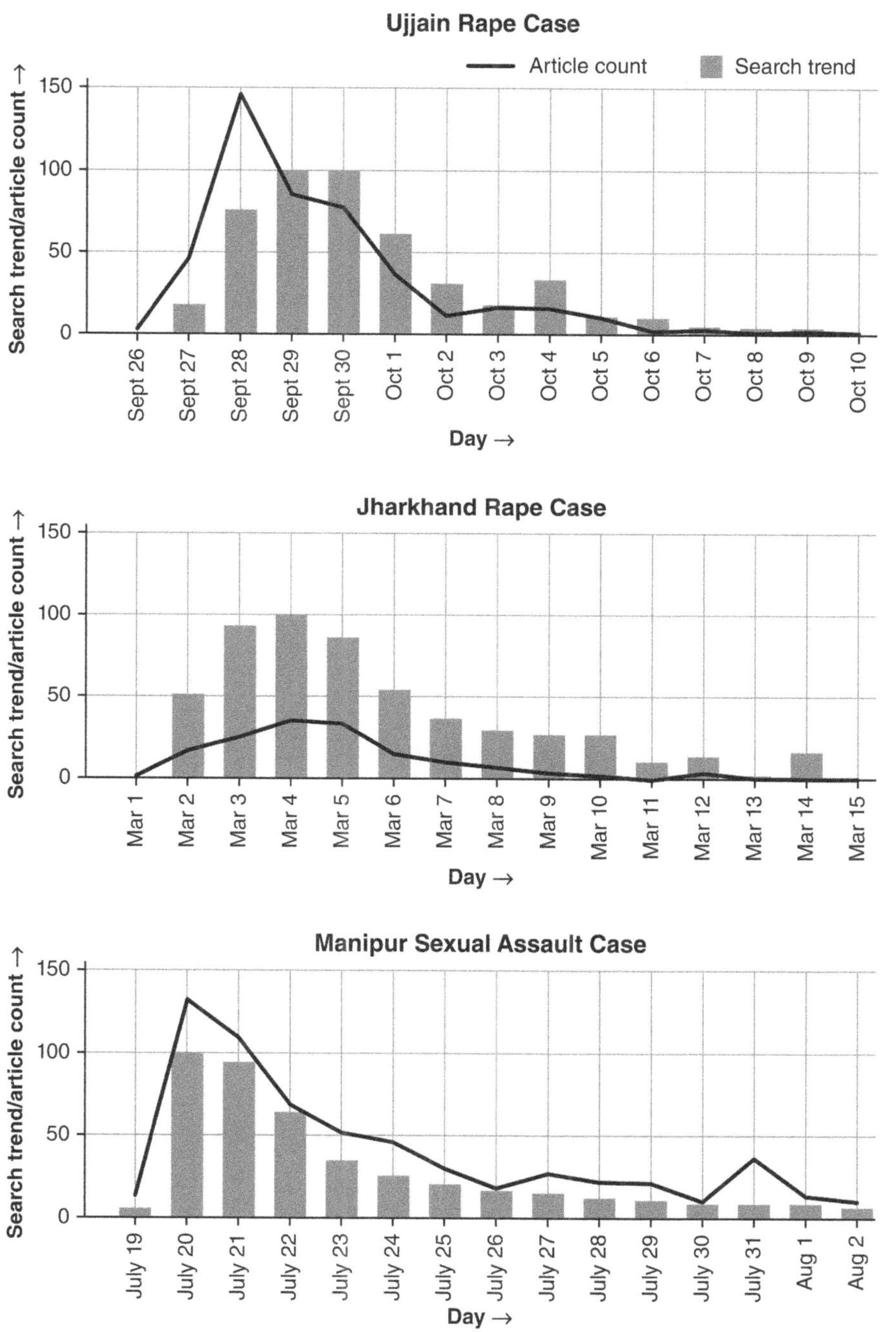

Figure 6.2 Time-series plots for the three cases: Search trends and articles published

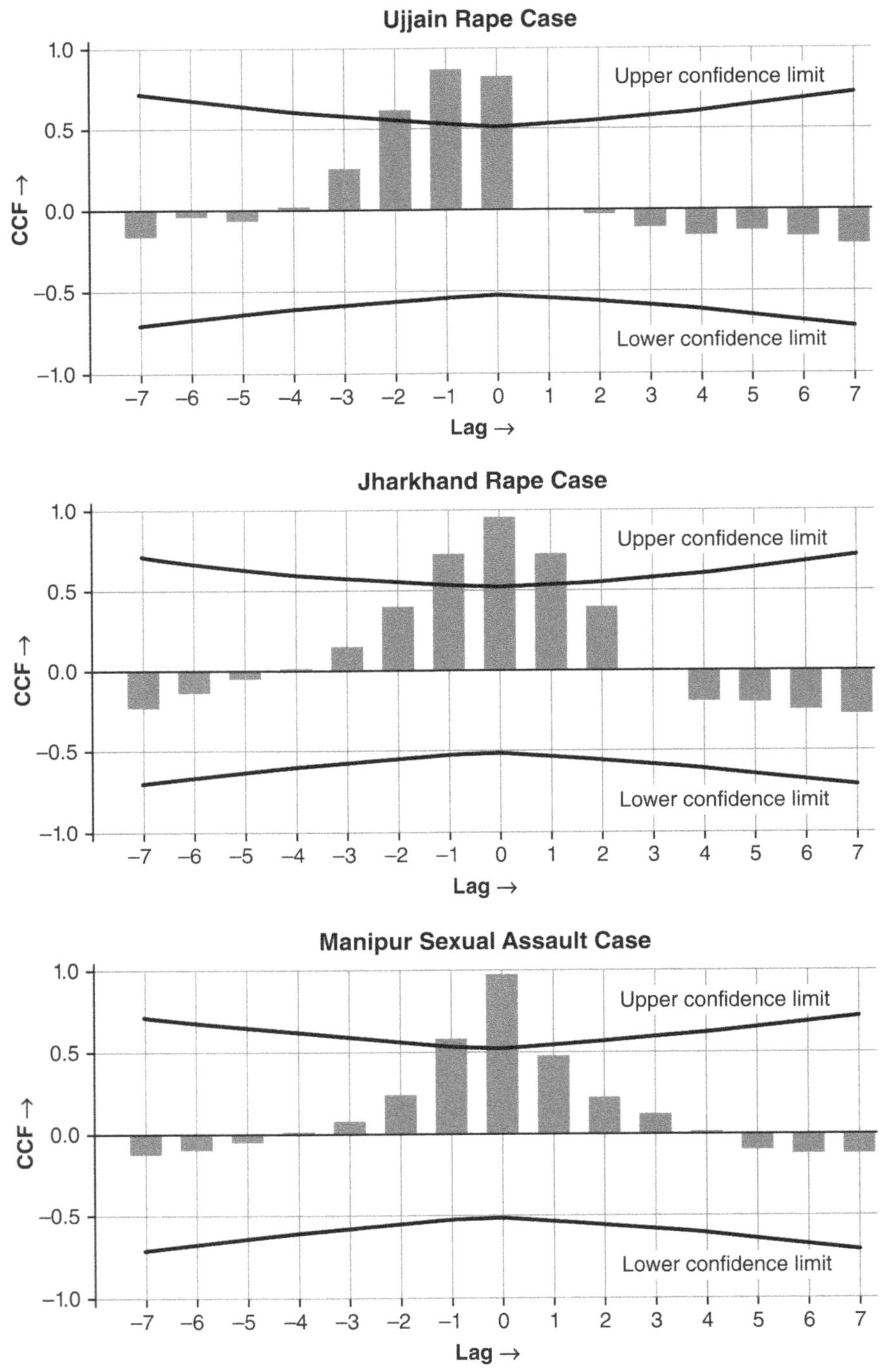

Figure 6.3 Cross-correlation between search trends and article counts

Meanwhile, in the case of the Manipur sexual assault, both the public interest surge when it was reported and the media response to news demand in the case were immediate, indicated by the strongest positive correlation at lag zero (0.976). Strong signs of the press influencing public interest (generative demand) and vice-versa (response to episodic demand) were also witnessed with a correlation of 0.572 at lag −1 and 0.478 at lag 1 (refer to Figure 6.3).

While in the case of the Manipur sexual assault, video footage of the atrocity recorded by the perpetrator of the attack went viral, in the case of the Ujjain minor rape, leaked CCTV footage of the victim walking on the road seeking help in vain after the assault were circulated along with several news reports. The immediate upsurge in public interest in these cases, as indicated in the time-series plots of Figure 6.2, may be caused by this factor, while the public interest witnessed a gradual gain in the case of the Jharkhand assault.

While the time-series analysis provided a snapshot into how the news media responds to public news demands or generates it while reporting sexual violence, to identify information and source-related issues and discuss how they align with or become a part of predatory editorial practices, a qualitative content analysis is performed using the variables identified for the study (refer Table 6.1) on a sample of online news articles published on these three cases.

Case analysis [I] Fanning public fear

News item [1] Dwary (2023, September 29) published at 8:29 pm

Headline: *"In Ujjain Rape Case, Those Who Didn't Help Teen May Face Charges: Police"*

News item [2] Shankar (2023, September 30) published at 8:18 am

Headline: *"Ujjain Rape Case: 'Failing to Report or Register', People Who Didn't Help Survivor May Face Charges"*

News item [3] Banerjee (2023, September 30) published at 1:21 pm

Headline: *"Ujjain Rape Case: People who failed to assist 12-year-old rape survivor may face charges"*

News item [1] (Dwary, 2023, September 29), attempts to fan public fear, speculating that people who had failed to "help" the Ujjain minor rape victim or report the crime may face charges under the Protection of Children from Sexual Offences (POCSO) Act.

Nevertheless, the later parts of the article publish contradicting claims. Further, the news report provides details about the case, apart from clubbing side stories about people offering to help the victim, the chief minister of the state promising severe punishment and the father of the main accused in the case wanting capital punishment for his son. This case study also examines two other news stories, news item [2] which seems to be churned out of news item [1] while news item [3] is strikingly similar to news item [2].

Locus: Here news item [2] carries a byline, naming the person who has "curated" this report, along with the location where the crime was reported to have happened (Ujjain, India), news item [3] is presented as a special byline story (which, in all probability, is a copy of a copy). Though it is presented as a curated report, the news item [2] mentions the location, which could lead to a misconception that it is reported from the mentioned location. News item [3] avoids location. Locus of both these "churned" news articles is, hence, obscure, as they are curated and not reported from the location of the occurrence of the crime.

Information and source-related issues

A major portion of news item [2] (about 77 per cent) and item [3] (about 81 per cent) are borrowed from the NDTV report, which was published a day earlier. Nevertheless, both the news items [2] and [3] cite the original article only once, making most of the reportage appear original.

Further, news item [1] itself seems to circulate improbable speculation (of police action under the POCSO Act) with the skilful (and wilful?) misrepresentation of the quotes of a police officer to indicate that the members of the public may be arrested, the churned news reports duplicate this distortion, perhaps to draw reader attention. Consequently, both the news reports use borrowed but rewritten content from news item [1], lacking any kind of original journalistic endeavour and could be termed as regurgitated content. While the news item [1] posts this improbable speculation through questions, "The question now is—will others who similarly refused to help her also face police action? Will they act against the people who saw and ignored a young girl bleeding and in clear distress?", in the middle of the article, the reports that are based on item [1] have omitted them, presenting action against the people who had failed to help as an imminent possibility, further distorting information. Another distortion can be identified here: Auto-rickshaw driver Rakesh Malviya, who had transported the survivor in his vehicle after the assault but failed to report the crime, is equated with the general public (will others who *similarly*…?). News item [1] also uses recycled content from other news articles, although from the same news outlet, and embeds links to those news articles within it.

While news items [1] and [2] use blurred screen grabs from the video showing the survivor after the assault, news item [3] uses a stereotypical representative image. All the images featured in these news articles lack proper photo captions and mention of sources of images. Exhibiting the issue of deficient information, the articles lack critical details while reporting such a sensitive news event. The news item [1] quotes an Additional Superintendent of Police in Ujjain as stating that "action has been taken" against the identified auto-rickshaw driver, the kind of action taken is not detailed. Also, the speculation (tactfully using the word "may") that people who "failed to help" may face "charges" is abstract and vague. The articles feature screenshots from the supposedly leaked CCTV footage (without proper sourcing) and offer indiscreet descriptions of how people reacted to the survivor based on the (unverified) footage.

All three news items [1], [2] and [3] are hyperdetailed, offering micro-details of the crime to stereotype and sensationalise it. Indicators of them are the recurring appearance of phrases such as "horrifying visuals", "semi-naked", "bleeding after rape" and "going door-to-door for help". Both the churned reports use sources quoted in the original but have been presented in a way to appear as original (re-sourced sources). These news reports are stereotypical in their coverage of sexual violence, presenting the crime as a heinous "horror" and framing the victim as "helpless".

While quoting the main accused's father, who demanded the "death penalty" for his son, news items [1] and [2] engage in a media trial. News item [1] also quotes an unnamed "police officer" who details how the main accused sustained injuries from a "cemented road" when he "tried to escape". News item [1] reported that the main accused "was taken to where he allegedly raped the girl" to "recover the clothes worn by the girl". A slew of other news reports had published contradicting versions of this particular incident (ABP News Bureau, 2023, September 28; Sharma, 2023, September 28; TNN, 2023, September 29), while a few of them even speculated that the main accused sustained a bullet injury in his leg in a police encounter (Outlook Web Desk, 2023, September 28; Sarkar, 2023, September 28; FPJ Web Desk, 2023, September 29)—indicating a lack of ground reporting and verification of information.

Case analysis [II] Popularising intrusive and prejudicial reporting

News item [4] (Navbharat Times, 2023, September 29)

Headline: *Ujjain Rape Case:* आरोपी *Bharat Soni* के
Father ने रोते कर दी बेटे को फांसी की मांग
(Ujjain Rape Case: Accused Bharat Soni's Father
Demands Death Penalty For Son While Crying)

News item [5] (India Today, 2023, September 29) published at 10:22 pm

Headline: *"'That could have been my child...':
Ujjain rape accused's father seeks death penalty"*

News Item [6] (PTI, 2023a, September 29) published at 11:19 pm

Headline: *"Ujjain minor rape case: Father of accused held seeks death penalty for son"*

News item [7] (Chitre, 2023, September 30) published at 2:01 pm

Headline: *"'Should be hanged': Ujjain rape accused's
father demands strict punishment"*

News item [8] (Outlook Web Desk, 2023, September 30) published at 04:09 am

Headline: "*Ujjain rape case: Father of accused demands death penalty, Those who didn't help teen may face charges under POCSO*"

News item [9] (Gaharwar, 2023, September 30) published at 7.49 am.

Headline: "*Ujjain rape horror: Shameful act, my son should be hanged, says father of accused auto driver*"

News item [10] (Livemint, 2023, September 30).

Headline: *"Ujjain rape case: 'She could have been my daughter', accused's father demands capital punishment for his son"*

News item [11] (Anand, 2023, October 1) published at 07:29 am.

Headline: *"'He should be hanged for his crime': Father of Ujjain rape accused"*

News item [12] (Free Press Journal, 2023, October 3) published at 04:00 pm.

Headline: "*Ujjain rape case: Hang him to death, says father of accused Autorickshaw driver*"

A day after the main accused in the Ujjain minor rape case was arrested and his name was published in the news, his father was interviewed and several news outlets published his comments (in the form of text and video), engaging in intrusive and prejudicial reporting.

Published on 29 September 2023, this interview video, posted by Navbharat Times (news item [4]) but recorded by ANI, shows the father of the accused, who is visibly ashamed (crying) and unable to venture out of his house due to the sexual assault and the publication of his son's name in the media. While he is unsure about whether his son has committed the crime or not, he is repeatedly quizzed about how he feels about it and what kind of punishment should be given. He is shown to say that "if his son is guilty, he deserves the capital punishment".

Another media report published on the same day (news item [5]) reflected similar sentiments.

> If my child had been in the victim's place, I would have said the same thing. Those who commit such crimes do not deserve to live… I can say that he [his son] couldn't have done this, but if he has, he should be given strict punishment.

The report said that the father "emphasised that swift action is needed in such horrific cases to deter potential offenders, saying, 'The police should just shoot them'". But several other (wire copy) media reports published on the same day (news item [6] for instance) were selective and partial in their coverage of this interview, reporting that he demanded "death for his son", indirectly suggesting that the accused was guilty and discussing the punishment the accused deserved. Building upon these biassed reports, a slew of news stories were published in the subsequent days, reflecting the same idea and a few of them carried the same quotes verbatim (news items [7]–[12]).

For instance, a wire copy (PTI, 2023b, September 29) published this quote on 29 September 2023, with a grammatical error in it:

> It is a shameful act. Neither have I gone to hospital to meet him, no[r] will I go to the police station or courts. My son has committed a crime, therefore he should be hanged.

On the following day, a slew of news reports (news items [8] and [9] for instance) were published carrying the same quote with the same grammatical error, but published as special or byline articles, showing explicit signs that they were churned (or recycled) news reports.

These churned reports had also aggregated content from other news sources, adding some masala (to spice up the report) with the use of popular phrases such as "widespread outrage", "horrifying video", "barely wearing anything", "wandering on the streets", "injuries to her private parts", "bleeding", "shameful" and "hanged".

Ignoring the presumption of innocence (where the law rules that a "person shall be presumed innocent until proven guilty beyond reasonable doubt"), news stories published the names and other details of the main accused in the case and those "detained for failing to inform the police" about the incident, even while a handful of news articles recorded responses from several quarters condemning the crime and the accused. Such reporting caused humiliation for their families, even though there were remote chances that the accusations framed were fabricated. A few of these news articles also published images of the accused and CCTV footage showing the victim after the assault, sending shock waves and creating hatred.

Engaging in intrusive journalism and conducting a media trial, the news reports also published interview statements of the father of the main accused, seeking capital punishment.

Further, the news reports informed that "the local bar association appealed that no lawyer should defend him in the court". Most of the news reports divulged the name of the father at the beginning of them. A few of the reports further stressed "shooting" the guilty (for instance, news item [5]) uttered by the father, favouring extra-judicial punishment. Such reporting fans the popular wave of demanding vandal-style justice, seeking "lynching" of the accused.

These similar online articles were published across days, pointing to a culture of churnalism. All of these stories have also used the statement of the father of the accused as their headline either exhibiting shame or demanding capital punishment for his son, distorting the messages of shame (because the media publicised their personal details) and capital punishment (if he was guilty) to suggest that the accused was indeed guilty, with the tactful (partial) use of statements and literary devices such as quotation to feed populist desires. For instance, news item [5], though it reports that the father did not believe that his son had committed the crime, uses the headline "'That could have been my child…': Ujjain rape accused's father seeks death penalty", suggesting that the accused was guilty, by avoiding the predicate.

Locus and information-related issues

While the original interviews may have adopted an obtrusive locus (indicating privacy intrusion when those [the victims of sexual assault or those associated with the victims or accused] suffering trauma are interviewed and their emotional responses are elicited, often using unethical means), the news copies that recycle the same content may have been adopting an obscure locus, mostly from Web-based desks. These interview reports feature contradictory statements from the father of the accused, with one of them (news item [10]) quoting the father saying "Police have made him accused. The truth will come out. I will support him because he is my child. I can say that he couldn't have done this. But if he has, he should be given strict punishment", casting a cloud over the credibility of a section of interview reports. This *Mint* news item, too, features a misleading headline and cites *India Today* as its original source.

Major portions of the churned news articles were borrowed and the sources were not properly mentioned. Most of them also used blurred screengrabs of the CCTV video and the image source was not cited, while a section of the news reports did not have proper bylines, reporting locations and used representational (stereotypical) images.

Case analysis [III] **"Rice bag" journalism**

After the news about the gang rape of a foreigner in the Indian state of Jharkhand was reported in March 2024, a slew of "churned" news articles relied on social media content.

News item [13] (Panigrahy, 2024, March 5)

Headline: *"What is the name of the accused arrested in the r*pe case of Fernanda 4ver Spanish woman biker in Jharkhand and what is their religion"*

While most (mostly recycled) news articles described the crime, named the victims, revealed their social media handles, published their images, tracked the investigation, recorded (emotional) public response and discussed whether the incident defamed the nation or not, this news article [13] was inquisitive about the names and religion of the accused arrested.

Mostly, this news report uses content and quotes published verbatim in other news sources as well. It also shares the name, age and social media handle of the survivor, apart from the names of the people arrested, reporting that they were "said to be members of Christian missionaries and Christian themselves by religion". It also featured an embedded X post that states that three arrested members belong to this minority religion, naming them. Further, another X post embedded within the news article carries a photograph of a person, which it claimed was one of the rapists, the most violent of them and shared by the survivor on social media.

An AltNews report (Majumder, 2024, March 8) debunked this social media claim from a section of users that three of the arrested were "rice bag converts", a derogatory term used to describe people belonging to a minority religious group. It also embedded an X post from a political leader that states "What faith or religion do people have who are sold for sacks of rice? They all should be given the death sentence", along with several other X posts that claim the accused in the case worked for Christian missionaries.

After performing a fact check, the report informed that one of the eight arrested was a Christian and none of them worked for a missionary. Yet another churned news report featured an X post embedded within it that discussed the religion of the accused, while it also published the X post (featured in a news item [13]) that sought public support (by sharing the social media post) to help the police nab the "most violent" of the rapists. It also shared the photographs of the victims, their names (along with those of the accused) and social media posts.

News item [14] (OpIndia Staff, 2024, March 4)

Headline: "*'Won't provide content to destroy Bharat's reputation': Jharkhand-based biker woman turns down Barkha Dutt's interview invite on Dumka gang rape case*"

Another news item [14] uses an obscure locus (without mentioning the location of the reportage) and social media content to churn out a news story related to the Jharkhand gang rape case. It builds a news story based on a social media claim that a local biker turned down an interview request from popular journalist Barkha Dutt after the gang rape was reported. It quoted from an X post of the biker and also had the social media post embedded.

It also adds some one-sided "*masala*" to the claim and the story that the biker was campaigning on X seeking "justice" for the gang rape victim and that the popular journalist had a "history of irresponsible journalism". It neither featured an explicit mention of permission to use social media material and more information (apart from the social media post) from the user nor the version of and confirmation from the popular journalist about the social media claim.

Though it duplicates the social media claim, this news article may also legitimise it, as this news report also gets circulated in other news sources (Web Desk, 2024, March 5).

Case analysis [IV] Sexualising the crime with salacious details

News item [15] (Saikia, 2023, July 19)

Headline: "*'If you don't take off your clothes, we will kill you':*
Kuki women paraded naked in Manipur"

In the case of Manipur sexual assault, a series of news reports assumed an obtrusive locus to invade the privacy of the victims and their families, zooming in on the salacious aspects, using crude words to describe the assault, sexualising the crime and exhibiting distasteful designs of exploitation—all to sell a story and earn from it under the garb of news reporting.

For instance, news item [15], which was published on the same day the assault video and news about it surfaced, interviewed one of the sexual assault victims.

Its headline played up the threat that commenced the crime "If you don't take off your clothes, we will kill you" and also accommodated the phrase "women paraded naked" that went on to become the most-favoured media preference to describe this kind of crime. It provides a narrative with crude words used to describe the actions and the salacious details, such as "strip off our clothes", "every item of clothing", "dragged to a paddy field", "asked by the men to lie down", "three men surrounded me", "One of them told the other, 'let's rape her'" and "grabbed my breasts", perhaps retraumatising the victim. Apart from the interview, it quotes a police complaint and unnamed police officers, to offer additional details about the crime, including the location of the crime (or victims) and their demographic details. Quotes from this interview were picked up and recirculated in a slew of curated news articles that followed (Ghosh, 2023, July 20; TNM Staff, 2023, July 20; CNBCTV18, 2023, July 21).

News item [16] (PTI, 2023, Jul 21) published at 02:53 PM IST

Headline: "*Fought For Nation But Could Not Protect My Wife. Husband Of Woman Paraded Naked In Manipur*"

News item [17] (Business Today Desk, 2023, Jul 21) published at 6:41 PM IST

Headline: *"Manipur parading incident: 'Fought for country but couldn't protect wife,' says Kargil veteran"*

News item [18] (Shandilya, 2023, July 23) published at 12.06 AM IST

Headline: "*Fought for India in Kargil, But Couldn't Protect Wife: Ex Army Man Rues After Manipur Woman Paraded Naked*"

News item [19] (Choudhury, 2023, July 24) published at 7:40 pm IST

Headline: *"'Served Country, Couldn't Protect Wife…': Ex-Soldier On Manipur Video Ratnadip"*

In a similar case, quotes from the husband of one of the Manipur sexual assault victims published in a news report (news item [16]) were lifted and reused within four hours (news item [17]) and in the following days as well (news items [18] and [19]). Though the news item [16] appeared to be the first among all to carry the quote,

> fought for the nation in the Kargil war and was also in Sri Lanka as part of the Indian Peace Keeping Force. I protected the nation but am dejected that after my retirement, I could not protect my home, my wife and fellow villagers… I am sad, depressed.

it was a wire copy that translated the quote from an unnamed "Hindi news channel". Stories churned based on this quote also used it verbatim and identified the husband of the survivor as a war veteran who had "served the Indian Army as a Subedar of the Assam Regiment" (item [19]). Sources are thus elusive in the churned news reports (devoid or delusive). Another quote, "I have seen the war fighting in the front at Kargil. And when I have returned home (after my retirement), my own place is more dangerous than the battlefield", published in the *Times of India* (Kalita, 2023, July 21) was found recurring in several news reports (news item [17]; OpIndia Staff, 2023, July 21). In most of these news articles, there were similarities in the lead paragraphs and headlines, with some of them reusing phrases such as "made to strip at gunpoint", "forced to dance" and "paraded naked".

While one of the news articles (item [19]) implied that the husband of the victim made the statement "at a press conference in state capital Imphal", it still used a three-day-old quote.

Meanwhile, the *ToI* article stated that it "spoke to the couple… in a relief camp".

While items [16] and [19] provide the location of reporting, [17] and [18] do not. Further, the sources of all four news items have not been properly identified or mentioned. There are indications of resourcing of content from wire copies (PTI) and other news sources (a Hindi channel) and usage of blurred images from video footage (without sources) or representational images without captions. Obscure and churned using online resources, these reports exploit the quotations of the husband to sensationalise the crime.

There had been a slew of such news interviews with victims of sexual assault that detailed their ordeals with indiscreet openness (for instance, Sabir, 2023, October 8), divulged personal-identification details and carried sexist statements (for instance, Arya, 2023, November 10), oblivious of the adverse effects that news statements and their word choices can have.

Sabir (2023, October 8) quoted a gang rape victim as saying, "One by one, they put their hands inside my blouse, and molested me as I struggled to free myself… They touched me in my private parts", while the other report reinforced archaic ideas:

> I was treated like an animal… It was hard enough to live with that trauma, but then two months later when the video of the attack went viral, I almost lost all hope to continue living… You know how Indian society is, how they look at women after such an incident. I find it hard to face other people, even in my own community. My pride is gone. I will never be the same again.

While the article underscores that the "video amplified their suffering", the flurry of news reports that followed and textually described their assaults in vividity could perpetually re-traumatise them.

While such intrusive news accounts invade the privacy of those who suffered the sexual assaults, the articles that are churned and circulated to reach a wider audience amplify their adversities. Both of these brands of problematic reporting (obscure and obtrusive) are riddled with issues related to credible information and proper citation of sources, as the analyses have indicated. Analysis of the sample of news articles published on sexual violence cases clearly points to the prevalence of an online culture of churnalism where news content is lifted and recycled with minimal edits and at terrific speeds, creating clouds of duplications and curtailing the scope for original reporting. When the goal of online journalism becomes filling the space with something interesting (in its own understanding) rather than offering credible and useful information to the readers, this fill-and-sell culture, mostly churning and recycling (sensational) muck, could jeopardise its own future, especially when it is facing challenges from all sides.

References

ABP News Bureau. (2023, September 28). *Ujjain Rape accused sustains injuries after "Falling while trying to flee" during crime scene inspection.* https://news.abplive.com. https://news.abplive.com/news/india/ujjain-minor-rape-case-accused-auto-driver-injured-while-escaping-crime-scene-madhya-pradesh-hospital-1632543

Anand, M. J. (2023, October 1). 'He should be hanged for his crime': Father of Ujjain rape accused. *The Indian Express*. https://indianexpress.com/article/india/he-should-be-hanged-for-his-crime-father-of-ujjain-rape-accused-8963183/

Angad, A. (2024, March 3). 'Something I wouldn't wish on anyone… 7 men raped me': Spanish travel vlogger on Jharkhand nightmare. *The Indian Express*. https://indianexpress.com/article/india/spanish-woman-gangraped-jharkands-dumka-3-detained-9191720/

Arya, B. D. (2023, November 10). Manipur women in naked assault video 'will not give up.' *BBC*. https://www.bbc.com/news/world-asia-india-67291370

Ayoob, A. (2024, January 13). Stifled voices, sensationalized stories: Churnalism's toxic touch. *Kashmir Observer*. https://kashmirobserver.net/2024/01/13/stifled-voices-sensationalized-stories-churnalisms-toxic-touch/

Banerjee, A. (2023, September 30). Ujjain rape case: People who failed to assist 12-year-old rape survivor may face charges. *Firstpost*. https://www.firstpost.com/india/ujjain-rape-case-people-who-failed-to-assist-12-year-old-rape-survivor-may-face-charges-13188202.html

Baruah, S. (2023, July 19). Women paraded naked in Manipur were forcibly taken away from police custody by mob. *The Indian Express*. https://indianexpress.com/article/india/tension-manipur-hills-areas-may-4-video-two-women-paraded-naked-surfaces-8849063/

Business Today Desk. (2023, July 21). Manipur parading incident: 'Fought for country but couldn't protect wife,' says Kargil veteran. *Business Today*. https://www.businesstoday.in/latest/in-focus/story/manipur-parading-incident-fought-for-country-but-couldnt-protect-wife-says-kargil-veteran-390817-2023-07-21

Chitre, M. (2023, September 30). 'Should be hanged': Ujjain rape accused's father demands strict punishment. *Hindustan Times*. https://www.hindustantimes.com/india-news/should-be-hanged-ujjain-rape-accuseds-father-demands-strict-punishment-101696051631085.html

Choudhury, R. (2023, July 24) 'Served Country, Couldn't Protect Wife…": Ex-soldier on Manipur video. *NDTV.com*. https://www.ndtv.com/india-news/served-country-couldnt-protect-wife-ex-soldier-on-manipur-video-4237327

CNBCTV18. (2023, July 21). *Manipur video: Grabbed my breasts, threatened to kill, police didn't help – Survivors share harrowing details.* CNBCTV18. https://www.cnbctv18.com/india/manipur-video-survivors-share-harrowing-details-grabbed-breasts-threatened-to-kill-police-didnot-help-17279101.htm

Dwary, A. (2023, September 29). In Ujjain rape case, those who didn't help teen may face charges: Police. *NDTV.com*. https://www.ndtv.com/india-news/ujjain-rape-case-news-in-ujjain-rape-case-those-who-didnt-help-teen-may-face-charges-4436074

FPJ Web Desk. (2023, September 29). Ujjain rape case: Main accused auto driver shot by police while attempting to flee from police custody, taken. *Free Press Journal*. https://www.freepressjournal.in/indore/ujjain-rape-case-main-accused-auto-driver-attempts-to-flee-police-custody-cops-end-chase-with-gun-shot

Free Press Journal. (2023, October 3). Ujjain rape case: Hang him to death, says father of accused Autorickshaw driver. *Free Press Journal*. https://www.freepressjournal.in/ujjain/ujjain-rape-case-hang-him-to-death-says-father-of-accused-autorickshaw-driver

Gaharwar, S. (2023, September 30). *Ujjain rape horror: Shameful act, my son should be hanged, says father of accused auto driver*. News9live. https://www.news9live.com/crime/ujjain-rape-horror-shameful-act-my-son-should-be-hanged-says-father-of-accused-auto-driver-2304469

Ghosh, S. (2023, July 20). Manipur video: Kuki survivor recounts 'take of your clothes, or will kill you….' *Mint*. https://www.livemint.com/news/india/manipur-women-paraded-naked-kuki-survivor-recounts-take-of-your-clothes-or-will-kill-you-11689819879592.html

Harcup, T. (2004). Journalism: principles and practice. London: Sage.

Harcup, T. (2007). The Ethical Journalist. London: Sage.

Hindustan Times. (2024, March 13). *"India Rape Capital": War over "What's wrong with India" trend; Netizens call out West's "Hypocrisy"* [Video]. YouTube. https://www.youtube.com/watch?v=faiDIkDp4rY

HT Correspondent. (2024, March 3). Spanish woman gangrape: Jharkhand CID, special branch, forensic team begin probe. *Hindustan Times*. https://www.hindustantimes.com/cities/ranchi-news/jharkhand-cid-special-branch-forensic-team-begin-probe-in-dumka-rape-case-101709482140129.html

Hussain, S. T. (2024, March 10). Fakedia, churnalism, and churnalists. *The Nation*. https://www.nation.com.pk/10-Mar-2024/fakedia-churnalism-and-churnalists

IANS. (2023, July 19). Smriti Irani dubs video showing 2 women paraded naked in Manipur as "downright inhuman". *Deccan Herald*. https://www.deccanherald.com/india/smriti-irani-dubs-video-showing-2-women-paraded-naked-in-manipur-as-downright-inhuman-1238809.html

India News Desk. (2024, March 13). 'What's wrong with India?' Trends on X, government joins netizens with interesting response. *Financial Express*. https://www.financialexpress.com/india-news/whats-wrong-with-india-trends-on-x-government-joins-netizens-with-interesting-response/3424203/

India Today. (2023, September 29). 'That could have been my child…': Ujjain rape accused's father seeks death penalty. *India Today*. https://www.indiatoday.in/india/story/ujjain-rape-accused-father-seeks-death-penalty-2442476-2023-09-29

Jackson, D., & Moloney, K. (2016). Inside churnalism: PR, journalism and power relationships in flux. *Journalism Studies*, *17*(6), 763–780. https://doi.org/10.1080/1461670X.2015.1017597

Jagran. (2023, September 26). Ujjain Rape Case: MP के उज्जैन मे 12 साल की बच्ची के साथ दरिंदगी, पुलिस ने खंगाले 400 CCTV footage. *Jagran*. https://www.jagran.com/videos/news/madhya-pradesh-ujjain-girl-raped-and-left-bleeding-news-12-400-cctv-footage-mp-17786.html

Johnston, J., & Forde, S. (2017). Churnalism: Revised and revisited. *Digital Journalism*, *5*(8), 943–946. https://doi.org/10.1080/21670811.2017.1355026

Kalita, P. (2023, July 21). Manipur women paraded naked: Made to strip, dance at gunpoint, says wife of Kargil war veteran. *The Times of India*. https://timesofindia.indiatimes.com/city/guwahati/made-to-strip-dance-at-gunpoint-kargil-war-veterans-wife/articleshow/102001472.cms

Klikauer, T. (2022, May 31). Churnalism's manipulation of the news. *Countercurrents*. https://countercurrents.org/2022/05/churnalisms-manipulation-of-the-news/

Livemint. (2023, September 30). Ujjain rape case: 'She could have been my daughter', accused's father demands capital punishment for his son. *Mint*. https://www.livemint.com/news/india/ujjain-rape-case-she-could-have-been-my-daughter-accuseds-father-demands-capital-punishment-for-his-son-11696046526170.html

Majumder, S. (2024, March 8). *Spanish vlogger's rape: Only one of eight arrested is a Christian; crime given false communal spin*. Alt News.
Miró-Llinares, F., & Aguerri, J. C. (2023). Misinformation about fake news: A systematic critical review of empirical studies on the phenomenon and its status as a 'threat'. *European Journal of Criminology*, *20*(1), 356–374. https://doi.org/10.1177/1477370821994059
Mishra, A. (2023, September 26). उज्जैन मे 12 साल की लड़की से रेप, दरिंदगी के बाद सड़क किनारे फेंका; हालत गंभीर. *Hindustan*. https://www.livehindustan.com/madhya-pradesh/story-12-year-old-minor-girl-of-up-raped-in-ujjain-condition-critical-admitted-into-hospital-8763101.html
Mohan, A. J. (2023, September 27). CCTV shows bleeding 12-year-old rape victim in Ujjain seeking help, being shooed away. *The Indian Express*. https://indianexpress.com/article/cities/bhopal/cctv-rape-victim-ujjain-help-shooed-away-8958289/
Moore, M. (2011, March 3). Churnalism exposed. *Columbia Journalism Review*. https://www.cjr.org/the_news_frontier/churnalism_exposed.php
Mukesh, A. (2024, March 2). Jharkhand shocker: 8–10 men gang-rape Spanish woman in Dumka. *The Times of India*. https://timesofindia.indiatimes.com/city/ranchi/jharkhand-shocker-spanish-woman-gang-raped-in-dumka/articleshow/108155549.cms
Navbharat Times (2023, September 29). *Ujjain Rape Case: आरोपी Bharat Soni के Father ने रोते रोते कर दी बेटे को फांसी की मांग (Accused Bharat Soni's Father Demands Death Penalty For Son While Crying)* | NBT [Video]. YouTube. https://www.youtube.com/watch?v=mviW2941PHw
NDTV News Desk. (2023, July 19). *After Manipur sexual assault video, opposition wants PM in Parliament*. NDTV.com. https://www.ndtv.com/india-news/after-manipur-sexual-assault-video-opposition-wants-pm-narendra-modi-in-parliament-4223678
NDTV News Desk. (2024, March 3). *"Rotten Society": Actor after Spanish woman gang-raped in Jharkhand*. NDTV.com. https://www.ndtv.com/india-news/rotten-society-actor-richa-chadha-after-spanish-woman-gang-raped-in-jharkhand-5166221
NDTV. (2023, July 19). *In Manipur horror, 2 women paraded naked on camera, allegedly gang-raped*. NDTV. https://www.ndtv.com/video/manipur-violence-in-manipur-horror-2-women-paraded-naked-on-camera-allegedly-gang-raped-712448
OpIndia Staff. (2023, July 21). *Made to strip at gunpoint, forced to dance, paraded naked: Victim seen in Manipur viral video, wife of a Kargil war veteran, narrates her dreadful tale*. OpIndia. https://www.opindia.com/2023/07/manipur-viral-video-wife-of-kargil-war-veteran-narrates-her-ordeal/
OpIndia Staff. (2024, March 4). *'Won't provide content to destroy Bharat's reputation': Jharkhand-based biker woman turns down Barkha Dutt's interview invite on Dumka gang rape case*. OpIndia. https://www.opindia.com/2024/03/wont-provide-content-to-destroy-bharats-reputation-jharkhand-based-bikerwoman-turns-down-barkha-dutts-interview-invite-on-dumka-gang-rape-case/
Outlook Web Desk. (2023, September 28). Ujjain rape case: Auto-rickshaw driver detained, tried to escape police custody. *Outlook India*. https://www.outlookindia.com/national/ujjain-rape-case-72-hours-later-no-arrests-made-details-unclear-sit-formed-news-321195
Outlook Web Desk. (2023, September 30). Ujjain rape case: Father of accused demands death penalty, those who didn't help teen may face charges under POCSO. *Outlook India*. https://www.outlookindia.com/national/ujjain-rape-case-father-of-accused-demands-death-penalty-those-who-didn-t-help-teen-may-face-charges-under-pocso-news-321539
Panda, S. (2024, March 5). *3 accused in gang rape of Brazilian-Spanish Biker Fernanda 4ever identified*. Unique News Online. https://www.uniquenewsonline.com/3-accused-in-gang-rape-of-brazilian-spanish-biker-fernanda-4ever-identified/
Panigrahy, R. (2024, March 5). *What is the name of the accused arrested in the r*pe case of Fernanda 4ver Spanish woman biker in Jharkhand and what is their religion*. The SportsGrail. https://thesportsgrail.com/what-is-the-name-of-the-accused-arrested-in-the-rpe-case-of-fernanda-4ver-spanish-woman-biker-in-jharkhand-and-what-is-their-religion

Ponsford, D., & Davis, A. (2022, October 7). Churnalism 2022: Where do UK's leading news websites get their stories from? *Press Gazette*. https://pressgazette.co.uk/news/churnalism-2022/

PTI. (2023, July 21). *Fought for nation but could not protect my wife. Husband of woman paraded naked in Manipur*. Zee News. https://zeenews.india.com/india/fought-for-nation-but-could-not-protect-my-wife-husband-of-woman-paraded-naked-in-manipur-2638408.html

PTI. (2023a, September 29). Ujjain minor rape case: Father of accused held seeks death penalty for son. *The New Indian Express*. https://www.newindianexpress.com/nation/2023/Sep/29/ujjain-minor-rape-casefather-of-accused-held-seeks-death-penalty-for-son-2619430.html

PTI. (2023b, September 29). *He should be hanged: Father of accused held in MP for 12-yr-old's rape*. Rediff.com. https://www.rediff.com/news/report/he-should-be-hanged-father-of-accused-held-in-mp-for-12-yr-olds-rape/20230929.htm

Rajagopal, K. (2023, July 20). Manipur sexual violence video | Supreme Court 'deeply disturbed', orders Centre, Manipur government to act. *The Hindu*. https://www.thehindu.com/news/national/manipur-sexual-assault-using-women-as-instruments-of-violence-is-unacceptable-says-cji/article67100560.ece

Rich, P. R., & Zaragoza, M.S. (2020). Correcting misinformation in news stories: An investigation of correction timing and correction durability. *Journal of Applied Research in Memory and Cognition*, *9*(3), 310–322. https://doi.org/10.1016/j.jarmac.2020.04.001

Sabir, A. (2023, October 8). *'I have thought of taking my life': A Meitei woman recalls how she was raped by a mob*. Scroll.in. https://scroll.in/article/1057135/i-have-thought-of-taking-my-life-a-meitei-woman-recalls-how-she-was-raped-by-a-mob

Saikia, A. (2023, July 19). *'If you don't take off your clothes, we will kill you': Kuki women paraded naked in Manipur*. Scroll.in. https://scroll.in/article/1052938/video-shows-kuki-women-being-paraded-naked-by-a-mob-manipur-police-confirm-fir-filed

Saridou, T., Spyridou, L.-P., & Veglis, A. (2017). Churnalism on the rise? *Digital Journalism*, *5*(8), 1006–1024. https://doi.org/10.1080/21670811.2017.1342209

Sarkar, S. (2023, September 28). MP: Ujjain minor rape case accused arrested; gets injured in a bid to escape custody. *The Week*. https://www.theweek.in/news/india/2023/09/28/mp-five-suspects-detained-in-ujjain-minor-rape-case-tribal-girl-belongs-to-satna.html

Shandilya, S. (2023, July 22). 'Fought for India in Kargil, but couldn't protect wife': Ex-Army man rues after Manipur woman paraded naked. *English Jagran*. https://english.jagran.com/india/manipur-woman-paraded-naked-fought-for-india-in-kargil-but-couldnt-protect-wife-ex-army-man-rues-after-10089296

Sharma, H. (2023, September 28). Accused in Ujjain minor rape tries to escape police, then… *India Today*. https://www.indiatoday.in/india/story/ujjain-minor-rape-accused-auto-driver-tries-to-escape-shot-in-leg-by-police-2441923-2023-09-28

Sikdar, S. (2023, September 28). Auto driver arrested in Ujjain rape case. *The Hindu*. https://www.thehindu.com/news/national/auto-driver-arrested-in-ujjain-rape-case/article67358588.ece

Singh, V. (2023, July 19). Women face sexual violence in Manipur, video clip surfaces. *The Hindu*. https://www.thehindu.com/news/national/video-of-sexual-violence-on-women-in-manipur-emerges-police-promise-arrests-soon/article67098429.ece

The Quint. (2023, July 19). *"Turning blind Eye": AAP, Congress slam Modi Govt over shocking Manipur video*. The Quint. https://www.thequint.com/news/politics/manipur-video-kuki-women-paraded-naked-aap-congress-reactions-rahul-gandhi

TNM Staff. (2023, July 20). *FIR details the horrors three Manipuri women were subjected to, no arrests yet*. The News Minute. https://www.thenewsminute.com/news/fir-details-horrors-three-manipuri-women-were-subjected-no-arrests-yet-179966

TNN. (2023, September 29). Ujjain minor rape accused arrested; tries to flee police custody, injured. *The Times of India*. https://timesofindia.indiatimes.com/city/indore/ujjain-rape-case-accused-injured-in-bid-to-flee/articleshow/104027074.cms

Web Desk. (2024, March 3). Dulquer Salman expresses shock at rape of Spanish woman in Jharkhand. *The Week*. https://www.theweek.in/news/entertainment/2024/03/03/dulquer-salman-express-shock-over-rape-of-sapnish-woman-in-jharkhand.html

Web Desk. (2024, March 5). 'Won't provide content to destroy Bharat's reputation': Jharkhand-based biker woman turns down Barkha Dutt's. *HinduPost*. https://hindupost.in/crime/wont-provide-content-to-destroy-bharats-reputation-jharkhand-based-biker-woman-turns-down-barkha-dutts-interview-invite-on-dumka-gang-rape-case/

Weiss, R. (2017). Nip misinformation in the bud. *Science*, *358*(6362), 427–427. https://doi.org/10.1126/science.aar2683

Part III

Taming the Beast

7 The Social Dilemma

Rise and Impact of Social Media News Channels

Digital penetration may have reached prolific levels in India—the seventh-largest nation in terms of area and proclaimed to be the world's largest democracy with an estimated population of 1.44 billion as of June 2024 (Worldometer, 2024, June 30)—with 1.24 billion (86 per cent) accessing the Internet (Statista, 2024) and 862 million (59.9 per cent) users on online social media applications (Behera, 2024, June 13). A majority of them access the Internet using their smartphones and spend an average of 150 minutes a day on those applications (Behera, 2024, June 13). Thanks to this scale of connectedness, social media use has transformed and multiplied news dissemination and consumption, perhaps appropriating some control from mainstream news outlets over their content (Aneez et al., 2017; Kumar et al., 2019).

After a susceptible slump in newspaper circulation and revenues when the COVID-19 pandemic struck, Indian print media has been posting a gradual rise. A forced focal shift towards the digital space during the lockdown period, along with advertisement opportunities in the Internet domains, may have encouraged the adoption of technologies to meet online demands (Aneez et al., 2017; Kaur, 2024, February 13; Statista, 2024, May).

Kaur (2024, February 13) also noted that the print media share of advertising revenue had declined from 35 per cent in 2016 to 18 per cent in 2024 in the post-pandemic period. Nevertheless, the digital shift has helped offset the print loss (Kaur, 2024, June 26).

According to RNI (2022), India had 1,46,045 registered publications as of March 2022, with 20,821 newspapers among them. While Hindi had 56,052 registered publications, English recorded the second-largest number of newspapers and periodicals at 19,929. Similarly, Hindi publications claimed a combined circulation of 191 million (19.10 crore), while English publications claimed 36 million (3.64 crore) and the total claimed circulation was pegged at 391 million (39 crore). Per the RNI report, *Dainik Bhaskar* claimed the largest daily circulation of 3.45 million (34.47 lakh) with 44 editions, with *The Times of India* claiming the second-largest circulation with 33 editions at 2.65 million (26.47 lakh). Nevertheless, daily newspapers posted a minuscule drop in combined circulation (0.06 per cent), with 225.72 million during 2021–2022, against the 225.85 million copies per publishing day in 2020–2021 (RNI, 2022). While Hindi dailies (103 million copies) accounted for 45.84 per cent of the total newspaper circulation, their English counterparts (20.91 million copies) claimed a share of 9.26 per cent.

DOI: 10.4324/9781003468042-11

As media outlets across the globe take a digital-first turn to monetise news, the paper-pulp media and public-interest journalism are finding it challenging to sustain themselves and maintain news diversity and quality (Pedersen, 2021, December 22). A Dalberg report (Gupta et al., 2021) forecasts that "digital news will reach 700 million users in India by 2026" and that an average Indian news consumer will spend 49 minutes a day in 2026 (against 44 minutes in 2020; Pedersen, 2021, December 22). A Reuters Institute annual survey (Krishnan, 2024, June 17) pointed to the emergence of a new generation of Indians who have online social media as their main source of news, with 54 per cent accessing YouTube for news, apart from other popular platforms such as WhatsApp (48 per cent), Facebook (35 per cent) and Instagram (33 per cent). While showing a generic across-media decline in news interest over the past few years, the latest data showed that 71 per cent of the respondents sourced news online, while 46 per cent of them viewed television for news and 40 per cent read printed publications.

Further, outlining the offline news trend, the survey found that 32 per cent of the respondents viewed NDTV (a 24-hour television news channel) at least once a week, while 27 per cent read *The Times of India* once a week. Traditional media outlets were also found to dominate the digital space, with NDTV Online leading the race (Krishnan, 2024, June 17).

These trends point to a converged news milieu in India where traditional news outlets dominate the digital space and online social media circulate their online-offline produce.

Meanwhile, the overall trust in news, per the Reuters Institute survey, was found to vary from 38 to 41 per cent in the past few years. Among the popular media channels, All India Radio, BBC News, CNN, DD News, *Economic Times*, *Hindustan Times*, *India Today* and NDTV were adjudged as the most credible, with 60–65 per cent of the respondents trusting them (Krishnan, 2024, June 17). Bhattacharya and Ram (2016) noted that online social media has led to a shift in the competitive landscape of news providers, with different news sources exhibiting distinctive news propagation patterns. Further, Bhattacharya and Ram (2016, p. 719) found online news more detailed and engaging than their traditional counterparts with space constraints. Though traditional news media are time-bound, they are still popular in contemporary times as the online space is overcrowded and viewed as less credible.

Social media as a source of news

For decades now, online social media has been discussed as a source of news: From brainstorming and generating news ideas and identifying sources to learning about events first announced on social media and opinion-mining. These apart, generating news stories from social media content (for instance, using posts from verified social media handles of celebrities or churning a piece of entertainment news out of Instagram posts) has also been popular (Farhi & Chettah, 2020). Online avenues are also used to crowdsource information for news (Poell & Borra, 2012; Akagi & Linning, 2013, April 29). Akagi and Linning (2013, April 29) defined crowdsourcing as "obtaining data, information, or ideas from a group of people—can quickly bring up vast quantities of information that might otherwise be unavailable". Akagi and Linning (2013, April 29) also raised concern that crowdsourcing often fails to provide verified information due to its obscurely sourced and speculative information. Ferrucci (2017) noted that online social media can be used in a plethora of ways for news production, from idea generation, research, source identification, opinion procurement and information verification to announcement and promotion of news. What more? Social media can also offer insights into news consumption (readership trends) and reader response (likes, comments and shares). Through these, social media can influence journalism and dictate their priorities (Tandoc, 2014). Often, reporters are expected to tweet curtain-raisers for their news stories even before writing them and promote them again on social media once they are published (Tandoc, 2014). Creating news stories based on social media content, however, could be problematic as chances are less for information verification. Using such platforms for reporting on sexual crime (or crowdsourcing information to write sexual crime stories) could thus be problematic (Miró-Llinares & Aguerri, 2023), as newsroom competition and the race for reporting also limit the scope for information verification (Rich & Zaragoza, 2020).

Social media as a channel of news

Apart from being a source for news generation, online social media has also evolved to become a prime channel of news, with traditional media outlets dominating these people's media spaces and the rise of social media-only news channels run by individuals or small groups.

While the online space has brought down the cost of establishing a news channel to a pittance, social media platforms such as YouTube and Instagram have brought that cost further down to nothing. *Does this bother traditional journalism?* Though social media has been helpful in connecting traditional media houses with their audiences, it has created several conceptual and practical issues for journalists (Hermida, 2012; Farhi & Chettah, 2020), altering the relationship between the producers and consumers of news. In the online space, the power imbalance between the journalists and the audience is abridged and both decide what is newsworthy (Hermida et al., 2012; Chung, 2017). Besides, online social media has also blurred the line between producers and consumers of news (Barclay, Boobalakrishnan & Anushiya, 2022a). Now, anyone with a smartphone—which has also become affordable—can become a journalist on social media—which supports imagery (photographs and short videos shot with ease on smartphones) and micro-news content that can be composed with relative ease.

As news consumers (especially the millennials) expect near-immediate delivery of news and favour short-video formats (Desani, 2024)—as their attention span is diminishing (Kohler, 2023) thanks to online social media—traditional media outlets are forced to alter their content and strategies on digital platforms to remain relevant and cater to the changing news needs. Such social media pressures could force editorial aberrations (shortcomings or overstepping) and compromise the quality of news, leading to a loss of credibility (Safori, Rahman & Mohammed, 2016; Farhi & Chettah, 2020; Barclay, Boobalakrishnan & Anushiya, 2022c). Scholars have studied the positive and negative impacts of smartphone addiction (Barclay, Boobalakrishnan & Anushiya, 2022b), the culture of clicking (photographs) and social media (Barclay, 2022; Barclay et al., 2022a) on news dissemination and allied information consumption.

For instance, Hermida (2012) observed that the popularity of social media was based on its ability to broadcast information live from disaster spots where journalists were absent or yet to arrive. Hermida (2012) saw the consolidation of news in "real-time" tweets, "eyewitness (Facebook) accounts" and "cellphone (YouTube) videos" (p. 314).

These phenomena have also affected both sexual violence—with an associated culture of recording the crime and transmitting it online (or using social media)—and its reportage—sharing links (of news) and popularising them, tracking developments and capturing imagery and posting opinions (or reactions on social media) and consolidating them (using hashtags). Hasnat (2014) highlighted the importance of accuracy, trustworthiness and journalistic ethics in ensuring the credibility of news on social media channels.

A paradoxical situation is perceivable in the convergence of (online-offline) news production and social media emergence, as the latter aids in the generation and dissemination of news and poses a challenge as an adversary (Chadwick, 2011). Technology-driven news production techniques that may be replacing traditional strategies in the newsroom may be more efficient but low on quality, may pay attention to algorithmic nuances but circumvent established ethics, may be market-driven but steer away from responsible journalism and may focus on human interest and sideline public interest.

While there is a generic concern that social media-circulated information lacks depth, a section of users view it as an alternative media adding breadth to the available information.

Pursuing this perspective, Sharma (2014, December 1) wrote:

> … our data suggested that news consumers (social media users)… believe their social circles provide them with a broader range of news and information than if they relied solely on traditional media… The steady, uncelebrated process of newsgathering also makes the media an essential invigilator of power.

In contemporary times, the challenges that online social media poses to traditional journalism are manifold and intense (Haque, 2023, May 3), especially when reporting sexual violence against women. When several recent cases were reported, we witnessed a flurry of social media channels (mostly fringe) recirculating content and imagery from other social media channels and news sources, essentially engaging in Predatory Journalism. Such social media reporting could come without formal journalism education and training or disregard traditional publication ethics. A handful of research has studied the use of online social media for news reporting and discussed allied issues, but specifically, reporting on sexual violence on those platforms remains unexplored or understudied. For instance, Barberá, Vaccari and Valeriani (2017, p. 29) observed an excessive reliance on social media among journalists and examined how it contributes to the "personalisation of journalism on social media".

Nevertheless, in connected newsrooms, if mainstream media outlets value traditional journalistic ethics and practices, then they will be able to combine "new approaches with old principles" and retain their "institutional and cultural significance" in the digital space (Belair-Gagnon, 2015, p. 114) and those practices include verification, maintenance of accuracy and balance and emphasis on ground reporting and face-to-face interviews.

Analysing threats and opportunities in using social media for conflict reportage, Sacco and Bossio (2015, p. 59) found that though these Internet-based applications aid instant news broadcast and widen view variations, "reporters must also negotiate the complexities that fast, multi-medium and multi-sourced information create for reportage, especially in terms of the verification and contextualisation of information", making it critical to analyse how "journalists position themselves and their practices within this new media ecosystem".

Investigative journalism is another critical area that emboldens and animates news reporters and that news consumers value. Analysing the effect of social media use on investigative journalism, Abdenour (2017) found no evidence of improvement. Jewitt (2009) noted that social media journalism enables netizens (some sans professional journalism training) with diverse backgrounds to comment on and analyse topical news events.

Similarly, unregulated social media could be used to share content that invades privacy and carries misinformation (Sreedharan, 2023, May 30). Such participatory or networked journalism could become predatory when the primary aim is to capitalise on a current news topic, that has managed to garner public curiosity for clicks and views instead of information and opinion dissemination. This chapter conducts a case study to identify predatory practices while reporting on sexual violence on social media channels.

For the case study, the chapter chooses a recent controversial case that involved an "alleged MMS leak". On 17 September 2022, female hostel students of a private university in Mohali in the Indian state of Punjab complained that another female student from the same hostel had recorded and shared washroom videos of them without their knowledge. An inconclusive conversation between the warden and the accused student was leaked on social and news media (Singh, 2022, September 18; Sehgal, 2022, September 19). Though the university administration and police investigation maintained that the accused student did not record videos of other students, rumours and speculations (Mahanagar Times, 2022, September 20; Zee Media Bureau, 2022, September 18) were rife on social and news media, leading to massive protests (India.com News Desk, 2022, September 22), which forced the police to arrest the female student and three other males (PTI, 2022, September 24) and her identity, the conversation footage and pictures of one of the accused males were widely shared on social media (Kanthwal, 2022, September 20; Sehgal, 2022,

September 26). It turned out to be a classical case of "social media reporting" that was mostly a sham.

Mainstream media embraced social media journalism, picking up (lending credence to) their rumours, editorialising (sensationalising) them, using the conversation footage for credibility (though unverified and inconclusive) and adding unverified quotes (which were loaded with misinformation). For instance, social media claims and news media reports (backed by student quotes) that informed of mass student suicides over the issue were found to be untrue (Zee Media Bureau, 2022, September 18). As the investigation proceeded and matured, there was no evidence to suggest that videos of other students were recorded and shared (Zee News, 2022, September 20). Charges were also dropped against two of the accused males (Times News Network, 2022, November 18).

When information about the "MMS leak" in an educational institution spread across social and news media, it circulated nationwide inquisitiveness, triggering the production of a slew of imagery and content across media to feed and monetise the collective curiosities.

Using the conversation footage that was widely circulated on social media and student versions grabbed from television reports, social media accounts and channels spun speculations and conspiracy theories (which were also recycled in the mainstream media): 60 girls were victimised (Telangana Today, 2022, September 19), hundreds of their washroom videos were shared and monetised and the scandal had international connections.

Though there were contradictions in the case, which several reports acknowledged and reported, the mainstream media still tended to be biassed, sensationalising the issue and capitalising on the curiosities (FPJ Web Desk, 2022, September 18; Sehgal, 2022, September 26; Zee Media Bureau, 2022, September 20). On this media mayhem, Bajpai (2022, September 22) wrote:

> Faithfully, news channels recorded the allegations and anger, but mercifully, we saw none of the alleged offending videos. What did we see? A warden scolding the student who apparently shared the videos, another clip of a warden-student face-off over whom to blame for the entire sorry episode, and interviews with students and the police. The latter said they had found no evidence, thus far, of videos that outraged anyone's modesty. In the absence of any clear picture, the news channels looked at the 'dirty picture'.

Picking up cues from social media, news reports used terms such as "spine-chilling", "dirty picture" (a popular movie title), "*mahapaap*" (a great sin) and "that will shock you" to sensationalise the issue (Zee News, 2022, September 18; Aaj Tak, 2022, September 18; Singh, 2022, September 20). Highlighting how unthinkingly relying on social media data and unverified claims could be problematic, Baliarsingh (2022, September 19) reported that "Twitter thread on Chandigarh University MMS will shock you" and "as per a Twitter thread, at least eight students have tried to end their lives. One of them breathed her last while seven of them are under treatment" and Times Now Navbharat (2022, September 18) quoted students saying: "There are four more girls associated with the main female accused… yes it is made… videos of more than 60 female are there… we have seen the videos". When the reporter asks, "Where are these posted?", the female students respond in unison, "in some site. She was sending the videos to her male friend. She used to take money and send videos to boys. She was sending to boys' hostels also… videos of more than 60 females". Several YouTube videos also used this interview with Times Now Navbharat (2022, September 18). In this case study, a sample of three YouTube video posts from non-legacy media sources on this issue is purposively chosen to examine unethical editorial practices and indications of Predatory Journalism.

Video item [1] (Priyaashi, 2022, September 19) posted on 19 September 2022 discusses the MMS leak case using borrowed footage of student interviews from television channels and the conversation video between the hostel warden and the accused female student, along with apparent representative images, for a duration of 19:58 minutes.

Video item [2] (StudY LoveR- VeeR, 2022, September 18) posted on 18 September 2022 on the YouTube channel "StudY LoveR- VeeR" for 7:19 minutes discusses the MMS leak case, beginning with a video of a girl demanding justice for female students. Then, it presents a compilation of screengrabs, Google Trends reports and borrowed video footage from news channels to offer an "expert" analysis.

Video item [3] (Mojo Story, 2022, September 18) posted on the YouTube channel Mojo Story recycles the footage of the conversation between the warden and the accused student without additional information or source citation, though the channel, led by popular journalist Barkha Dutt, takes pride in being "non-partisan in a hyper-polarized world. Neither 'Chamcha' nor 'Morcha' we promise you content that puts #PeopleFirst" in the channel description.

Inexperience. Priyaashi, the YouTube channel that published the video item [1] on the MMS scandal, described itself as a "channel that makes videos on fashion, makeup, challenge related videos, review videos, clothing haul. other than that… daily vlogs and many other contents". A pair of women run and present in this channel. Launched in 2017, this channel had 476,000 subscribers and posted 599 videos as of 3 July 2024. Similarly, the YouTube channel "StudY LoveR- VeeR" that had posted video item [2] claims to aid preparation for competitive examinations. Launched in 2016, this channel has 1.24 million subscribers (as of 3 July 2024).

Sensationalism and sexualisation. Video item [1] uses a thumbnail image which features the pair of women who present the video content, along with a back view of a girl in the shower (representative image?), along with the text "THE BIGGEST SCANDAL: MMS LEAKED" and an icon of danger, showing clear signs of sensationalism (exaggeration) and sexualisation of the issue. At the beginning of video item [1], a collage of short videos is presented, where the warden is shown raising her hand to slap the accused female, followed by the blurred (apparently borrowed from a news report [Times Now Navbharat, 2022, September 18]) footage of protesting female students, one of whom demands "justice", recycling the misinformation published in the news report about the involvement of four more girls and student deaths.

Following the video collage, the two women running the channel appear to introduce themselves and the topic at hand, which is "quite different" from their usual topics of "horror" and "entertainment". Starting their conversation on the "social issue", one of the presenters presents a "popular saying from childhood", which states that "a woman is an enemy of woman".

In between conversations, the video presented slides of images showing the accused girl and protesting students with captions such as "Chandigarh University incident is an absolute horror" and "don't spread [those] videos because she is someone's sister or someone['s] daughter". They also request the viewers watch the video until the end "for the safety of all of us and our loved ones". *Privacy invasion.* Publishing edited and unverified images and videos of those involved in the case and branding the event using the name of the educational institution, the video item [1] invades their privacy. While it was still unclear whether the accused girl was a victim, video item [1] published her photographs, along with one male accused, causing irreparable damage to them. Further, the video item condemns the act.

Plagiarism and misinformation. Video item [1] based its presentation on video footage borrowed from news channels and circulated on social media. Nevertheless, the sources from which the footage was used are not identified. Though there was no evidence to suggest or information from trusted sources that indeed the accused girl recorded and transmitted videos of fellow students, it presented arguments and expressed emotions, along with suggestions and warnings, under the premise that washroom videos were indeed recorded and shared. Video item [1] also shared footage of students misinforming about 60 victims and mass suicides. Though video item [1] has borrowed footage from news reports and social media without proper attribution and explanation, it, ironically, states in the video description that "All the content and image on this channel belongs to us and are protected under copyright law. Kindly don't copy or reproduce content without my prior explicit permission". Video item [2] also resorts to recycling screengrabs (from *The Times of India*) without attribution of source.

Prejudicial reporting. Video item [1] divulged the images of both the accused female and her alleged male partner (the male shown in the image was later found to be not involved in the case and his profile picture was used in the WhatsApp profile of her male friend). Drawing from the rumours circulating on social media, the presenters claimed that washroom videos of more than 60 female students went viral, leading to panic attacks and fainting, while eight among them attempted to commit suicide. Further, the presenters also claim, without attributing it to any source, that the warden of the girl's hostel had instructed all the inmates to delete videos from their mobile phones. Similarly, news item [2] also appears to be prejudicial and biassed as it is posted with a thumbnail carrying the picture of the female accused and the kicker "*Chandigarh me sharmnak kand*" (shameful incident in Chandigarh), inciting a sense of disgust among the audience about the incident. The video then starts with a clip of a female describing the scandal and demanding justice for the victims. The later part of the video carries a male voiceover who presents an analysis of the incident, taking cues from media reports. It points to inaction, despite "protestors demanding action against the accused" and an institutional cover-up to "save its reputation", apart from spreading misinformation about student suicides. It indirectly supports the scandal theory that suggested that videos were recorded and shared, apart from fanning conspiracy theories about police inaction and institutional cover-up based on unverified rumours. Based on the unverified information provided, it also asks the viewers to judge if strict action should be taken or if the matter should be suppressed.

Reviewing the case and the sample YouTube videos on it, it can be understood that though social media is a critical-democratic tool that can be used as an alternative medium to voice opinion suppressed in the mainstream media, the inexperience (as journalists) of social media influencers can be problematic without understanding editorial principles, especially when reporting on a sensitive topic. Unverified and biassed information and inconclusive footage were used to fan conspiracy theories about the case, forcing unwarranted arrests and indiscriminate sharing of photographs and identification details of the accused, causing irreparable social damage to them. On the other hand, mainstream media picked up social media rumours and embraced its suggestions to lend credence to those theories. This reciprocal relationship between mainstream and social media exhibited how reporting a sensitive sexual issue could be erroneous. Social media channels were also found to engage in churnalism to cash in on the trending topic. When information gets passed, at times, it gets sensationalised and distorted, creating a cloud of misinformation. In this case, such a media cloud led to massive student protests, drew political criticism and created nationwide curiosity.

In several cases, the mainstream media was also found to use social media to crowdsource information, leading to the publishing of biassed and prejudicial misinformation. YouTube was also found to become a mainstream news channel, with users resorting to it for news. Inexperienced churnalists, both on social and mainstream media, were also unable to separate fact from fiction and present (recycled) information with proper attribution and objectivity. In their reports, there were cues of sexualisation and sensationalism, perhaps to draw views and popularise their channels. Further, apparently, representative washroom images of girls were in thumbnails of both news reports and YouTube videos. In those speculative and sensationalised stories, cues of victim-blaming and slut-shaming were identified.

As Chapter 4 discusses, publishing critical footage and identification of the accused infringes upon their rights to a fair trial. In the present case, the names of the male accused, their professional details and the photograph of the female accused were widely circulated both on social and news media, apart from unverified student versions that spread through word-of-mouth. Among the widespread imagery related to this case, there were images of female students in the hostel, the warden, the female accused, her alleged male friend and the washrooms of the hostel "where the crime took place". Among the tactics that YouTube channels used to churn content on the issue and garner views were the use of explicit imagery of female bodies, images of the accused and victims circulated online and blurring or cropping of borrowed videos from news sources. Most of those churned videos came with additional emotional outrage and warnings, branded as for public interest. Here, this trend raises a critical question: Are these (un)professional journalists and social media influencers really oblivious to the social damage that unverified information passed can cause?

Social media is a powerful tool that must be used cautiously. Predatory (even if unmindful) use could cause serious social damage to stakeholders. These findings resonate with the views of Tandoc and Vos (2016), who argued that social media trends influence journalistic decisions and directions. More often than not, journalists tend to give in to social media pressures, whether to report a particular story or take a specific side. Recording and sharing of videos, which smartphones have simplified, is another critical aspect in sexual crime and reporting, as witnessed in the present case as well, where at the core of the scandal were videos—the (unrecorded?) washroom videos of incognisant girls, the conversation video of the warden and the news videos of protesting students blurting (word-of-mouth?) information.

Though it lasted for just about a week, the Mohali episode had all the essential ingredients to make an interesting story: Massive student protests providing spectacular visuals, enraged students offering hysterical comments, conspiracy theories of police inaction and institutional cover-up, comments and criticism from the political elite, inside visuals that went viral, a *femme fatale* who had online friendship with low-profile men, mass suicides, voyeurism in a hostel washroom, 60 victims and hundreds of videos sold to popular pornographic websites, blackmail and threats, foreign connection and all of these creating nationwide public interest and social media furore—just that most, if not all, of them were either blatantly baseless or utterly untrue, which, seemingly, did not bother career-oriented journalists and social media content creators who were in a rat race striving to capitalise on the controversial scandal.

About a month later, investigations concluded and found no evidence to suggest that the accused female had recorded videos of fellow hostel mates and charges against one of the arrested were dropped as another accused had misused his photograph as his profile photo (Sharma, 2022, November 17). Even after the initial allegations and allied exaggerations were found to be baseless, the inaccurate news and social media posts still remain online (even after two years), along with the photographs of the accused and their details—accumulating views and increasing profits. Exhibiting duplicity, the news and social media hardly bothered to cover the acquittals and uncover (or correct) their past inaccuracies, lending some credence to our argument of Predatory Journalism in this book. It also explains how the public sphere of social media can be a convenient and compelling space to exploit news on sexual violence and the audience who are interested in it—at times, even corrupting the mainstream media with feeble ethical foundations.

A contemporary trend—in the post-pandemic phase that has propelled the uncultivated commoners to launch YouTube channels and monetise their videos—is exploring hot trending topics (including crime) and viral videos (including sexual) and engaging in analysis and activism. Online social media, already at the crossroads of affirmative use, maleficent misuse and calls for regulation, needs to tread with extra caution and sensitiveness when the topic is at the intersection of sex and crime (sexual crime) as covering it comes with serious consequences. Social media provides opportunities both for practising Predatory Journalism and inventing ways to check unethical reporting. As the laws are becoming tighter, media outlets using social media and online content creators may have to be more aware of issues, such as sensationalism, sexualisation, plagiarism, misinformation and prejudicial reporting, to avoid unfortunate legal and penal actions. Not just for the new-age journalists and social media activists (as several scholars [Hasnat, 2014; Sacco & Bossio, 2015] have stressed), fact-checking becomes hypercritical even for the passive consumers of online social media content.

References

Aaj Tak. (2022, September 18). *Mohali MMS case: Chandigarh University MMS कांड के बाद छात्राओं के परिवार में मचा हड़कंप! | AAJTAK* [Video]. YouTube. https://www.youtube.com/watch?v=-7hjB3IGyKA

Abdenour, J. (2017). Digital gumshoes: Investigative journalists' use of social media in television news reporting. *Digital Journalism*, *5*(4), 472–492.

Akagi, K, & Linning, S. (2013, April 29). Crowdsourcing done right. *Between the Spreadsheets*. http://www.cjr.org/between_the_spreadsheets/crowdsourcing_done_right.php

Aneez, Z., Chattapadhyay, S., Parthasarathi, V., & Nielsen, R. (2017). *Indian news media and the production of news in the age of social discovery*. ORA - Oxford University Research Archive. https://ora.ox.ac.uk/objects/uuid:b8c05879-6655-4096-aa0c-47affa3c8468

Bajpai, S. (2022, September 22). *'Mumbai se Mohali' – How TV news covered Chandigarh University 'MMS kand.'* ThePrint. https://theprint.in/opinion/telescope/mumbai-se-mohali-how-tv-news-covered-chandigarh-university-mms-kand/1138124/

Baliarsingh, C. (2022, September 19). *Twitter thread on Chandigarh University MMS will shock you*. Twitter Thread on Chandigarh University MMS Scandal Will Send Chills Down Your Spine. https://odishatv.in/news/national/twitter-thread-on-chandigarh-university-mms-scandal-will-send-chills-down-your-spine-185851

Barberá, P., Vaccari, C., & Valeriani, A. (2017). Social media, personalisation of news reporting, and media systems' polarisation in Europe. In M. Barisione, & A. Michailidou, (Eds.), *Social media and European politics*. Palgrave Studies in European Political Sociology. Palgrave Macmillan (pp. 25–52). https://doi.org/10.1057/978-1-137-59890-5_2

Barclay, F. P. (2022). Social media policy in the age of misuse and misinformation. In Francis P. Barclay & N. Boobalakrishnan (Eds.), *Social media in India: Regulatory needs, issues and challenges*. Sage. ISBN-978-93-5479-075-1 (HB).

Barclay, F. P., Boobalakrishnan, N. and Anushiya, K. (2022a). Balancing social media autonomy, privacy and regulation. In Francis P. Barclay & N. Boobalakrishnan (Eds.), *Social media in India: Regulatory needs, issues and challenges*. Sage. ISBN-978-93-5479-075-1 (HB).

Barclay, F. P., Boobalakrishnan, N. and Anushiya, K. (2022b). Social media dependence and the loss of distinction and detachment. In Francis P. Barclay & N. Boobalakrishnan (Eds.), *Social media in India: Regulatory needs, issues and challenges*. Sage. ISBN-978-93-5479-075-1 (HB).

Barclay, F. P., Boobalakrishnan, N., & Anushiya, K. (2022c). Credibility of social media messages and user awareness. In Francis P. Barclay & N. Boobalakrishnan (Eds.), *Social media in India: Regulatory needs, issues and challenges*. Sage. ISBN-978-93-5479-075-1 (HB).

Behera, T. R. (2024, June 13). *Social media users statistics in India 2024*. GrabOn's indulge – Online shopping tips, buying guide, savings. https://www.grabon.in/indulge/tech/social-media-statistics/#:~:text=India%20has%20862.08%20million%20social,list%20with%201.06%20billion%20users

Belair-Gagnon, V. (2015). *Social media at BBC News: The re-making of crisis reporting*. Routledge.

Benedict, H. (1993). Virgin or vamp: How the press covers sex crimes. Oxford University Press.

Bhattacharya, D., & Ram, S. (2016). Understanding the competitive landscape of news providers on social media. In P*roceedings of the 25th International Conference Companion on World Wide Web (WWW '16 Companion). International World Wide Web Conferences Steering Committee, Republic and Canton of Geneva.* CHE (pp. 719–724). https://doi.org/10.1145/2872518.2890097

Chadwick, A. (2011). The political information cycle in a hybrid news system: The British Prime Minister and the 'Bullygate' affair. *The International Journal of Press/Politics*, 16(1), 3–29. https://doi.org/10.1177/1940161210384730

Chung, M. (2017). Not just numbers: The role of social media metrics in online news evaluations. *Computers in Human Behavior*, *75*, 949–957. https://doi.org/10.1016/j.chb.2017.06.022

Desani, A. (2024). Reels to the real world-assessing the effects of watching short-form video on the attention span of children and parents. *Journal of the Indian Society of Pedodontics & Preventive Dentistry*, *42*.

Farhi, F., & Chettah, M. (2020). Social media as news sources for TV news channels–A study in the newsrooms. *Talent Development & Excellence*, *12*(3).

Ferrucci, P. (2017). Are you experienced? How years in field affects digital journalists' perceptions of a changing industry. *Journalism Studies*, *19*(16), 2417–2432. https://doi.org/10.1080/1461670X.2017.1349550

FPJ Web Desk. (2022, September 18). Explainer: What is the MMS scandal that has rocked Chandigarh University? *Free Press Journal*. https://www.freepressjournal.in/india/explainer-what-is-the-mms-scandal-that-has-rocked-chandigarh-university

Gupta, G., Walia, K., Goyal, S., Marks, J., Sunavala, N., Doshi, A., Bhatnagar, R., Dahiya, R., Hobbs, C., Khakhar, D., & Dalberg Advisors. (2021). *The future of the news in India [Report]*. https://dalberg.com/wp-content/uploads/2021/12/The-Future-of-News-in-India_Dec.pdf

Haque, E. (2023, May 3). Navigating new-age challenges of news: AI-generated content, algorithm bias, and deepfake menace. *Times of India Blog*. https://timesofindia.indiatimes.com/blogs/thebigd/navigating-new-age-challenges-of-news-ai-generated-content-algorithm-bias-and-deepfake-menace/

Hasnat, M. O. (2014). Credibility of social online media: in the eyes of Finnish professional journalists. *Comunicação E Sociedade*, *25*, 220–235. https://doi.org/10.17231/comsoc.25(2014).1870

Hermida, A. (2012). Social journalism: Exploring how social media is shaping journalism. In E. Siapera & A. Veglis (Eds.). *The handbook of global online journalism*. (1st ed.). John Wiley & Sons, Inc.

Hermida, A., Fletcher, F., Korell, D., & Logan, D. (2012). Share, like, recommend. *Journalism Studies*, *13*(5–6), 815–824. https://doi.org/10.1080/1461670X.2012.664430

India.com News Desk. (2022, September 18). *Chandigarh University case: Statements, claims of CU ADMN and police raise more questions*. India.Com. https://www.india.com/news/india/chandigarh-university-case-statements-claims-of-cu-admn-and-police-raise-more-questions-details-inside-5639248/

Jewitt, R. (2009). The trouble with twittering: Integrating social media into mainstream news. *International Journal of Media and Cultural Politics*, *5*(3), 233–240.

Kanthwal, G. (2022, September 20). Chandigarh University video 'leak': Suspect's identity remains exposed. *The Tribune*. https://www.tribuneindia.com/news/chandigarh/chandigarh-university-video-leak-suspects-identity-remains-exposed-433754

Kaur, C. (2024, February 13). Print's Ad share drops 15% in last 7 years. *Exchange4media*. https://www.exchange4media.com/media-print-news/prints-ad-spend-share-drops-from-35-to-20-in-last-7-years-132494.html

Kaur, C. (2024, June 26). Print's Q2 bears good news for ad revenue. *Exchange4media*. https://www.exchange4media.com/media-print-news/prints-q4-bears-good-news-for-ad-revenue-135222.html

Kohler, T. J. (2023). *Caught in the loop: the effects of the addictive nature of short-form videos on users' perceived attention span and mood* [Bachelor's thesis]. University of Twente.

Krishnan, A. (2024, June 17). *India*. Reuters Institute for the Study of Journalism. https://reutersinstitute.politics.ox.ac.uk/digital-news-report/2024/india

Kumar., N., Nagalla, R., Marwahc, T., & Singha, M. (2019, August 23). Sentiment Dynamics in Social Media News Channels. *Online Social Networks and Media*. https://arxiv.org/pdf/1908.08147

Mahanagar Times. (2022, September 20). Chandigarh University MMS scandal: Girls are getting threats after video leaked, messages like "Your video is also there, I have..." *Mahanagar Times*.https://www.mahanagartimes.com/post/chandigarh-university-mms-scandal-girls-are-getting-threats-after-video-leaked-messages-like-your-video-is-also-there-i-have

Miró-Llinares, F., & Aguerri, J. C. (2023). Misinformation about fake news: A systematic critical review of empirical studies on the phenomenon and its status as a 'threat'. *European Journal of Criminology*, *20*(1), 356–374. https://doi.org/10.1177/1477370821994059

Mojo Story. (2022, September 18). *Chandigarh University MMS leak | Accused girl arrested, says "Sent videos to a boy in Shimla"* [Video]. YouTube. https://www.youtube.com/watch?v=PJTiX50deuQOOSGA.

Pedersen, M. (2021, December 22). *The future of news in India*. Dalberg. https://dalberg.com/our-ideas/the-future-of-news-in-india/

Poell, T, & Borra, E. (2012). Twitter, YouTube, and Flickr as platforms of alternative journalism: The social media account of the 2010 Toronto G20 protests. *Journalism*, *13*(6), 695–713. https://doi.org/10.1177/1464884911431533

Priyaashi. (2022, September 19). **CHANDIGARH UNIVERSITY Girls Hostel* Scandal* ✖ ⚠ [Video]. YouTube. https://www.youtube.com/watch?v=5XIsEG3CB5Y

PTI. (2022, September 24). Chandigarh University video case | Army man held from Arunachal Pradesh, fourth arrest in case. *The Hindu*. https://www.thehindu.com/news/national/other-states/chandigarh-university-video-case-army-man-held-from-arunachal-pradesh-fourth-arrest-in-case/article65931453.ece

Rich, P. R., & Zaragoza, M. S. (2020). Correcting misinformation in news stories: An investigation of correction timing and correction durability. *Journal of Applied Research in Memory and Cognition*, *9*(3), 310–322. https://doi.org/10.1016/j.jarmac.2020.04.001

RNI. (2022). Press in India. *RNI*. Retrieved July 7, 2024, from https://rni.nic.in/all_page/PIN2021_22.html

Sacco, V., & Bossio, D. (2015). Using social media in the news reportage of war & conflict: Opportunities and challenges. *The Journal of Media Innovations*, *2*(1), 59–76.

Safori, A. O., Rahman, N. A. A., & Mohammed, R. (2016). Perspectives and attitudes on the credibility of news on social networking (SNSS) sites: urgent need of research work. *Journal of New Media and Mass Communication*, *3*(1), 25–33.

Sehgal, M. (2022, September 19). Chandigarh University row: Accused girl made video of another student, says her lawyer. *India Today*. https://www.indiatoday.in/india/story/chandigarh-university-row-accused-girl-made-video-of-another-student-lawyer-says-2002126-2022-09-19

Sehgal, M. (2022, September 26). Woman who filmed Chandigarh students was dating arrested Army man. *India Today*. https://www.indiatoday.in/india/story/woman-who-filmed-chandigarh-university-students-dating-arrested-army-man-2004973-2022-09-26

Sharma, N. (2022, November 17). Chandigarh University video leak case| No objectionable photos of other girl students found, Mohali police say in chargesheet. *Hindustan Times*. https://www.hindustantimes.com/cities/chandigarh-news/chandigarh-university-video-leak-case-no-objectionable-photos-of-other-girl-students-found-mohali-police-say-in-chargesheet-101668641833200.html

Sharma, S. (2014, December 1). Will newsgathering survive the proliferation of online media? *The Caravan*. https://caravanmagazine.in/perspectives/minority-report

Singh, N. (2022, September 18). Chandigarh University girl held for 'leaking' obscene videos, varsity says clip was personal. *India Today.* https://www.indiatoday.in/india/story/chandigarh-university-girl-arrested-leaking-obscene-videos-punjab-police-rumours-2001675-2022-09-18

Singh, S. (2022, September 20). Spine-chilling MMS scandal in Chandigarh University; girl hosteller, two men held. *Krishi Jagran.* https://krishijagran.com/news/spine-chilling-mms-scandal-in-chandigarh-university-girl-hosteller-two-men-held/

Sreedharan, S. (2023, May 30). The changing dynamics of modern media in India. *Businessworld.* https://businessworld.in/article/the-changing-dynamics-of-modern-media-in-india-478429

Statista. (2024). *Number of internet users in India from 2010 to 2023, with estimates until 2050 (in millions)*, Statista. https://www.statista.com/statistics/255146/number-of-internet-users-in-india/

Statista. (2024, May). *Print newspapers & magazines – India.* Statista. https://www.statista.com/outlook/amo/media/newspapers-magazines/print-newspapers-magazines/india

StudY LoveR- VeeR. (2022, September 18). *Chandigarh University girl viral video news | Protest in Chandigarh University* [Video]. YouTube. https://www.youtube.com/watch?v=cfV5XMtxao4

Tandoc, E. C. (2014). Journalism is twerking? How web analytics is changing the process of gatekeeping. *New Media & Society*, *16*(4), 559–575. https://doi.org/10.1177/1461444814530541

Tandoc, E. C., & Vos, T. P. (2016). The journalist is marketing the news: Social media in the gatekeeping process. *Journalism Practice*, *10*(8), 950–966. https://doi.org/10.1080/17512786.2015.1087811

Telangana Today. (2022, September 19). All about MMS scandal that has rocked Chandigarh University. *Telangana Today.* https://telanganatoday.com/all-about-mms-scandal-that-has-rocked-chandigarh-university

Times Now Navbharat. (2022, September 18). *60 छात्राओं के MMS वायरल होने का सच क्या ? | Chandigarh University MMS Scandal Case | Hindi News* [Video]. YouTube. https://www.youtube.com/watch?v=L3Fg8oNbwi4

Times News Network. (2022, November 18). Chandigarh University video leak case: Charges against 2 accused dropped. *The Times of India.* https://timesofindia.indiatimes.com/city/chandigarh/cu-video-leake-case-charges-against-2-accused-dropped/articleshow/95592438.cms#:~:text=MOHALI%3A%20Police%20have%20dropped%20charges%20against%20two%20of,seeking%20sexual%20stimulation%20by%20visual%20means%20and%20stalking.

Worldometer. (2024, June 30). India population. *Worldometer.* https://www.worldometers.info/world-population/india-population/#:~:text=The%20current%20population%20of%20India,of%20the%20total%20world%20population.

Zee Media Bureau. (2022, September 18). *'No student committed suicide, don't believe in rumours': Chandigarh University Vice Chancellor on girls video leak.* Zee News. https://zeenews.india.com/india/no-student-committed-suicide-don-t-believe-in-rumours-chandigarh-university-vice-chancellor-on-girls-video-leak-2511610.html

Zee Media Bureau. (2022, September 20). *DNA exclusive: Analysis of Chandigarh University video leak case and attempts to cover up students claims*. Zee News. https://zeenews.india.com/india/dna-exclusive-analysis-of-chandigarh-university-video-leak-case-and-attempts-to-cover-up-students-claims-2512491.html

Zee News. (2022, September 18). *Chandigarh:* डर्टी पिक्चर का मास्टरमाइंड कौन ? Zee News. http://54.251.163.26/hindi/india/video/chandigarh-who-is-the-mastermind-of-the-dirty-picture/1356947

Zee News. (2022, September 20). *Chandigarh University MMS scandal: What is the lawyer of the accused saying?* [Video]. Zee News. https://zeenews.india.com/video/news/chandigarh-university-mms-scandal-what-is-the-lawyer-of-the-accused-saying-2512351.html

8 Predatory Journalism

Consolidation, Criticism and Consequences

In recent times, reporting sexual violence has become a tricky business, with theoretical polemics, ethical dilemmas and consequential paradoxes surmounting several associated issues. Elemental of those doubleheader debates is the existential question of whether or not to report (or highlight) sexual violence against women in the news media (implying whether news reporting of sexual violence suppresses this social sickness or breeds it).

As sexual violence can be cataclysmic with severe physical, psychological and social consequences, the most-persistent insistence is that it is essential to report and educate the public about it. On the other side, there is a small-scale but growing discord that claims contemporary coverage of sexual crime is, in fact, cultivating a culture of rape.

On from where such concern stems from, Prasad (2019, June 23) writes:

> For at least 20 minutes on June 6, I was sitting in silence and darkness in my room, consumed with the breaking news of the brutal rape, torture, and murder of a two-year-old girl in Aligarh, India. The news and celebrities, journalists, media houses and armchair activists on social media painted a vivid picture: Two Muslim men raped the Hindu girl, gouged her eyes out, mutilated her body, threw acid on her and then murdered and discarded her in a garbage dump. Turns out, most of that never happened.

Assessing five cases, Prasad (2019, June 23) noted that a section of news reporting on sexual violence was stereotypical, sensationalist, sectionalist and inaccurate. On the apparent lack of media accountability, Prasad (2019, June 23) further observed that:

> Unverified sensationalization and unnecessary communalization aside, the minor victim's name was aggressively published and shared in headlines across the board; her photos, and a video of her before the incident went viral and was used extensively—all this when the media thought it was a rape case. When police reports came out inconclusive about the sexual assault and denied any acid being poured on her or her eyes being gouged out, most publications silently changed the narrative without issuing public clarifications or removing past inaccuracies.

DOI: 10.4324/9781003468042-12

Prasad (2019, June 23) finds the news reporting on sexual violence to be (mostly) short-sighted—focusing mainly on current crimes (viewing them as isolated events) and failing to explore the reasons—and sensationalist—distancing crime such as rape from social realities. She also identified hints of victim-blaming in the media coverage of sexual crimes that could perhaps advocate restrictions against the freedom of women and uphold the culture of rape.

A handful of recent studies have explored the connection between the media, victim-blaming and rape culture (Thacker & Day, 2017; Cusmano, 2018; Blumell & Mulupi, 2022). Thacker and Day (2017) identified the "problematic links" among the media, victim-blaming, rape culture—that normalises sexual violence—and legal-judicial practices. According to the researchers, sexist media coverage, while propagating a rape culture and sexual violence, affects how rape victims are perceived and treated, along with judicial trial outcomes. Thacker and Day (2017) also viewed the mass media as harbingers of rape myths—where the "language of rape" is used to frame such crimes as "normal" and "pleasurable" (both for the accused and victims) and accuse the victims of "provoking the abuse", "asking for it" or "enjoying it". Conducting case studies, Blumell and Mulupi (2022) identified "rape culture acceptance" in the news reporting in the form of popular tropes such as "dismissal of the event", "victim-blaming", "discrediting survivor" and "threats to survivor".

Bhandari (2021) noted that patriarchial rhetoric underlying media discourse could popularise a culture of rape. Further, sensationalist reporting of sexual violence could spawn stigma and discourage survivors from reporting the crime (Thiagarajan, 2017, December 16).

Jolly (2016, July 20) observed that India's English press was less sympathetic towards rape victims and that the Indian media reports rape as a "crime of lust and passion" where "sexually precocious women… provoke men to attack". In a feminist commentary that takes on the predominantly patriarchal Indian culture, Zaina (2024, February 1) notes that:

> This is simply another way to blame a woman for assault, by policing her body and decisions. Popular questions under this category would include "what was she wearing?", "were her clothes tight?" and more. In rape culture, women are told how to dress to avoid being catcalled or slut-shamed, as showing any skin is considered to be a sign of 'asking for it' or 'inviting trouble'. The focus must be on protecting victims and holding offenders accountable. Rape tells us nothing about the character of the victim, but the perpetrator.

Another dilemma that journalists and experts face while reporting sexual violence against women is whether such crimes should be sensationalised or not.

While a section of journalists believes it is necessary to trigger emotional outrage and garner public support in favour of the victim, another feels it could be counterproductive. Both victim-blaming and emotional outrage could be coping strategies in the face of exposure to news events of sexual (or extreme) violence because they threaten people's just world beliefs and provokes distress (according to the Just World Theory; Harber, Podolski & Williams, 2015).

In this issue, there are also ideological oppositions, where sensationalising sexual violence could be viewed as both feminist and sexist. While sensationalism of sexual violence against women may offer a myopic view that may support the cause of the survivor seeking justice, thereby being feminist, it could also be argued to be a sexist subterfuge to stress the criticality of chastity and magnify sexual assaults to monstrous magnitudes.

Chapter 1 (and its analysis), which measured the prevalence of stories on sexual violence on the front pages of the leading English newspaper in India, indicated that the media attention to assorted cases of sexual crime could be disparate. Extreme cases of sexual violence that included public, brutal or fatal assaults were the ones allotted the prime news spaces, while the "ordinary" rapes (and gangrapes) hardly secured a single column, mostly briefed. Those top stories were also politicised. Frequencies of sexual violence and sensationalisation of extraordinary crimes may have led to the trivialisation of even heinous sexual crimes such as rape (without extraordinary storylines) in the news and desensitisation of the media audience that is conditioned to react only when the crime is hyped or hyperdetailed. Of the cases that received prime coverage during June-December 2023 was the 2023 Manipur assault that involved crimes such as disrobing, public humiliation and video recording and transmission of the ordeal. It is in line with observations of past studies that severe forms of corporeal violence inflicted on female autonomy received sensationalist media treatment (Fadnis, 2017; Sreedharan & Thorsen, 2021). This indicates the gendered structure (van Zoonen, 1994) of news production that neglects certain stories of sexual crime for not fitting the news agenda (Skidmore, 1998, p. 215). Of the stories that received brief (news) attention on the front pages were stories on rape and sexual harassment that came with allied crimes such as blackmail, physical assault, illegal detention, extortion, acid attack, verbal abuse and robbery. Most of the front page articles that occupied top positions were politicised, highlighted conflicts or involved the power elite or celebrities.

While effect studies of fictional violence and explicit sexual content in media such as films are popular, the nuances of reporting real-world violence and the consequences of publishing explicit content in the mass media remain under-investigated. Each individual could have an exciting-disturbing threshold: where violent and sexual content within that trigger threshold could be exciting for that individual and when the nature of violence or level of explicitness crosses the threshold, it could be disturbing. Nicklin, Swain and Lloyd (2020) found gender and prior exposure affect reactions to violent and sexual content on social media.

Applying the theory of desensitisation in the context of media reporting of sexual violence, it can be understood that routine exposure to explicit imagery and detailed-sensationalised news on sexual violence can alter this threshold among the media audience, making events, which had earlier been unsettling, exciting.

This leads to yet another ethical dilemma while reporting sexual violence: Should it be clinical (vague) or specific (graphic)? Expositioning this dilemma while "writing incessantly about sexual violence", popular culture writer Grady (2017, November 30) comments:

> It's not that we don't have a vocabulary for talking about sexual violence, because we do. But that vocabulary is inadequate. It is confusing and flattening in ways that make it hard to talk about sexual violence without either trivializing it, obfuscating the systems that enable it, or getting so specific as to become salacious or triggering.

Several of the news items analysed in the previous chapters of this book belonged to the second category of salacious reporting. Grady (2017, November 30) informed that she intentionally chose the "specific" way of reporting to "make it clear that these acts are violent" but not without latent concerns: "And I have found that the less specific my language is, the more invisible the violence becomes. But I also worry that the more specific I get, the more sensationalized my language feels". Accessing the issue from the perspective of the victims (or survivors) of sexual assaults, salacious language could be troubling.

When it takes immense courage and conviction to report the sexual crime and seek justice, the survivors have little or no control over the information about the assaults the news media publish. It could be traumatising, especially when extremely private information is shared in a shaming culture, along with identification details such as demographics, triggering unwarranted consequences such as media publicity, societal judgements, fervent social media searches for imagery of the crime or the survivors and ostracisation. Moreso, when the event is sensationalised or the reporting spreads misinformation.

Chapter 3 identified illocutions that were sensationalist (exposive, evaluative, warning, extolling, trivialising and dehumanising), sexist (lambing), sexual (experiencing and sexualising) and sectionalist (branding). For sexual assault survivors, sensational coverage and over-detailed news reports can trigger or make them relive their own trauma. In the case of the survivor of the crime being reported, insensitive reporting can be highly triggering and re-traumatising.

In a recent case of rape, the survivor raised a complaint that a news website "intruded" into her "grief and shock by publishing details of her physical reaction to the attack" (Linford, 2024, June 5). In this case, a local UK news website, in its coverage, offered a detailed description of the sexual crime, including the accused's words during the act and the survivor's reactions to them. Though the news website defended itself, saying that the information published was part of the hearing in open court, the victim still felt it was insensitive and traumatising. Several Indian cases have witnessed similar issues.

For instance, in the case of the infamous Delhi gangrape, a convict blamed the victim for the fatal attack and several media outlets reported it along with several other sexist remarks (Sinha, 2015, March 2; Time Staff, 2015, March 2). Though the articles were intended to criticise the sexist comments of the convict, their headlines were not explicitly critical.

Chapter 5 identified hints of eroticism and sexualisation in hyperdetailed news narratives and exhibitions—in terms of explicit imagery—while reporting extreme sexual violence against women such as rape. On unwanted details in news reports, Bhateja (2018, January 17) writes:

> The time of the night; the place of assault; the clothes on her; the company she did or did not have. It is all immaterial! When you ask such questions, give these details, you are starting the blame game. The victim MUST have done something to bring it on, that's what your readers are playing in their head and you are enabling these thoughts. Don't pin it on her. You are feeding the patriarchal mindset when you talk of such things and that's helping no one. Focus on the perpetrator instead. What was he wearing? Where was he going? Who was he with? Why did he do it?

Analysing recent cases, Chapter 5 identified exploitation in rape reporting, where there is an excessive focus on graphic or lurid details that are in some way gratuitous, exploitative, eroticising and sexualising the crime (through direct descriptions of the sexual acts and avoiding euphemisms). Several news reports are found to feature explicit imagery and a tendency to narrate the crime (presenting it as a first-person account [or witness] while it is not the case). Such hyperdetailing, divulging unwarranted information about the crime and victims, coupled with exhibitionist imagery may evoke erotic responses rather than an empathetic attitude towards the victim. News sensationalism has often been associated with a lack of gender sensitivity in newsrooms (Fadnis, 2017; Chattopadhyay, 2022a; 2022b; 2022c). Fadnis (2017) and Rao (2014) found patriarchal perspectives influencing the coverage of news stories on sexual assaults.

To name the victim (or survivor) or not? It is yet another dilemma while reporting sexual crimes. While it is a punishable offence to reveal the identity of sexual assault survivors (intended to protect their privacy and save them from unwarranted consequences), in certain cases, the survivors are named in the news reports and, in several others, the survivors choose to disclose their identities. In the Jharkhand gangrape case, discussed in Chapter 6, the survivor used Instagram to announce the assault. In another case of rape, the survivor chose to make her identity public, as "…to keep my name hidden makes me feel like I have something to be ashamed of and if I am certain of anything it is that none of the shame is mine" Butalia, 2018, April 26). Even in the case of the 2012 Delhi gangrape, the victim's mother was "not ashamed" to reveal her daughter's name. "Whoever has suffered should not hide their name. It is the offenders who should be ashamed and hide their name" (Angre, 2015, December 16). Popular cases in which the victims are unnamed are mostly named after places.

It is also usual to witness populous-sexist tropes—that blanket those places as dangerous (triggering fears and imposing restrictions) and suggest that the safety of women solely remains in the hands of governments (implying that women are incapable of handling their own safety)—doing the rounds when sensational "horrors" break out (Awasthi, 2023, August 4; Mishra, 2023, August 28; Singh, 2023, December 16).

Sexual crime stories were found to often identify the accused, detailing their occupation, social status and acquaintance with the victim. Chapter 1 found that stories identifying the victims or accused, divulging their familial details, were prioritised and given more editorial space while the anonymised ones were downplayed.

Is it appropriate and essential for the news media to debate sexual assault matters under trial? Chapter 4, in its analyses of news articles on two recent cases of sexual violence (2019 Hyderabad gangrape-murder and the 2017 Kerala actress abduction-molestation case involving actor Dileep), found the news media extolling news events (India rises in anger over), sensationalising cases (Hyderabad horror), dictating political action (instigating Parliamentary debate) and conducting media trials to advocate extra-judicial punishments (lynch the "rapists") and exonerate the accused (congratulating and praising the "heroes" [Telangana government and police] for the fake encounter; supporting the "scapegoat" [actor who was accused in the molestation case]; blaming the survivor [and her alleged professional connection with the main accused] for the sexual assault in a moving car)—most of which seem populous.

Though these dilemmas are understandable, the fear is that behind the facade of reporting in the public interest, the news media could be engaging in exploitation, focusing mainly on surviving (or minting money) from miseries (incidents of sexual violence). Voices against the contemporary style of reporting sexual violence against women are loud and clear.

On the need to sensitise journalists on these issues, Bhateja (2018, January 17) writes:

> Want to bring a change in the society? Start with the newsroom. It's time to educate every reporter on the sensitivity of the matter and how to proceed with it. How much should you talk about her life if it's irrelevant to the case? Do you really need to dissect every bit of her personal life? Do your readers have to know about the graphic details of the crime? It is disturbing, for us, for your readers, for those who have lived this reality, and their family members.

Most of these dilemmas would disappear when the news media adopts a sensitive victim-first stance, highlighting their concerns and supporting them in ways that will avoid invading their privacy, sexualising the crimes, re-victimising them and exploiting their cases for gain. This book introduces and conceptualises Predatory Journalism to foreground and bring together unethical editorial practices that exploit both the victims in cases of sexual violence and the media audiences. Employing scientific research methods to analyse news content and isolate problematic practices, this book helps in understanding the scope of this phenomenon, which makes inventing solutions to the problem (guidelines and policy recommendations) tangible.

In all these issues, linguistics plays a critical role. In accordance with this understanding, this book adopts pragmalinguistics and discourse analysis as its predominant conceptual and analytical strategy. Exemplifying this notion on discourse, Pal (2018, April 13) writes that:

> ...there is little understanding of the complexity of these issues, and one such realm that has been largely left out from these conversations is the linguistics of representation of sexual violence in the media. The media constitutes a key arena in which rape is defined, shaping perceptions about how sexual violence is viewed in the society and who is held accountable and what assumptions are being conveyed to the audiences about the victims and the perpetrators. Here I aim to explore aspects of news coverage to reveal how the language used in texts, legitimises, sustains and condones violence against women.

Systematic analysis of word choices and semantic structures, along with discussions about their situated meanings, underlying ideologies and social implications, are primordial for the identification and analysis of a phenomenon (Predatory Journalism) this comprehensive and convoluted. For instance, persistent exposure to the words "rape" and "gangrape" and intermittent news related to them may have drained those words and crimes of all their seriousness as a formidable level of invasion of privacy and preserved modesty. In contemporary times, indications are that rape (or gangrape) *per se* does not seem so daunting (at least in the news). In a view, these words and crimes may be now normalised.

As the analysis has also shown in Chapters 5 and 6, news reports on sexual violence are rife with sexual vocabulary. On the linguistic linkage between sex and violence, Grady (2017, November 30) writes: "We are already primed to read violence as erotic because our erotic vocabulary is a violent one. Our words for sex are violent... and our expressions for violent anger are sexual... Our language treats violence and sex as near-equivalents, so there is constant slippage around our vocabulary for violence that occurs in the arena of sex: It is far, far too easy to make it sound sexy." Lack of understanding about sensitive issues related to reporting sexual violence and the time to stop and think before writing and publishing may be behind this abhorrent use of language to describe such crimes in news reports and inappropriate topic selection. In the case of the 2023 Manipur sexual assault that drew international attention, the news media used the phrases "stripped naked" and "paraded naked" to describe the incident, which popularised the phrases as veritable diction to denote such a crime (refer to Chapters 3 and 5). Now, "paraded naked" is a familiar news headline in India (Pandey, 2023, December 26) and fears are that it is becoming a contemporary method of punishing women.

"Paraded naked" has been an anaphoric reference to the act of mob-public sexual assault where the victim is disrobed and, sometimes, this act is video recorded and transmitted or used to threaten the survivor. In the case of the Manipur sexual assault, against the backdrop of communal violence, mobs of men committed the crime (Baruah, 2023, July 20) and video footage of it was shared online drawing international media attention. In the 254 news headlines analysed, "paraded naked" appeared 43 times (refer to Chapter 3). A slew of similar cases of sexual violence was reported after the Manipur incident (India Today Video Desk, 2023, September 2; PTI, 2024, April 7; ETV Bharat, 2024, April 6, to name a few).

It was a similar case to the 2012 Delhi gangrape, after which a string of "iron rod" rapes were reported (India.com News Desk, 2016, May 2; Express News Service, 2017, August 2; Mishra, 2017, October 13; DC Correspondent, 2018, February 20; Mirror Now Digital, 2018, October 31; PTI, 2020, January 28; Singh, 2021, January 11).

There have also been consequential paradoxes associated with reporting on sexual violence. Technology has been one of them. While digital applications could ease source identification, news composition, data sourcing and fact verification, among others, Chapter 6 analysis indicates technology-assisted churnalism, where news recycling thrives online. The analysis identified digested and sensationalist news content being recirculated online forming clouds of stereotypical and similar stories. Such "churned" stories were also found to be infested with information and sources-related issues.

Though, thanks to the Internet, it is effortless to identify duplicate news content, the digital news media space seems to nurture such an unscrupulous culture.

Similarly, while there is increasing awareness about sexism and self-criticism against media sensationalism, unethical editorial practices are prospering like never before. Reporting on sexual violence is a delicate issue that needs to factor in several issues, including stringent laws, opposing ideologies, feminist campaigns, media power, political powerplays, guidelines, regulations, the diversity of cultures and a close watch on crime trends. These apart, media convergence, online applications and social media orientations need to be viewed critically as they have altered almost all walks of life—including news production, dissemination and consumption. For instance, news production and YouTube content generation, in contemporary times, are based on search and social media trends: On any given day, you may find digital content being expeditiously generated and published on top topics as they start trending.

Online social media is used to spread sensational news stories and also used as an allied source to fetch additional information. Chapter 5 discussed how the reportage of sexual violence, especially rape, triggers online searches for imagery. For instance, after the sensationalist reporting of the Kathua case, along with the divulgence of critical details, the victim's name became "the most searched item on a popular pornographic website" (Roy, 2018; Pande, 2021).

Thanks to the over-smart search engines, identification of and understanding maniacal curiosities that sensational sexual violence coverage generates among the public has also become easier. Google searches throw up lists of questions that "People also ask". During our Google investigations when this book was written, queries related to the 2012 Delhi gangrape case that we came across were: Was Nirbhaya's boyfriend involved? Who is the real girl in the Nirbhaya case? What were the last words of Nirbhaya? What happened to Nirbhaya's intestine? Who inserted the iron rod? Who among the rapists was the most notorious? A review of search trends also identified spikes when "sensational" rape cases are reported.

Further, news in 2018 reported that Google's auto-complete and related search functions were revealing the identities of rape victims. Google said "it had removed all examples it had been 'made aware of'". But even in 2024, we find the issue persisting.

Indeed, journalism is at a crossroads in the current era facing a plethora of challenges and a dire need to draw readers and retain readership—young and old. But insensitive sensationalism and other exploitative editorial practices could, in the long run, curtail credibility and threaten readership. If it is linguistics where the problem of sexual violence starts in India (Pande, 2023, August 6), then the resolution must start from the newsrooms.

References

Angre, K. (2015, December 16). "My daughter's name is Jyoti Singh": Nirbhaya's mother 3 years after Delhi Gang-Rape. *NDTV.com.* https://www.ndtv.com/india-news/my-daughters-name-is-jyoti-singh-mother-of-delhi-braveheart-1255660#:~:text=Whoever%20has%20suffered%20should%20not,%22%20she%20said%2C%20fighting%20tears

Awasthi, A. (2023, August 4). "India's New Rape Capital": In Rajasthan, five men abduct and gangrape minor. *Firstpost.* https://www.firstpost.com/india/indias-new-rape-capital-in-rajasthan-five-men-abduct-and-gangrape-minor-12957422.html

Baruah, S. (2023, July 20). Women paraded naked in Manipur were forcibly taken away from police custody by mob. *The Indian Express.* https://indianexpress.com/article/india/tension-manipur-hills-areas-may-4-video-two-women-paraded-naked-surfaces-8849063/

Bhandari, A. (2021). Indian Media Narratives in Gang Rape (Master's thesis, Old Dominion University). Retrieved from https://digitalcommons.odu.edu/cgi/viewcontent.cgi?article=1055&context=sociology_criminaljustice_etds

Bhateja, A. (2018, January 17). Dear Indian media, we need to be more sensitive about how we cover rape. *India's Largest Digital Community of Women | POPxo.* https://www.popxo.com/article/insensitive-indian-media-coverage-on-rape-647124/

Blumell, L. E., & Mulupi, D. (2022). Investigating rape culture in news coverage of the Anita Hill and Christine Blasey Ford cases. *Violence Against Women, 28*(2), 487–509. https://doi.org/10.1177/10778012211021129

Butalia, U. (2018, April 26). Healing myself: A woman recounts her struggles after a court acquitted the man she accused of rape. *Scroll.in.* https://scroll.in/article/876788/healing-myself-a-woman-recounts-her-struggles-after-a-court-acquitted-the-man-she-accused-of-rape

Chattopadhyay, D. (2022a). Journalism in an Online-First Era. In *Indian Journalism and the Impact of Social Media.* 11–35. Palgrave Studies in Journalism and the Global South. Palgrave Macmillan. https://doi.org/10.1007/978-3-031-07318-2_2

Chattopadhyay, D. (2022b). Emerging Challenges and the Way Ahead. In: *Indian Journalism and the Impact of Social Media.* 175–193, Palgrave Studies in Journalism and the Global South. Palgrave Macmillan. https://doi.org/10.1007/978-3-031-07318-2_7

Chattopadhyay, D. (2022c). Implications. In: Indian Journalism and the Impact of Social Media. 195–221, Palgrave Studies in Journalism and the Global South. Palgrave Macmillan. https://doi.org/10.1007/978-3-031-07318-2_8

Cusmano, D. (2018). Rape culture rooted in patriarchy, media portrayal, and victim blaming. *Writing Across the Curriculum. 30.* https://digitalcommons.sacredheart.edu/wac_prize/30

DC Correspondent. (2018, February 20). Deccan Chronicle. *Deccan Chronicle.* https://www.deccanchronicle.com/nation/crime/200218/wb-men-insert-iron-rod-inside-tribal-womans-private-part-gangrape.html

ETV Bharat. (2024, April 6). Woman paraded naked, beaten after son married his girlfriend in Punjab; FIR registered. *ETV Bharat News.* https://www.etvbharat.com/en/!state/woman-paraded-naked-beaten-after-son-married-his-girlfriend-in-punjab-fir-registered-enn24040601047

Express News Service. (2017, August 2). 'Iron rod inserted into private parts.' *The Indian Express*. https://indianexpress.com/article/cities/kolkata/iron-rod-inserted-into-private-parts-4778245/

Fadnis, D. (2017). Uncovering rape culture: Patriarchal values guide Indian media's rape-related reporting. *Journalism Studies*, *19*(12), 1750–1766. https://doi.org/10.1080/1461670X.2017.1301781

Grady, C. (2017, November 30). The complicated, inadequate language of sexual violence. *Vox*. https://www.vox.com/culture/2017/11/30/16644394/language-sexual-violence

Harber, K. D., Podolski, P., & Williams, C. H. (2015). Emotional disclosure and victim blaming. *Emotion*, *15*(5), 603–614. https://doi.org/10.1037/emo0000056

India.com News Desk. (2016, May 2). Nirbhaya-like rape repeated in Kerala: Law student raped and brutally murdered, reveals autopsy. India.Com. https://www.india.com/news/india/nirbhaya-like-rape-repeated-in-kerala-law-student-raped-and-brutally-murdered-reveals-autopsy-1153690/

India Today Video Desk. (2023, September 2). Rajasthan woman beaten, stripped, paraded naked by husband, in-laws - India Today. *India Today*. https://www.indiatoday.in/india/video/rajasthan-woman-beaten-stripped-paraded-naked-by-husband-in-laws-2429998-2023-09-02

Jolly, J. (2016, July 20). Rape in India: Is the English-language press falling back on stereotypes? *Columbia Journalism Review*. https://www.cjr.org/analysis/india_rape_journalism.php

Linford, P. (2024, June 5). Rape case report intruded into victim's grief and shock, IPSO rules. *HoldTheFrontPage*. Retrieved from https://www.holdthefrontpage.co.uk/2024/news/rape-case-report-intruded-into-victims-grief-and-shock-ipso-rules/

Mirror Now Digital. (2018, October 31). Woman brutally gang-raped by relative and accomplices, iron rod found inserted in private parts. *Times Now*. https://www.timesnownews.com/mirror-now/crime/article/west-bengal-woman-brutally-gang-raped-by-relative-and-accomplices-iron-rod-inserted-in-private-parts-in-jalpaiguri/304972

Mishra, A. (2023, August 28). Parliament watch | Decoding the BJP blame game over mishandling Of Manipur crisis. *Frontline*. https://frontline.thehindu.com/politics/parliament-watch-decoding-the-bjp-blame-game-over-mishandling-of-manipur-crisis/article67213186.ece

Mishra, G. (2017, October 13). Bihar woman dies as man thrusts iron rod in her private parts. *IBTimes India*. https://www.ibtimes.co.in/bihar-woman-dies-after-rapist-thrusts-iron-rod-into-her-private-parts-745494

Nicklin, L. L., Swain, E., & Lloyd, J. (2020). Reactions to unsolicited violent, and sexual, explicit media content shared over social media: Gender differences and links with prior exposure. *International Journal of Environmental Research Public Health*, *17*(12): 4296. https://doi.org/10.3390/ijerph17124296

Pal, S. (2018, April 13). Blame and Shame: Examining the media coverage of a Dalit rape victim in India. *South Asia@LSE*. https://blogs.lse.ac.uk/southasia/2018/04/13/blame-and-shame-examining-the-media-coverage-of-dalit-rape-victim-in-india/

Pande, M. (2023, August 6). The problem with India's violence against women starts at the linguistic level. *World Crunch*. Retrieved from https://worldcrunch.com/women-worldwide/hindi-language-women-rape-culture

Pande, S. (2021). The ethics of reporting rape in India: A case study. In L. T. Price, K. Sanders & W.N. Wyatt (Eds.). *The Routledge companion to journalism ethics* (pp. 237–244). Routledge. https://doi.org/10.4324/9780429262708

Pandey, B. G. (2023, December 26). Woman paraded naked: A familiar headline in India. https://www.bbc.com/news/world-asia-india-67769453

Prasad, P. (2019, June 23). News reporting of sexual violence is propagating rape culture. *The Swaddle*. https://www.theswaddle.com/news-reporting-of-sexual-violence-is-propagating-rape-culture

PTI. (2020, January 28). Nagpur Teen choked, raped in unconscious state, iron rod inserted in privates: *Police*. NDTV.com. https://www.ndtv.com/nagpur-news/nagpur-teen-choked-raped-in-unconscious-state-iron-rod-inserted-in-privates-police-2170743

PTI. (2024, April 7). 55-year-old Punjab woman assaulted, paraded semi-naked; 4 held. *The Indian Express*. https://indianexpress.com/article/cities/chandigarh/punjab-woman-assault-paraded-semi-naked-9255632/

Rao, S. (2014). Covering rape in shame culture: Studying journalism ethics in India's New Television News Media, *Journal of Mass Media Ethics*, *29*(3),153–167. https://doi.org/10.1080/08900523.2014.918497

Roy, K. (2018, April 16). How perverted is India? Kathua victim's name becomes top trending search on porn websites. *Outlook India*. https://www.outlookindia.com/society/how-perverted-is-india-kathua-victims-name-becomes-top-trending-search-on-porn-w-news-311055

Singh, A. (2021, January 11). MP twin shocker: Widow raped, iron rod inserted in private parts; 13-year-old raped and murdered. *The New Indian Express*. https://www.newindianexpress.com/nation/2021/Jan/11/mp-twin-shocker-widow-raped-iron-rod-inserted-in-private-parts-13-year-old-raped-and-murdered-2248748.html

Singh, N. (2023, December 16). Numberspeak | 11 Yrs of Nirbhaya horror: How Delhi continues to be most unsafe city for Women in India. *News18*. https://www.news18.com/india/numberspeak-11-years-of-nirbhaya-horror-how-delhi-continues-to-be-most-unsafe-city-for-women-in-india-8705954.html

Sinha, K. (2015, March 2). Nirbhaya gang-rape convict blames victim for the fatal assault. *The Times of India*. https://timesofindia.indiatimes.com/city/delhi/nirbhaya-gang-rape-convict-blames-victim-for-the-fatal-assault/articleshow/46433506.cms

Skidmore, P. (1998). Gender and the Agenda. In S. Allan, G. Branston, & C. Carter, (Eds.). *News, gender and power* (1st ed., pp. 204–218), Routledge.

Sreedharan, C. & Thorsen, E. (2021). Sexual violence and the news media: Issues, challenges, and guidelines for journalists in India. UNESCO. ISBN: 978-81-89218-78-2, Retrieved from https://eprints.bournemouth.ac.uk/35830/7/MAAR%20REPORT%20PDF%20Online%20.pdf

Thacker, L. K. & Day, L. (2017). Rape culture, victim blaming, and the role of media in the criminal justice system. *Kentucky Journal of Undergraduate Scholarship*, *1*(1), 8.

Thiagarajan, K. (2017, December 16). In interviews with 122 rapists, student pursues Not-So-Simple question: why? *NPR*. https://www.npr.org/sections/goatsandsoda/2017/12/16/570827107/in-interviews-with-122-rapists-student-pursues-not-so-simple-question-why

Time Staff. (2015, March 2). Delhi Gang-Rape convict blames victim for brutal attack. *TIME*. https://time.com/3728061/delhi-gang-rape-blames-victim/

van Zoonen, L. (1994). *Feminist media studies*. SAGE Publications.

Zaina, N. (2024, February 1). 'What was she wearing?': Rape culture and the thriving narrative of victim shaming. *Feminism in India*. https://feminisminindia.com/2022/07/13/what-was-she-wearing-rape-culture-and-the-thriving-narrative-of-victim-shaming/

9 The Way Forward

Building a Sensitive and Ethical Media Landscape

Though press freedom has come under critical scrutiny in recent times—thanks to certain censurable cases of excessive (and reckless) exercise of media privileges, often leading to inimical outcomes—the sociopolitical roles of news media as a cradle of credible information, an agency of investigation, a nontotalitarian sentinel upholding democracy and an influential institution managing public information and opinion cannot be undermined. There have also been reasonable fears that any move aimed at pruning its prerogatives or keeping it under constraints could be counterproductive. When it comes to reporting on and regulating public opinion about sexual violence, too, the news media plays a decisive role.

Nevertheless, as the empirical analyses of the earlier chapters have uncovered, there are a plethora of predacious problems while reporting on sexual crime in India and a sizeable scope for improvement—from changes in linguistic cultures and assuming imagery awareness to avoiding unethical-exploitative practices such as churnalism and prejudicial reporting.

While it is pressing to bring the perpetrators of sexual crime to books and also ensure the sustenance of journalism through the engagement of readers, it is also imperative to ensure that the privacies of the victims are intact and the readers, their concerns, curiousness and other emotions are not exploited in the process. To victims of sexual violence who have already suffered tremendous trauma and those falsely accused of such crimes, over-reporting and misreporting could (re) traumatise them and cause irreversible social damage.

Even though news reporting on sexual violence may be in good faith, reporters and editors need better sensitivity and renewed awareness about the long-term social consequences that their word and visual choices may have. Certain exploitative practices assembled under Predatory Journalism in this book have raised alarms in the recent past. For instance, the call to cull sensationalism is centuries old. But now, the cries and criticisms are loud and clear, as the all-embracing Internet and online social media have accelerated and escalated existing issues. Along with those raised before, this book foregrounds several unexplored issues and presents intuitive research methods to conclusively identify all of them.

This chapter identifies ways in which the practice of Predatory Journalism can be contained, arguing for a comprehensive regulatory framework for promoting responsible reporting that will be based on a balance of legal mechanisms,

DOI: 10.4324/9781003468042-13

independent regulatory bodies and self-regulation to promote greater accountability, transparency and public trust in the media. Further, it prescribes ethical guidelines and codes of conduct that can guide journalists and media organisations in their reporting on cases of sexual violence.

A policy to advocate ethical reporting

As clear-sightedness suggests, the first step in moderating an issue is concurring its existence and then resolving to repeal it. For, it is discernible that unethical practices are thriving in newsrooms as a cultivated culture, mainly, due to a lack of awareness or a delusion that those deeds are warranted for the common good. With this insight, it becomes imperative for the establishments (the government, media organisations and other established stakeholders) to undertake initiatives and encourage research aimed at issue identification and awareness generation.

It may also be hard and inaccurate to pin the blame on any one stakeholder for the sinister side of journalism today. For instance, while a section of narrow news outlets practises it, a section of the audience shows an appetite for it and a section of establishments and elites (say police and political leaders) fodder it. A policy aimed at curtailing this editorial epidemic, hence, needs to be all-inclusive, starting from the government and leading to the people. A multifaceted regulatory framework thus involving all stakeholders from the government, independent regulatory bodies, media outlets, social media intermediaries and the media audience is prescribed at three levels: Proactive, simultaneous and reactive.

Proactive measures to impede Predatory Journalism could start with the constitution of a firm and detailed policy and include undertaking awareness campaigns and encouraging research on issues such as sensationalism, sexism, sexualism, misinformation and prejudicial reporting in the news and social media. Further, the legal frameworks can be strengthened to define and tackle Predatory Journalism and the issues aggregated under it. In the media houses, several initiatives can be undertaken to prevent unethical practices while reporting on sexual crimes, from the selection of ideal (and adequate number of) reporters and editors for the job, offering specific reporting guidelines and organising training programmes to enforcing field reporting, inculcating a culture of fact-checking and cross-verification of information at the desk-level and encouraging responsible reporting in a gender-neutral newsroom. Self-regulation through the Press Council of India, the News Broadcasters and Digital Association, the News Broadcasters Federation (NBF) and their ilk need to be strengthened (Khan & Ahsan, 2023, November 14).

Simultaneous regulation could encompass engendering self-regulation at the media level, with well-informed and more aware and sensitive reporters and editors avoiding language that could be sensationalist, sexist (propagating rape myths) and sectionalist (divisive) and information that invades privacy or deprives the victims or accused chances of a fair trial, apart from according due editorial space to stories of sexual violence instead of sensationalising and cashing in on a select few. Similarly, social media platforms and online search engines need to institute mechanisms to identify and thwart the spread of fake news, explicit imagery of sexual assaults such as gang rape and details of rape victims as and when they are reported and flagged off. On the other hand, news consumers, too, need to be vigilant about sensationalism and the spread of fake news, engaging in fact-checking before reacting or sharing.

Reactive regulation would entail the creation of a robust remedial legal framework that responds to complaints of editorial inaccuracies or misuse of media liberties and ensures prompt action. Further, the news media needs to act responsibly and be more accountable, amending its missteps and removing content that is found to be incorrect or inappropriate.

This regulatory framework outlines the avenues to reproach the issues from several sides. Based on the findings of the studies conducted in the earlier chapters, this book prepares a set of guidelines for journalists to consider while reporting on rape and other forms of sexual violence. These guidelines point to assorted micro-issues identified to be unethical or exploitative in this book. Viewing news as a discursive culture and Predatory Journalism as a pragmalinguistic problem, the main focus is on the choice of words, which are cues to the underlying ideologies, sociopolitical stands and illocutionary intentions. For instance, in a rape news story, a person can be addressed as "accused" or "rapist", each of those words representing different social language and legal stances. Along with the bags of words used to report an event of sexual violence, journalists also need to pay attention to their social semantics and political consequences before choosing them. To guide contemporary journalists, this section highlights the following issues:

Content and trigger warning. When sensitive issues such as rape are reported on online platforms such as news websites and social media, content and trigger warnings could precede the news reports. It should be mandatory when there are detailed graphic descriptions and explicit imagery. On the other hand, traditional forms of news media such as newspapers, magazines and television may face practical difficulties in carrying such warnings and may best avoid content that could trigger or upset people, especially victims of sexual assault.

Demand-driven journalism. Contemporary tech-driven newsrooms and social-media-equipped journalists tend to prioritise currently-trending news topics based on social media and search trends. Choosing and composing news articles based on episodic social media and online trends can be detrimental, prioritising hits over information. At times, it could also dictate news angles and could be even more detrimental when the case being reported is sexual violence. For instance, when a violent sexual assault (such as rape) is reported, it could trigger a voluminous online search for images of the assault or the victim and for sensitive details about the crime. Despite temporary gains, attempts to tap into such news demands could hurt the news media image in the long term and soft-pedal the interests of the survivors seeking justice.

An associated dark trend showed the news media missing follow-up stories when the media audience lost interest in the case. Several sexual assault cases remain inconclusive in the online domain. For instance, Chandigarh's "MMS scandal" (refer to Chapter 7).

News media engage in hypercoverage of top news stories, leading to the churning of trash news to sustain continuous coverage and feed temporal news demands.

It is important for the news media to set delivering informative and useful content as its leading agenda.

Selective exposure. When it comes to reporting on sexual violence, there are concerns that news editors prioritise violent (brutal) cases and selective genres of sexual assaults reported from certain regions of India. These apart, caste bias is also said to influence news selection and prioritisation. Chapter 1 of this book identifies from an analysis that the stories that had named the victims, divulged their familial details or had well-known personalities as the victims and accused were prioritised more. However, news that had underprivileged victims and accused that were either young or were acquainted with the victim were relatively downplayed. Eventually, this selective exposure could lead to selective retention, societal bias and stereotyping, diminishing the credibility of the media as an impartial source of information.

Dehumanisation and demonisation. While reporting sexual violence, such as gang rape, in the present times, there is an overarching editorial tendency to term it as "horror" that dehumanises and associates social stigma to the crime, especially in the headlines. Further, there is also a propensity to describe the accused as "monsters" or "animals". Here are two headline examples: "Brother turns monster: Man along with four friends rapes sister; kills her in Odisha" (Dar, 2023, December 4) and "Shakti Mills monsters convicted; their families continue to suffer" (Mumbai Mirror, 2014, March 20), and a simple online news search would yield many more. In all probability, you may have also come across the Manipur horror (Raj, 2024, April 30), Hyderabad horrors (Mallick, 2019, December 5; Pillai, 2024, July 4; TNN, 2024, July 4), Assam horror (Web Desk, 2024, June 25), Jharkhand horror (Outlook Web Desk, 2024, March 3), Rajasthan horrors (Press Trust of India, 2024, June 27; Sharma, 2024, March 14) and definitely at least one of the Delhi horrors (Tripathi, 2024, March 28; Shahid, 2024, May 10)—triggering a temporary feeling of outrage. After speaking to 100 rapists lodged in Delhi's Tihar Jail, Madhumita Pandey told the Washington Post (Doshi, 2021, December 1):

> When I went to research, I was convinced these men are monsters. But when you talk to them, you realize these are not extraordinary men, they are really ordinary. What they've done is because of upbringing and thought process.

Echoing similar views in a media commentary, Mukherjee (2014, March 21) observes that calling rapists "monsters" could be problematic as it alienates them from an "otherwise perfect society" and covers the bigoted ideologies and societal issues that stimulate the culture of rape and other sexual violence. On it, Mukherjee (2014, March 21) wrote:

> Whenever a rape occurs it has become pretty common to hear people dismiss it by saying, 'They are monsters. No human being could ever do something like that. They have some mental disorder.' I have said that. I am sure you have heard that. Calling it an "act of monsters" helps men—and those of us who know, trust, and love the men in our lives—distance themselves from rapists.

In contemporary times, terms such as "horror" and "monsters" are used to sensationalise news stories on sexual violence and journalists need to be perceptive about the sociopolitical implications of this linguistic culture and be judicious about its application.

Metalepsis of sexual lingo. As the Chapter 3 analysis shows, there is also an editorial tendency to use sexual language in the context of reporting sexual crimes. In the case of the 2023 Manipur sexual assault of three women, the act was popularly described as "stripped naked" and "paraded naked" (Ellis-Petersen, 2023, July 21; HT News Desk, 2024, May 1), perhaps normalising the crime which is now becoming another popular way of punishing women (India Today Video Desk, 2023, September 2; PTI, 2024, April 7; ETV Bharat, 2024, April 6, to name a few). Metalepsis is understood as the use of words and phrases in new contexts. When 254 news headlines on the Manipur news headlines were analysed, the words paraded and naked appeared 45 and 49 times, respectively. The use of the words paraded (popularly used in the context of the military) and stripped (as in strip clubs or a voluntary sexual act) to describe an incident of disrobing and public humiliation normalises heinous acts. Similarly, post the 2012 Delhi gangrape, there has been a slew of "iron-rod rapes" and headlines carrying the phrase (India.com News Desk, 2016, May 2; Express News Service, 2017, August 2; Mishra, 2017, October 13; DC Correspondent, 2018, February 20; Mirror Now Digital, 2018, October 31; PTI, 2020, January 28; Singh, 2021, January 11). A sensible newsroom needs to be cautious of the language used to describe sexual crimes and which discourse it belongs to.

Extolling and exaggeration. Analysis has shown that illocutions, news frames and literary-rhetorical devices such as extolling, exaggeration (hyperbolising) and generalisation are used to sensationalise sexual violence. Media exaggeration and news distortion could come with consequences (Pinker, 2018, February 17). In Chapter 4, news stories analysed reveal the use of hyperbolising language to describe the crime and stimulate public outrage.

Video news reports resorted to terms such as "vicious" (for emphasis on violence and cruelty; Republic World, 2019, November 30) and "this incident has sent shockwaves across the country" (WION, 2019, December 6). Further, attempts to exaggerate and generalise news events ("protests across India" and "India rises in anger" [Republic World, 2019, November 30]) were also identified. Reporters and editors need to prefer accuracy over exaggeration, generalisation and extolling (presenting the event as extraordinary when it is not the case).

Quoting means (partially) stating. While publishing controversial statements and presenting conspiracy theories, it is also usual for the news media to tactfully use grammatical contraptions such as quotations and question marks to evade blame. Journalists need to understand that as editorial gatekeepers filtering information passing through them to the readers, quoting means, at least partially, stating, as readers may perceive that the questions raised, speculations made and the statements quoted have some substance as the news media has prioritised them. For instance, when the news media published the victim-blaming submissions of one of the rapists in the 2012 Delhi gangrape case, the reports that have not outrightly criticised those statements offer scope for a misinterpretation that the media endorses those sexist views (Sinha, 2015, March 2; Time Staff, 2015, March 2).

Journalists should desist from publishing ideas or statements that are unverified or lack substance merely because they are interesting, as this culture could spread misinformation and conspiracy theories that could divert cases of sexual assault.

Eroticism through voyeurism. News reports on sexual violence often take erotic and voyeuristic turns when they describe the crimes in hyperdetail and use sexual-explicit language and imagery. Presentation of voyeuristic narratives of sexual assaults in news stories could breach the privacy of the victims and re-traumatise the survivors. Further, the sexualisation of sexual violence could desensitise the media audience and normalise e heinous crimes such as gang rape. Carter (1998, p. 220) noted that sexual crime reporting had remained "explicit and lurid in detail… sometimes inducing 'moral panics' amongst news audiences". Several news items analysed in the previous chapters of this book identified salacious reporting.

For instance, in the Hyderabad veterinarian rape-murder case, several news reports were hyperdetailed ("They punctured her scooter & waited" — how 4 men executed horrific Hyderabad rape-murder [Poonam, 2019, December 3], "Accused showed no mercy, put liquor in Hyderabad vet's mouth while raping her": Cops [HT Correspondent, 2020, July 31], "Hyderabad veterinary doctor murder: 'They raped her in lorry cabin even after she died'" [The New Indian Express, 2019, December 2]). Sexual crime reporting in India is often titillating, triggering online searches for more information and imagery related to the crime. For instance, Prasad (2024, June 29) noted that the news media preferred to call a case of sexual assault (rape) the "obscene video" or "sex video" case and a "sex scandal". This can be an outcome of inherent sexism in the newsroom and among the audience. Further, eroticism in news stories, intentional or habitual, denotes moral depravity and a lack of sensitivity to the trauma that the victims suffer. It is, hence, recommended that journalists avoid hyperdetailing of sexual crimes and explicit imagery as they could also propagate a culture of rape.

Indian news media has drawn widespread criticism for being insensitive, especially while reporting on sexual violence. On reformations needed, Jolly (2016, July 20) writes:

> There are signs that India's English-language press may be reflecting a less sympathetic view towards rape victims …much could be done to improve how publications tackle this issue. There could be better press regulation to prevent salacious and sensationalized coverage, greater sensitivity in reporting… the appointment of specially-focused gender reporters and the reframing of rape from a lust crime to a political, economic, and social phenomena.

Breach of privacy. While covering sexual violence, privacy gets breached in many an aspect: In identifying (and locating) the victims and accused, sharing their images, sexualising and detailing the assaults, hounding them (victims and their families) for (exclusive) interviews and publishing personal (irrelevant) information without consent.

Jain (2023, September 26) suggested that journalists covering sexual crimes be cautious about not exploiting the victim's emotions. The consent and privacy of the survivors are primordial while reporting explosive and explicit details of sexual crimes.

Privacy breaches may also invite harm to the survivors and their kin, creating a non-conducive environment in their immediate neighbourhood, thereby obstructing other survivors from reporting such crimes and seeking justice. Manglik (2017, March 1) noted that disclosure of the identity of a survivor of sexual assault is a serious criminal offence under section 228A of the Indian Penal Code, which prevents persons from publishing or printing the name(s) or details of a person against whom the offences of Section 375 [Rape], 376A, 376B, 376C, 376D have been committed or alleged. Manglik (2017, March 1) argued that the objective of this law is to provide the survivor "a right to their privacy, peace and dignity and to prevent her from victimization and ostracism from the public". Although divulging the identity of a survivor of a sexual crime is prohibited by the Supreme Court of India (Agnihotri, 2016, October 25), the graphic and demographic details, semi-blurred images and the nature of acquaintance with the perpetrator often lead to victim identification.

The Dart Center for Journalism and Trauma laid down principles of reporting sexual assault, noting that insensitive reporting and invading the privacy of the survivors of sexual crime could cause re-traumatisation. Insensitive reporting could trigger painful memories of trauma. When *sensational* cases of sexual violence are reported, the news media conducts exclusive interviews with distressed survivors and their families to craft *interesting* (insensitive) stories, exploiting their pain and emotions. Several of the earlier chapters have identified such breaches of privacy and analysed them in detail, offering examples.

Reporters and editors, hence, need to prioritise privacy.

Romanticism of violence. Quite often, the news media tend to cinematise and romanticise cases of sexual violence, presenting the accused as the faces of evil monsters while lambing the victim (or survivor, who is portrayed as a hapless innocent) and celebrating the ones (sometimes, the police) that decimate those "monsters". For instance, in this news report (McCoy, 2021, October 25), check the description given to the victim and the accused:

> A young woman, 23, had just completed a four-year study program and was about to begin an internship when she ventured out one December night to see a movie at a local Delhi cineplex with a male friend. Her family had high hopes for her. If anyone had the gumption and pluck to escape the three-bedroom basement apartment where she had been raised without running water—it was her. Those dreams were shattered that night in late 2012… they encountered a pack of five drunk men on the lookout for sex.

In this case, the rapists are described as rabid animals (with the use of the word "pack") who shattered the high hopes of a poor family. Philipose (2020,

September 12) noted that "some of the most discomfiting aspects of today's news journalism, especially television news journalism, draw from formulae tried, tested and deployed by the cinema-centric publications of yesteryear" and identified the "daily churning out of heroes and villains" as part of that formulae. Sexual language and cinematic-narrative forms are used to describe cases of sexual assault. When the police executed the accused in the Hyderabad gangrape-murder case in an extra-judicial encounter, the media tended to, literally, "celebrate" their "heroes" (PTI, 2019, December 6; Pandey, 2019, December 6). Sensitive journalists need to steer clear of romanticising and cinematising sexual crime stories.

Sexism. Sexism is a critical aspect that needs scrutiny while reporting on sexual violence. It is because sexism is an inherent culture that could manifest in news reporting and the news media could also adopt (intentionally or otherwise) sexist (selling) strategies to woo and mollify the patriarchal mindset predominant among the (male) readers.

Apart from spreading sexual-explicit imagery of the crime, news stories on sexual crime use sexist-stereotypical representative images showing the victim (often semi-clad or disrobed) injured and alone in the dark, lacking agency, expressing fear, taking a submissive position, curled or bowing down in shame and being pinned down or stamped upon by monstrous males (or surrounded by their hands). Such imagery accompanying sexual crime stories could propagate patriarchial ideals and encourage sexual violence. Ghosh (2020, January 13) noted that these images spread sexism, presenting women as helpless, passive and scared victims. To counter these representative images, FII Team (2020, February 20) curated stock images that are gender-sensitive. Similarly, news stories on sexual violence engage in victim-blaming, apart from spreading several other rape myths. For instance, there have been complaints that the use of passive rather than active voice in headlines also propagates victim-blaming.

Bhandari (2021, p. 68) argued that when media associates "rape within a particular time of the day, the location of the crime, and personal enmity between the victim and the perpetrator, it establishes some blame on the victim". Dalton (2018) also noted that it could encourage victim-blaming. Bhandari (2021) observed that the news media needs to focus on systemic oppression and gender-based issues rather than graphically detailing the crime and focus on the perpetrators instead of the survivors. Prasad (2024, June 29) noted that:

> Patriarchal notions of victim-blaming always seek to displace blame onto the victims of sexual violence. Women are routinely held accountable for the crimes committed against them and the onus of preventing violence is shifted onto them… Whether the framing is intentional or not, it is still damaging. This highlights how Indian media outlets don't utilise appropriate vocabulary when reporting on sexual violence against women.

Good (2023, February 22) noted that sexist language, objectification of women and the "glamorisation" of sexual violence in news reports propagate rape myths and encourage a culture of rape, pinning the blame on the victims, normalising sexual violence and exonerating the perpetrators. It is important for contemporary journalists to pay attention to language and ensure that their writings are not sexist and do not propagate rape myths.

Sectionalism. It is also critical to ensure that news reports are not divisive, such as highlighting gender differences, playing the caste card, emphasising regional or religious dissociations, pinning the blame on the police or government as a custom sans substance, using communal reference and engaging in biassed reporting. In several recent cases, the caste card was used to politicise sexual assaults (Pal, 2019, June 15; Shinde, 2020, October 12).

Politicisation. It is also a current practice to politicise "sensational" cases of sexual assaults, reporting political blame games. It is usual for the Opposition parties and leaders to blame the government (and the police) for the acts of sexual violence and the ruling parties to respond with counterarguments and diversions. It is unbidden for two reasons: Exploiting sexual violence for political mileage is insensitive and unethical and holding the authorities responsible for the safety of women could propagate sexist ideas that women are incapable of ensuring their own safety and they need the help of others for protection. For example, in the case of the 2023 Manipur sexual assault, the Opposition blamed the ruling government for the sexual crimes (Singh, 2023, July 22; NDTV News Desk, 2023, July 19; The Hindu Bureau, 2023, July 19) and, in response, the government cited several other states run by the Opposition party that has seen a surge in sexual crime (Staff Writer, 2023, July 22; The Hindu Bureau, 2023a, July 22; The Hindu Bureau 2023b, July 22). Such blame-game trivialises and diverts the issue, apart from portraying the issue through a sexist prism and relegating women as devoid of agency and ability. Editors and reporters, hence, need to be extra careful about politicising sexual violence.

Prejudicial reporting. Prejudicial reporting and conducting media trials are a recurrent phenomenon in sexual crime reporting in India, especially in cases that have become popular. Chapter 4 details the nuances of such unethical editorial behaviours by analysing a sample of video news. News channels, in their prime-time debates, exclusive posts and sensationalised reports, tend to convict or exonerate the accused and engage in victim-blaming based on unreliable information and without proper citation of sources. Such reporting could invade privacies and hinder the opportunities for a fair trial. Chapter 4 analysis exposed media trial cues in the reportage of the Hyderabad rape-murder and the Kerala actor molestation cases.

News media also publish sensitive material that could hinder the investigation and judicial trial, influencing public opinion. News reporters and editors need to be mindful of the legal and judicial implications of their news when reporting on sexual violence.

Churnalism and information distortion. Distortion in the news can belong to disparate levels, from the outrightly synthetic (fake news) to the ones hard-to-identify (hyped and opinionated). Several chapters of this book analysed news and identified misinformation that a set of casual eyes could overlook. There was also a tendency to base the news on unreliable and unverified material and present it without proper source identification. In television journalism, the header and footer space were found to be the most misused to present quotes and opinions as facts without proper citation of sources. Using news samples and analysis, this book identified news stories based on unverified CCTV footage (News18 Debate & Interview,, 2023, September 29; NDTV, 2022, June 8), Twitter threads (Baliarsingh, 2022, September 19) and viral videos (India Today Video Desk, 2023, July 21).

Though Chapter 6 finds churnalism trending in online newsrooms, it is not restricted to online media. Recycling content is now omnipresent across news media and widening the scope for information distortion and sensationalism, presenting the problem of sourcing and, at times, lending credence to conspiracy theories and media speculations.

Instead of viewing cases of sexual violence as isolated incidents and inundating the news space with sensational episodic news coverages, the news media needs to focus on the larger picture, exploring underlying issues, and aim at preventing such crimes from occurring, engaging in responsible reporting and encouraging survivors to report such crimes. Both the prevention of sexual crimes and editing of unethical reporting practices need a comprehensive approach involving the people, practice and policy. Outlining problematic issues, this book encourages journalists to engage in self-reflection and concur that the rise of Predatory Journalism is a threat.

It is crucial to provide guidelines and increase awareness to check exploitative journalism while reporting on sexual crime and gender-based violence. While media education in India prescribes avoidance of the identification of victims of sexual crimes, the importance of avoiding publishing personal information such as caste, age, location and occupation is often overlooked. The onus of expunging predatory journalistic practices rests not only with policymakers, media houses and regulatory authorities but also relies on self-regulation and public discernment of news information, which dictates news spread. Media-information literacy also becomes imperative to encourage media consumers to read news content with a critical lens.

Journalism, on the other hand, needs to be more responsible and made accountable, providing a safe space for the victims to share their stories. While attention-grabbing headlines may be necessary, journalists need to balance this need with accuracy and empathy, at least while reporting sexual violence. Anand (2019, June 25) noted that survivors often believe that the news media will support them in their fight for justice:

> the press can cover cases in which the police refused to help… Sometimes these reports have real power to put pressure on the police to act. But these benefits are often negated when the reporting involved isn't sensitive to the survivor's needs. Journalism has the power to hold a space of compassion and dignity for the trauma that survivors are denied elsewhere; we must make sure that it does.

Pointing to the "breaking news" culture and the daily "search for the villain", in a commentary, Tharoor (2024, January 19) expressed concern over the "fourth estate" slipping from "its true place in a democracy" but was positive that "there's much to do to set things right again". Journalism is a powerful tool that can inform about and help expunge sociopolitical disorders. With great power comes greater responsibility and journalists, whether working in traditional media or on social media, have a duty to uphold ethical standards and avoid engaging in predatory practices. Through this book, we aim to encourage sensitive news reporting with renewed awareness about ethical issues. We hope that it will help the profession rebuild eroding public trust in journalism and serve the greater public interest.

References

Agnihotri, S. (2016, October 25). *7 FAQs on law, sexual violence and section 375 & 376 of the Indian Penal Code*. Feminism in India. https://feminisminindia.com/2016/08/22/faqs-law-sexual-violence-section-375-376/

Anand, A. (2019, June 25). *How I got a major Indian media outlet to change the way they depict sexual violence*. Women's Media Center. https://womensmediacenter.com/fbomb/how-i-got-a-major-indian-media-outlet-to-change-the-way-they-depict-sexual-violence

Baliarsingh, C. (2022, September 19). *Twitter thread on Chandigarh University MMS will shock you. Twitter Thread on Chandigarh University MMS Scandal Will Send Chills Down Your Spine*. https://odishatv.in/news/national/twitter-thread-on-chandigarh-university-mms-scandal-will-send-chills-down-your-spine-185851

Bhandari, A. (2021*). Indian media narratives in gang rape* [Master of Arts (MA) thesis]. Sociology & Criminal Justice, Old Dominion University. https://digitalcommons.odu.edu/sociology_criminaljustice_etds/55

Carter, C. (1998). When the 'extraordinary' becomes 'ordinary': Everyday news of sexual violence gender and the Agenda. In S. Allan, G. Branston, & C. Carter (Eds.), *News, gender and power* (1st ed., pp. 219–232). Routledge.

Dalton, M. (2018, October 26). Is the news media complicit in spreading rape culture? *Columbia Journalism Review*. https://www.cjr.org/analysis/news-study-rape-culture.php

Dar, J. (2023, December 4). *Brother turns monster: Man along with four friends rapes sister; kills her in Odisha*. News9live. https://www.news9live.com/crime/brother-turns-monster-man-along-with-four-friends-rapes-sister-kills-her-in-odisha-2367975

DC Correspondent. (2018, February 20). *Deccan Chronicle*. https://www.deccanchronicle.com/nation/crime/200218/wb-men-insert-iron-rod-inside-tribal-womans-private-part-gangrape.html

Doshi, V. (2021, December 1). A woman interviewed 100 convicted rapists in India. This is what she learned. *Washington Post*. https://www.washingtonpost.com/news/worldviews/wp/2017/09/11/a-woman-interviewed-100-convicted-rapists-in-india-this-is-what-she-learned/

Ellis-Petersen, H. (2023, July 21). India: Four men arrested after women stripped naked and paraded in Manipur. *The Guardian*. https://www.theguardian.com/world/2023/jul/21/india-arrest-women-stripped-naked-paraded-manipur

ETV Bharat. (2024, April 6). *Woman paraded naked, beaten after son married his girlfriend in Punjab; FIR registered*. ETV Bharat News. https://www.etvbharat.com/en/!state/woman-paraded-naked-beaten-after-son-married-his-girlfriend-in-punjab-fir-registered-enn24040601047

Express News Service. (2017, August 2). 'Iron rod inserted into private parts.' *The Indian Express*. https://indianexpress.com/article/cities/kolkata/iron-rod-inserted-into-private-parts-4778245/

FII Team. (2020, February 20). *Dear media, use these new stock images to depict rape instead! | #GBVinMedia*. Feminism in India. https://feminisminindia.com/2020/02/20/new-stock-images-rape/

Ghosh, A. (2020, January 13). *The media needs to use better images when it reports rape | #GBVinMedia*. Feminism in India. https://feminisminindia.com/2020/01/13/stock-images-rape-reportage/#google_vignette

Good, L. (2023, February 22). *The language of rape culture normalizes violence*. The Chimes. https://chimesnewspaper.com/52853/opinions/the-language-of-rape-culture-normalizes-violence/

HT Correspondent (2020, July 31). 'Accused showed no mercy, put liquor in Hyderabad vet's mouth while raping her': Cops. *Hindustan Times*. https://www.hindustantimes.com/india-news/accused-showed-no-mercy-put-liquor-in-hyderabad-vet-s-mouth-while-raping-her-cops/story-vWiH3jtwfkn2CD3BAQJz9I.html

HT News Desk. (2024, May 1). 'Manipur women, who were paraded naked, approached police Gypsy but…': CBI chargesheet. *Hindustan Times*. https://www.hindustantimes.com/india-news/manipur-women-who-were-paraded-naked-approached-police-gypsy-but-what-cbi-said-101714440464729.html

India Today Video Desk. (2023, July 21). Manipur viral video case: 4 accused sent to 11-day police custody. *India Today*. https://www.indiatoday.in/india/video/manipur-viral-video-case-4-accused-sent-to-11-day-police-custody-2409971-2023-07-21

India Today Video Desk. (2023, September 2). Rajasthan woman beaten, stripped, paraded naked by husband, in-laws. *India Today*. https://www.indiatoday.in/india/video/rajasthan-woman-beaten-stripped-paraded-naked-by-husband-in-laws-2429998-2023-09-02

India.com News Desk. (2016, May 2). *Nirbhaya-like rape repeated in Kerala: Law student raped and brutally murdered, reveals autopsy*. India.Com. https://www.india.com/news/india/nirbhaya-like-rape-repeated-in-kerala-law-student-raped-and-brutally-murdered-reveals-autopsy-1153690/

Jain, A. (2023, September 26). Unveiling the Indian media's approach to reporting rape cases: A critical analysis. *Medium*. https://medium.com/@aadhya_jain2019/unveiling-the-indian-medias-approach-to-reporting-rape-cases-a-critical-analysis-335b693bc0ee

Jolly, J. (2016, July 20). Rape in India: Is the English-language press falling back on stereotypes? *Columbia Journalism Review*. https://www.cjr.org/analysis/india_rape_journalism.php

Khan, A. & Ahsan, S. (2023, November 14). *Media trial conundrum: Experts say sensationalism generates good TRPs, not good outcomes*. Bar And Bench. Indian Legal News. https://www.barandbench.com/columns/media-trial-conundrum-experts-say-sensationalism-generates-good-trps-not-good-outcomes

Mallick, A. (2019, December 5). Week after Hyderabad horror, fear forces 8pm 'curfew' in village. *The Times of India*. https://timesofindia.indiatimes.com/india/week-after-hyderabad-horror-fear-forces-8pm-curfew-in-village/articleshow/72392067.cms

Manglik, T. (2017, March 1). *The Underlying sexism in the media reportage of the Malayalam actor's rape case*. Feminism in India. https://feminisminindia.com/2017/03/01/sexism-media-malayalam-actor/

McCoy, T. (2021, October 25). The chilling reason the Delhi bus gang-rapist blames his victim. *Washington Post*. https://www.washingtonpost.com/news/morning-mix/wp/2015/03/03/the-chilling-reason-the-new-delhi-bus-gang-rapist-blames-his-victim/

Mirror Now Digital. (2018, October 31). Woman brutally gang-raped by relative and accomplices, iron rod found inserted in private parts. *Times Now*. https://www.timesnownews.com/mirror-now/crime/article/west-bengal-woman-brutally-gang-raped-by-relative-and-accomplices-iron-rod-inserted-in-private-parts-in-jalpaiguri/304972

Mishra, G. (2017, October 13). Bihar woman dies as man thrusts iron rod in her private parts. *IBTimes India*. https://www.ibtimes.co.in/bihar-woman-dies-after-rapist-thrusts-iron-rod-into-her-private-parts-745494

Mukherjee, S. (2014, March 21). *Why rapists are not monsters, and calling them so can be harmful*. Women's Web. https://www.womensweb.in/2014/03/why-rapists-are-not-monsters-and-calling-them-so-can-be-harmful/

Mumbai Mirror. (2014, March 20). Shakti Mills monsters convicted; their families continue to suffer. *Mumbai Mirror*. https://mumbaimirror.indiatimes.com/mumbai/cover-story/shakti-mills-monsters-convicted-their-families-continue-to-suffer/articleshow/32379191.cms

News18 Debate & Interview. (2023, September 29). *Ujjain Rape Case CCTV footage: उज्जैन रेप कांड का नया CCTV Video आया सामने, दहल जाएगा दिल! |MP News* [Video]. YouTube. https://www.youtube.com/watch?v=ch82UOLeBAk

NDTV. (2022, June 8). *Hyderabad gang-rape: The 6-hour horror*. NDTV. https://www.ndtv.com/video/hyderabad-rape-hyderabad-gang-rape-the-6-hour-horror-636745

NDTV News Desk. (2023, July 19). *After Manipur sexual assault video, opposition wants PM in Parliament*. NDTV.com. https://www.ndtv.com/india-news/after-manipur-sexual-assault-video-opposition-wants-pm-narendra-modi-in-parliament-4223678

Outlook Web Desk. (2024, March 3). *Jharkhand horror: "Beaten and robbed, they wanted to rape me", says Spanish women, three arrested*. Outlook India. https://www.outlookindia.com/national/jharkhand-horror-beaten-and-robbed-they-wanted-to-rape-me-says-spanish-women-three-arrested

Pal, S. (2019, June 15). *Linguistics of blame: Rape reporting remains sensationalist*. NewsClick. Retrieved April 25, 2023, from https://www.newsclick.in/linguistics-blame-rape-reporting-remains-sensationalist

Pandey, G. (2019, December 6). *Hyderabad case: Why Indians are celebrating the killings*. https://www.bbc.com/news/world-asia-india-50683615

Philipose, P. (2020, September 12). *Backstory: Everything wrong with the media is reflected in the Sushant Singh Rajput coverage*. The Wire. https://thewire.in/media/back-story-indian-media-sushant-singh-rajput-coverage

Pillai, J. (2024, July 4). *Hyderabad horror: 10-year-old kidnapped, gets pregnant after being raped by 10 men*. India.Com. https://www.india.com/telangana/hyderabad-horror-10-year-old-kidnapped-gets-pregnant-after-being-raped-by-10-men-7059969/

Pinker, S. (2018, February 17). The media exaggerates negative news. This distortion has consequences. *The Guardian*. https://www.theguardian.com/commentisfree/2018/feb/17/steven-pinker-media-negative-news

Poonam, S. (2019, December 3). 'They punctured her scooter & waited' — how 4 men executed horrific Hyderabad rape-murder. *ThePrint*. https://theprint.in/india/they-punctured-her-scooter-waited-how-4-men-executed-horrific-hyderabad-rape-murder/329459/

Prasad, P. (2024, June 29). *Prajwal Revanna and the politics of language while reporting rape*. The Wire. https://thewire.in/gender/prajwal-revanna-and-the-politics-of-language-while-reporting-rape

Press Trust of India. (2024, June 27). Rajasthan horror: MBBS student undergoes dialysis 4 times after ragging, 7 booked. *News9live*. https://www.news9live.com/india/rajasthan-horror-mbbs-student-undergoes-dialysis-4-times-after-ragging-7-booked-2594318

PTI. (2019, December 6). Global media gives prominent coverage to police action in Hyderabad rape-murder case. *The Times of India*. https://timesofindia.indiatimes.com/india/global-media-gives-prominent-coverage-to-police-action-in-hyderabad-rape-murder-case/articleshow/72403328.cms

PTI. (2020, January 28). *Nagpur teen choked, raped in unconscious state, iron rod inserted in privates: Police*. NDTV.com. https://www.ndtv.com/nagpur-news/nagpur-teen-choked-raped-in-unconscious-state-iron-rod-inserted-in-privates-police-2170743

PTI. (2024, April 7). 55-year-old Punjab woman assaulted, paraded semi-naked; 4 held. *The Indian Express*. https://indianexpress.com/article/cities/chandigarh/punjab-woman-assault-paraded-semi-naked-9255632/

Raj, V. (2024, April 30). Manipur horror: Women assaulted, paraded naked after police denied help, reveals CBI chargesheet. *English Jagran*. https://english.jagran.com/india/manipur-violence-horror-women-assaulted-paraded-naked-after-police-denied-help-reveals-cbi-chargesheet-10157315

Republic World. (2019, November 30). *Hyderabad horror: 4 Accused in the vicious gang-rape-murder sent to judicial custody for 14 days [Video].* YouTube. Retrieved June 13, 2024, from https://youtu.be/RQo1Uy4BsxQ?feature=shared

Shahid, G. A. (2024, May 10). *Delhi HORROR: 8-YR-Old Nepal girl kidnapped, sexually abused for 24 hours in Kotla Mubarakpur; Bite Marks Foun.* India.Com. https://www.india.com/news/delhi/delhi-horror-8-year-old-nepal-girl-kidnapped-sexually-abused-for-24-hours-kotla-mubarakpur-mehrauli-delhi-police-crime-6919482/

Sharma, G. (2024, March 14). *Rajasthan horror: 20 women gang-raped on pretext of jobs in anganwadi.* Oneindia. https://www.oneindia.com/jaipur/rajasthan-horror-20-women-gang-raped-on-pretext-of-jobs-in-anganwadi-3748335.html

Shinde, R. (2020, October 12). From indifference to victim-blaming: Why the mainstream media's coverage of Hathras is unsurprising. *Newslaundry.* https://www.newslaundry.com/2020/10/12/from-indifference-to-victim-blaming-why-the-mainstream-medias-coverage-of-hathras-is-unsurprising

Singh, A. (2021, January 11). MP twin shocker: Widow raped, iron rod inserted in private parts; 13-year-old raped and murdered. *The New Indian Express.* https://www.newindianexpress.com/nation/2021/Jan/11/mp-twin-shocker-widow-raped-iron-rod-inserted-in-private-parts-13-year-old-raped-and-murdered-2248748.html

Singh, S. S. (2023, July 22). BJP, Trinamool trade charges over assault on women in West Bengal. *The Hindu.* https://www.thehindu.com/news/national/other-states/assault-on-women-in-west-bengal/article67108838.ece

Sinha, K. (2015, March 2). Nirbhaya gang-rape convict blames victim for the fatal assault. *The Times of India.* https://timesofindia.indiatimes.com/city/delhi/nirbhaya-gang-rape-convict-blames-victim-for-the-fatal-assault/articleshow/46433506.cms

Staff Writer. (2023, July 22). Manipur horrific video: BJP targets opposition, says, 'crime against women increasing in other states.' *Mint.* https://www.livemint.com/news/india/manipur-horrific-video-rape-against-women-ncrb-data-malda-rajasthan-bengal-crime-congress-bjp-opposition-parties-11690014254974.html

Tharoor, S. (2024, January 19). *Indian Media: Quo Vadis?* https://www.thehindu.com/opinion/lead/indian-media-quo-vadis/article67753206.ece/amp/

The Hindu Bureau. (2023, July 19). Opposition outraged by Manipur viral video. *The Hindu.* https://www.thehindu.com/news/national/opposition-outraged-by-manipur-viral-video/article67099278.ece

The Hindu Bureau. (2023a, July 22). Under opposition attack over Manipur, BJP highlights crimes in Rajasthan, West Bengal. *The Hindu.* https://www.thehindu.com/news/national/under-opposition-attack-over-manipur-bjp-highlights-crimes-in-rajasthan-west-bengal/article67110295.ece

The Hindu Bureau. (2023b, July 22). Gehlot hits out at Modi for making reference to Rajasthan in Manipur comments. *The Hindu.* https://www.thehindu.com/news/national/other-states/gehlot-hits-out-at-modi-for-making-reference-to-rajasthan-in-manipur-comments/article67109915.ece

The New Indian Express. (2019, December 2). Hyderabad veterinary doctor murder: "They raped her in lorry cabin even after she died". *The New Indian Express.* https://www.newindianexpress.com/cities/hyderabad/2019/Dec/01/hyderabad-veterinary-

Time Staff. (2015, March 2). Delhi gang-rape convict blames victim for brutal attack. *TIME.* https://time.com/3728061/delhi-gang-rape-blames-victim/

TNN. (2024, July 4). Horror on wheels: Woman drugged, gang-raped by colleagues in car in Hyderabad, 2 held. *The Times of India.* https://timesofindia.indiatimes.com/city/hyderabad/woman-drugged-gang-raped-by-colleagues-in-car-2-held/articleshow/111470718.cms

Tripathi, P. (2024, March 28). Delhi horror! 30-year-old tenant rapes 3-year-old in Peergarhi, accused absconding. *Times Now.* https://www.timesnownews.com/mirror-now/crime/delhi-horror-30-year-old-tenant-rapes-3-year-old-in-peergarhi-accused-absconding-article-108855330

Web Desk. (2024, June 25). *Assam horror: Islamist abducted & gang-raped minor girl; Police arrest five accused of gang rape in Udalguri district.* Organiser. https://organiser.org/2024/06/25/244341/bharat/assam-horror-islamist-abducted-police-arrest-five-accused-of-gang-rape-in-udalguri-district/

WION. (2019, December 6). *Hyderabad rape and murder case: Huge crowd gather at encounter site* [Video]. YouTube. Retrieved June 13, 2024, from https://youtu.be/vzXy2-G04Ok?si=oEv5qZ_Ru3568JiX

Index

Note: Bold page numbers point to text within tables.

2017 Kerala actress abduction-molestation case 3, 63, 69–74, 132, 146
2017 Unnao rape 4, 9, 46, 79, 81–82
2018 Kathua rape case 4, 9, 79, 81–84, 134
2020 Hathras gangrape-murder 9, 43, 79, 83

addiction 85, 116
advertisement 12, 19, 113
advertising *see* advertisement
All India Radio 114
allied crimes 2, 12, 14–17, 129
alliteration 50, 54
anaphora 50, 54
Appraisal Theory 24, 34, 51

BBC News 114
branding 19, 34, 51, 55, 57, 69, 120, 130

celebrities *see* celebrity
celebrity 11–13, 15, 17, 18, 30, 44, 50, 54, 62, 69, 93, 94, 114, 127, 129–30
character assassination frame 64
chastity 129
churnalism 89–93, 95, 97, 99, 101, 105–109, 121, 134, 138, 146–147
CNN 114
communal reference 45–47, 56, 146–147
conflict 12–13, 15–16, 17, 19, 24, 50, 73, 79, 117
content warning xiv, 140
convergence 116, 134
convictive discourse 64
COVID-19 33, 113; pandemic 62, 113, 122; lockdown 113
critical discourse analysis 3, 63–64
crowdsourcing 115

DD News 114
decriminalisation frame 64, 71
dehumanisation *see* dehumanising
dehumanising 15, 34, 51, 55, 57, 74, 83, 141
Delhi gangrape 28, 77, 130–131, 134, 142; case 10–11, 68, 134, 142
delusive 32, 92, 105
demonisation *see* demonising
demonising 15, 34, 51, 55, 141
demand 3, 10, 28, 33–34, 46, 50, 65–66, 72, 74, 81, 90, 92–94, 97, 99–101, 106; demand-driven 28, 33, 92, 140
detailing 50, 54–55, 77, 78, 132, 143, 145
devices 3, 28, 29, 33, 48–51, 55–57, 77, 101, 142
devised 32, 92
devoid 32, 92, 105, 146
diagnostic 50, 54,
digested 32, 92, 134
digital penetration 113
digital news 3, 114; media 79, 134
Discordant Locus 4, 28, 91–92; obscure 4, 28, 30, 91–93, 102–103, 105, 115; obtrusive 4, 28, 30, 91–93, 102–103, 105, 115
Dissonant Composition 4, 28, 32, 91–92
distorted 19, 28, 32, 92, 121, 134

Economic Times 114
emotional frame 64, 66, 68, 70–71
emotive 15, 28, 35
entertainment value 24–25, 43–44
episodic 9, 28, 147
erotic 35, 133, 143; eroticisation 84; eroticising 4, 78, 131; eroticism xii, 3, 77–85, 131, 143; exhibitionism 31; responses 4, 28, 34, 79, 85, 131
establishment frame 64, 66
evaluative 15, 34, 37, 48, 51, 55, 57
evidence frame 64, 72
exhibitionism 4, 31, 79, 83

explicit imagery 2, 28, 34, 77–78, 121, 129, 131, 139–140, 143
exploitation ii, xi, 5, 26, 28, 34–36, 104, 131–132
exposive 15, 34, 51, 55, 130
extolling 15, 34, 51, 55, 57, 130, 132
extreme violence 50, 54–56

Facebook 45, 114, 116
frames 3, 19, 28, 33, 48–51, 54–57, 63–64, 67–68, 72, 142

gendering 34, 44, 51, 55, 139
generalising 15, 34, 51, 55
generative 28, 33, 92, 94, 97
Google Trends 10, 92, 119; Google News search trends 9, 10, 49, 92–94
governmental action 49, 52
grammatical structures x, 48, 49, 51–52, 55, 56

Hindustan Times 81–82, 94, 114
humour 50, 54
Hyderabad gangrape-murder 3, 63, 66, 76, 132, 145
hyperbole 50, 54–56
hypercoverage 9, 10, 30, 57, 140
hyperdetailing 2, 4, 62, 77–78, 81, 83, 85, 131, 143

identification iv, 12, 13, 47, 50, 54–56, 85, 105, 115, 121, 130, 133–134, 139, 144, 146–147
illocutions x, 3, 28, 34, 44, 47, 49, 51, 55–57, 130, 142; illocutionary issues 34; sexist illocutions 34, 47–57
imagery i, xiv, 2–4, 9, –10, 15, 24, 28, 31, 47, 77–79, 84–85, 115–116, 118, 121, 129–131, 134, 138–140, 143, 145
India Today i, 10, 20, 31, 37, 58, 75, 80, 85, 86, 99, 102, 107, 109, 114, 125, 126,134, 136, 142, 147, 149
Instagram 4, 90, 114, 115, 131
Instigation frame 64, 66
institution xiii, 14, 50,54,56,118,120,138; institutional action 13, 14, 18, 49, 52; institutional cover-up 121, 122
internet 4, 31, 32, 52, 53, 89, 90, 113, 117, 121, 126, 134
invasive journalism 4, 30, 126
investigative journalism 117

judicial action 13, 14, 18, 19, 49, 52, 62, 64, 69, 94

Kathua 4, 9, 79, 82–87, 134, 137
Kuki 47, **53**, 55, 57, 103

lambing 34, 51, 55, 57, 130, 144
legal action 3, 13, 14, 18, 19, 26, 49, 52, 63
locus x, 4, 28, 30, 91–93, 98, 102, 103
locution 30, 48; locutionary issues 30–32; locutionary topics 3

mainstream media 2,9, 33, 36, 60, 61, 74, 80, 117, 118, 121; traditional media 4, 35–36, 43, 114–116, 148
Manipur xi, 1, 3, 4, 15, 19, 46–49, 53–58, 80, 85, 88, 92, 94, 97, 103, 104, 106, 107, 109, 129, 133–136, 141–142, 146, 148, 150, 151; sexual assault 47, 55, 92, 97, 103, 104, 108, 133, 142, 146
marginalisation 50, 54–56
media trials i, vii, 2, 3, 31, 61–63, 67, 71–76, 132, 146
Meitei 47, 55, 80
metalepsis 50, 54–56, 142
metaphor 50, 54
millennials 43, 115
misinformation 4, 32, 33, 46, 73, 90–92, 104, 110, 117–121, 123, 125, 130, 139, 143, 146
MMS 117–118, 123, 125, 140, 148
monetise 114, 118, 122
morality 50, 54

NDTV 43, 57, 59, 74, 84, 85, 94, 98, 106, 108, 114, 135, 146, 147, 150
news prioritisation 2–3, 9–20, 23
news values 2, 3, 10, 12–14, 24, 45, 46, 16, 17, 20, 24
news trend 15, 114
newspapers 1, 11–12, 113, 140; American 73, 78; British national 45; English 10, 12, 129; Indian 11, 19, Korean 78; Malayalam 11; traditional 23

outrage of modesty 1, 9, 118, 133
oxymoron **50**, **54**

paper-pulp media 114
paraded naked **53**–54, 56–57, 80, 103–105, 133, 142
perlocution 30, 34, 48; perlocutionary effects 34
personification **50**, **54**
plagiarism 120, 123
pleonasm **50**, **54**–**56**
police connivance **50**, **54**

police inaction **50**, **54**, 82, 121–22
politicisation *see* politicising
politicising 11, 19, 25, 34, 43, 47, **51**, **55**, 146
pornography 85; pornographic 84, 122, 134
pragmalinguistics 3, 28–29, 48–49, 57, 132
prejudicial reporting 2–3, 61–74, 99–100, 120, 123, 138–139, 146
prognostic **50**, **54**
prompts 34
psychological impact **50**, **54**, 55
publications 113–114, 127, 143, 145; Hindi 113; English 10, 113
punishment frame **64**, 66–67

rape culture 5, 31, 57, 79, 83, 85, 128
resourced sources 32, **92**, 99
re-traumatisation xi, xii, 4, 35, 78, 105, 143–44
Reuters Institute annual survey 114
ridicule 27, 46, **50**, **54**
RNI 113
romanticise 81, 85, 145; romanticism 144

sarcasm **50**, **54**
schismatic 15, 34, **51**, **55**
sectionalist 2–3, 28, 34, 46, 48, 51, 55–57, 127, 130, 139
selective exposure 28, 31, 141
sexualisation *see* sexualise
sexualise 4, 34–35, **51**, **55**, 57, 77–78, 80, 103, 119, 121, 123, 130–132, 139, 143
smartphone 113, 115–116, 122
social impact **50**, **54**, 55, **56**
social media outrage 47
socio-cognitive CDA framework 63
speculative frame **64**
stereotyping xii, 34, **51**, **55**, 141; stereotypes 31, 35, 44–45, 65, 83, 99; stereotypical 90, 98–99, 102, 127, 134, 145
stigmatisation 25, 31, 34, **51**, **55**, 82
stimulating 28
stripped 54, 57; naked 56, 80–81, 133, 142

television news 25, 73, 114, 145
textual 4, 31, 79, 105; devices 48; patterns 29
The Times of India 1–2, 11–12, 31, 45, 99, 105, 113–114, 120, 141
thematic demand 28, 33, 92
Tribal Solidarity March 47
trigger warning xiv, 140
trivialisation 11, 34, **51**, 129
tropes 28, 31, 128; sexist 131

victim blaming 5, 11, **50**, **54**, **64**, 70, 77, 121, 128, 132, 142, 145–46
victim shaming 5, 121, 130
viral video 47, 52, **53**, 55, 80, 94, 122, 147
voyeurism 30, 122, 143

WhatsApp 114, 120

YouTube 4, 36, 63, 114–123, 134

For Product Safety Concerns and Information please contact our EU representative GPSR@taylorandfrancis.com
Taylor & Francis Verlag GmbH, Kaufingerstraße 24, 80331 München, Germany

www.ingramcontent.com/pod-product-compliance
Ingram Content Group UK Ltd.
Pitfield, Milton Keynes, MK11 3LW, UK
UKHW020002200926
475702UK00015B/2423

* 9 7 8 1 0 3 2 7 4 1 9 1 8 *